Paul on Baptism

Paul on Baptism

*Theology, Mission and Ministry
in Context*

Nicholas Taylor

scm press

© Nicholas Taylor 2016

Published in 2016 by SCM Press
Editorial office
3rd Floor, Invicta House,
108–114 Golden Lane,
London EC1Y 0TG, UK

SCM Press is an imprint of Hymns Ancient & Modern Ltd
(a registered charity)
13A Hellesdon Park Road, Norwich,
Norfolk NR6 5DR, UK
www.scmpress.co.uk

British Library Cataloguing in Publication data

A catalogue record for this book is available
from the British Library

978 0 334 05476 4

Typeset by Manila Typesetting Company
Printed and bound by CPI Group (UK) Ltd, Croydon

To James Dunn

with appreciation and respect

Contents

Preface

This book is born of experience both as a New Testament scholar and as a Christian minister. For one who is both an academic theologian and a priest, the fruit of scholarship must be brought to bear upon all aspects of church life and ministry, including the pastoral care of one's congregation, outreach to the local community, teaching the faith and administration of the sacraments. Practical pastoral issues, which arise from time to time in the communities we serve, raise questions about our received traditions of interpretation of Scripture and the influence of these traditions of interpretation on our denominational discipline. No Christian denomination is exempt from the challenge of practical pastoral realities to its heritage and to the seemingly endless quest for relevance in the world of today.

Thoughtful and conscientious Christian clergy, whatever their denominational affiliation and the nature of their education and formation for ministry, seek to live out their vocation in accordance with the gospel. This requires that they reflect theologically on their pastoral context and seek to respond appropriately to its needs and challenges, in the light of Scripture and their received tradition. The tools for doing this are often not readily available. Academic books are frequently inaccessible to the non-specialist and seem remote from specific pastoral situations. Many books tend also to reflect the compartmentalization of academic learning rather than connect the fruit of diverse disciplines to contemporary issues. Studies relating to Scripture or church doctrine seldom reflect upon the pastoral issues with which clergy are confronted in the course of their ministry. Books on pastoral care and other aspects of ministry, even if theologically well informed and astute in the guidance they offer, often do not equip their readers to reflect theologically upon the issues they discuss. This is a significant lack in the resources available for mission and pastoral ministry in and by the Church today.

In most Christian traditions the sacrament of Baptism confers Christian identity and church membership. Baptism is theologically and sociologically fundamental to Christian life, and its implications for the witness and ministry of the Church, and for the lives of its members, accordingly require continual theological reflection. Among the many aspects to its meaning and significance, Baptism symbolizes the boundary between the Church and the world: outsiders become insiders through Baptism. Most directly, perhaps, the Church encounters and intersects with the human family in complex ways and, through the family, with the wider society. Christian identity and membership of the Church, conferred in and through Baptism, do not negate the identity the person already holds as a member of a particular family or the relationships within and beyond the family by which its members are inextricably linked to each other and to the wider community of which they are a part. Baptism therefore adds a further dimension of identity to a person who is already a member of a family, and in the modern world almost certainly the citizen of a country, with inherited and potentially also acquired ethnic, cultural and social identity indicators, which relate to each other in complex and potentially conflictual ways and can potentially influence the course of his or her life.

Except in the case of adult converts, and outside of the Baptist, Pentecostal and non-sacramental traditions, it has traditionally been the family, represented by the parents and/or godparents, that has brought candidates to the Church for Baptism. The family is essentially a social and cultural institution, created and perpetuated within a specific social and cultural setting, living in accordance with the conventions generated within the broader social and cultural community. Family structures and relationships are therefore not uniform or static but diverse, culturally fashioned and dynamic. While professing the sanctity of the family and of family life, not least through the blessing of marriages, Christian churches have not always appreciated the complexity of the family as a social phenomenon or the diverse form the family takes in different or even the same cultural settings. This was particularly the case during the period of Western missionary endeavours in Africa, Asia and the Americas. Conversions, with the accompanying imposition of Western cultural conventions, occasioned widespread disruption in the lives of the families affected. The close association of Christian missions with the economic and political aspects of imperialism aggravated the social dislocation that resulted and has subsequently compromised the witness of the Church in ways still being worked through in different parts of the world. Christian ministry to families today accordingly has to acknowledge and address an ambiguous legacy in many places. Furthermore, in the rapidly changing world of today, the forces of globalization are impacting on cultures and therefore on the patterns of family life and relationships, in ways that often seem destructive and threatening to those who seek to maintain traditional values. This poses additional challenges for Christian ministry, not least to families.

Churches and other organizations have responded to the rapid spread of infectious diseases, as well as to the poverty, the displacement of people through conflict and famine and other humanitarian disasters aggravated by global economic and political forces, in ways that, however inadequate, have been both practical and theological. While there may be growing consensus on many issues of economic justice, global Christian communities are increasingly divided by issues that appear closer to the heart of their beliefs and values. Issues of doctrinal orthodoxy, sexuality, the role of women in society and in the Church and, perhaps less prominently, the rights of children occasion at times bitter and very public divisions in Christian bodies. This is especially the case in denominations that seek to maintain a global unity and common identity. It is immediately apparent that many of these issues concern the family, and therefore the ministry of the Church to the family, in direct and indirect ways.

It is of the nature of pastoral ministry that global issues are manifested on a much smaller and more personal, often intensely painful scale in the congregation. Among the most gratifying experiences of my own ministry have been those occasions on which I have baptized teenagers after months of catechetical instruction, shortly before presenting them to the bishop for confirmation. It has also been my joy and privilege to baptize the infant children of active and dedicated members of the parishes and chaplaincies in which I have served. But for many Christian clergy, whatever the baptismal discipline of our particular denomination, many of our experiences in this crucial aspect of our ministry have been far less satisfying. As occasions on which the life of the family and that of the Church intersect, it is perhaps inevitable that there will be conflicting expectations regarding Baptism. In increasingly secular societies, lay people not active in church life but who seek the sacrament and its ascribed benefits, are unlikely to understand the rituals of the Church and their meaning as they are understood by Christian ministers and the communities by whom and in which these rituals are administered. Still less are they likely to understand or attach any importance or commitment to the promises involved. Even within many Christian communities the level of understanding of Christian doctrine and church discipline among clergy and laity alike is sadly deficient. The consequences are pastoral situations in which it is almost impossible both to uphold the teaching and discipline of the Church and to exercise a sensitive and nurturing Christian ministry. Most common is the demand for Baptism of their child by parents who have not made and have no intention of making any meaningful Christian commitment, and whose understanding of Christian identity and the sacrament has over generations, perhaps centuries, become entirely divorced from the doctrine of the Church. Clergy face the dilemma of reducing Baptism to an all but secular social event that celebrates the birth of a child or rebuffing families who, notwithstanding expectations that may seem unreasonable, consumerist or superstitious, need to be drawn into the life of the Church. But pastoral problems associated with the administration of Baptism do not occur only when that ministry is sought by people on the fringes or outside the life of the Church altogether. Once again, I do not believe my own experiences have been at all unique, but use them to illustrate issues with which I believe many Christian ministers are all too familiar. When serving as interim priest in a rural parish (in a country in which I had only recently arrived and the rudiments of whose vernacular language I was only beginning to acquire), I have been confronted with children presented to me for Baptism by a local catechist, in the absence of any other adult responsible for their nurture. I could ascertain neither how much preparation these children had received for Baptism nor what continuing pastoral support and Christian nurture would accompany them and their families on their Christian pilgrimage in their remote community. Nor could I know how meaningful the rite would be to the children, particularly as the liturgy was not yet available in their language. At a time when many families in Africa are without adult members on account of the Aids pandemic, this cannot be a rare occurrence, and it raises enormous questions about the ministry of the Church in such situations. It has been my task also on occasion to baptize at the point of death adult Aids sufferers whose condition had deteriorated beyond the point where they were physically or mentally able to make any profession of faith. The idea that the rite on its own is meaningful, and confers intangible but certain benefits in the next world if not in this, is by no means limited to societies others might regard as primitive or superstitious. While pastoral and sacramental assurance at the point of death is not lightly to be withheld, when Baptism marks the beginning of a Christian life that will encounter significant challenges in the present world, it is essential the rite be accompanied and sustained by such nurture as will enable and encourage faith to grow and to mature.

The sacraments of Baptism and the Eucharist are the pre-eminent rituals of the Christian Church. The Great Commission (Matt. 28.16–20) and the Last Supper (Matt. 26.26–29 and parallels; cf. 1 Cor. 11.23–26) have traditionally been understood to institute the sacraments of Baptism and the Eucharist respectively. The symbolic actions in these rites express, in many ways and for many people far more profoundly than the words that accompany those acts, the essence of the gospel, and they link Christian believers directly with the heart of their faith and with the God whom they worship. During the centuries of Christian history the Church and the various denominations into which it has fragmented have developed doctrinal and liturgical traditions in the light of which clergy are called to proclaim the gospel, administer the sacraments and exercise pastoral care. Considerations of Christian doctrine, church discipline and responsible and sensitive pastoral care raise serious dilemmas for the Christian minister faced with the human condition in all its complexity, imperfection and sinfulness. It is entirely appropriate that thinking and caring pastoral ministers should wish to reflect upon the tradition they have inherited and of which they are custodians, to discover some insight that will illuminate the situation in which they are called to serve and to represent the Church. It is the aim of this book to provide a resource for such an exercise. We will look specifically to the apostle Paul as the source of teaching on the subject of Baptism. Of the many men and women who proclaimed the Christian gospel during its earliest period, Paul had a unique capacity, among those who have left any written record, to think theologically and to apply his theological insights to practical and often urgent pastoral and missionary contexts. Furthermore, he did so in documents, many of which we can still read today. This is not to suggest that the Pauline tradition represents the only valid source of teaching on this or any other subject or that it is necessarily representative of the breadth of early Christianity. Nevertheless, the pastoral orientation of the letters and the profundity of theological reflection underlying them have bequeathed to the Church a particularly useful and informative resource for our present task.

This book is an offering to others in pastoral ministry who seek to be true to Christian doctrine and the discipline of their particular denomination regarding Baptism, and at the same time to administer the sacrament in a manner that is pastorally responsible, so it can be an effective vehicle of God's love and saving power in a broken world. While my perspectives and experiences as an Anglican will undoubtedly influence my perception of many of the issues, I hope the exegesis of biblical texts at least will be informative and stimulating to readers of all persuasions.

Acknowledgements

My thanks are due to Professor James D. G. Dunn, Emeritus of Durham University, and Dr Ellen Juhl Christiansen of Aarhus, who generously read and commented on the manuscript. Their expertise on the subject has challenged and refined my understanding of several issues, and their influence will be evident in the interpretation of several texts. For their comments and suggestions I would also like to thank Canon John Suggit, Professor emeritus of Rhodes University, Grahamstown, Professor Charles A. Wanamaker of the University of Cape Town, the Revd Dr Phillip Tovey of Oxford and my former colleague Dr Elizabeth Parsons of Boston University, then Director of Lay Training in the Diocese of Manicaland. Earlier versions of material included in this book have been presented at conferences of the Society of Biblical Literature and the Society for Liturgical Studies, and to the Biblical Studies and Church and Academy Seminars in the University of Glasgow. I am grateful to colleagues for the helpful insights offered in discussion following these presentations and to Dr A. K. M. Adam and Dr Scott Robertson for the opportunity to participate in these seminars. This book was completed during a period of sabbatical leave at the Tantur Ecumenical Institute in occupied Palestine. I would like to thank the Rector, Fr Russell McDougall CSC, the Librarian, Jacqueline Mazoyer and the staff and community for their fellowship and encouragement at a time of stress and anxiety for all who live and work in the Land of the Holy One. Finally I must thank Canon Scott Robertson and other clergy and lay officers who have borne the burden of my absence from pastoral duties. Any errors in the text of course remain my own responsibility.

Introduction

The letters of the apostle Paul are among the earliest Christian documents that survive. They constitute a high proportion of the New Testament canon and are the most substantial body of texts overtly seeking to regulate the lives of the earliest Christian communities. From the earliest centuries of what became orthodox Christianity, Paul has been particularly influential in defining doctrine and discipline. His evident theological acumen and application of his theological insights to pastoral and missionary situations, in documents available to be read today, render Paul's letters a particularly useful source of early Christian teaching. A study of early Christian Baptism, therefore, cannot be undertaken without reference to the scattered allusions to the rite in the Pauline letters. These are not the only statements on Baptism in the New Testament, and Paul may not in all respects be representative of early Christian teaching and practice. We should be aware that 1 Peter contains baptismal teaching and may incorporate an ancient baptismal liturgy.[1] The Gospel accounts of the ministry of John the Baptist, and the water rite to which Jesus himself submitted (Matt. 3.1–17; Mark 1.1–11; Luke 3.2–22; John 1.26–34; 3.23–36), reflect early Christian Baptism in complex ways,[2] as do the frequent symbolic occurrences of water in the fourth Gospel (John 2.1–11; 3.5–6; 4.5–26; 7.37–39; 13.3–17; 19.34–37).[3] In addition, the extra-canonical document known as the *Didache*, or Teaching of the Twelve Apostles, is regarded by an increasing number of scholars as more ancient than many canonical documents, or at least as incorporating more ancient oral or written traditions.[4] Nevertheless, the volume of teaching on Baptism in Paul's letters is considerably greater than that in any other documents in the New Testament or other first-century Christian writings. Furthermore, Paul has been uniquely important both in forging a Christian identity independent of ethnic Judaism, and in the development of Western Christian theology through the mediation of Augustine of Hippo. A millennium and more later, Paul was to be a formative influence on the Protestant reformers. His pre-eminent influence has continued to the present day, as is evident from the preponderance of citations of Paul, among all the New Testament writers, in the documents of the ecumenical movement of the last half century. A review of Paul's baptismal theology and practice is therefore crucial not only to our understanding of the early Church but also to contemporary issues relating to what is commonly known as Christian initiation.

Paul's theology has come down to the modern Church through letters he sent to Christian communities of his own day. Most of these were congregations he had established during the course of his missionary career and over which he exercised continuing pastoral oversight. Other letters were written to churches that Paul had not himself founded but with which he nonetheless found occasion to correspond. These churches, with the exception of that in Rome, were located in cities of the eastern Roman Empire, in areas that now lie in Greece and Turkey. There are also letters addressed to individuals, his companions and subordinates in mission and a Christian householder, church leader, and slave owner. These letters present their own particular issues, which we will need to consider in due course.

The specific circumstances in which Paul's letters were written present the contemporary reader, and the modern Church, with a series of challenges. First of all, we do not have access to any previous communications between Paul and the churches to which he sent letters; for example, we know from 1 Corinthians 5.9 that Paul had written a letter to the Corinthian church earlier than that we know as 1 Corinthians; we know also from 1 Corinthians 7.1 that the Corinthian Christians had addressed a letter to Paul, raising questions concerning their life as a church and their lives as disciples of Jesus in pagan society. We have not heard Paul's mission preaching and catechetical instruction to new converts, which, as we will discuss further, cannot be adequately reconstructed from the speeches attributed to Paul in the book of Acts. Nor have we had opportunity to seek his guidance on matters of faith and morals through letters or through verbal messages. We are, in short, not a party to the relationship within which Paul's letters were written. We can therefore know only incompletely the circumstances in which they were written and what particular considerations informed the apostle's teaching and guidance to the communities to which the letters were first addressed. We have only the texts of the letters.

Second, we live in a different age and are products of different cultures from those in which Paul and other Christians of his day lived and worked, and in terms of which they interpreted their experience of God and expressed the Christian gospel to which they had been converted. This raises questions as to what the letters mean for us as members of the Church, in and for which the New Testament documents are acknowledged as bearing authority as witnessing uniquely and definitively to the gospel of Christ, but are at the same time quite alien to our environment and culture. The authority of Scripture must by definition be relevant to the life of the Church today, but this requires that we seek to understand the text as its first recipients received and understood it.

Scholarship has developed various techniques for the interpretation of Paul's letters and other New Testament documents. First of all, the texts have been translated from the Greek original into various modern vernacular languages to make them accessible to contemporary readers. This is a complex process but one that modern Christians tend to take for granted, particularly those who live in societies in which vernacular Bibles have been available for centuries. Second, each age has developed methods of discerning what Paul is saying and applying it to its own context and to the challenges that confront Christians and Christian communities in their own cultural setting. This is much more problematic, and the assumptions and insights of one generation of scholars and interpreters are often challenged by the next. It is all too easy to project our own situation and concerns into the situations to which the biblical texts were addressed. While this may make the Scriptures appear more meaningful and relevant, it can also be misleading. If the text of the apostolic guidance is applied to a situation very different from that to which it was originally addressed, then the spirit of that message may be distorted or lost altogether. It is a constant danger in the life of the Church that the Bible can be misappropriated to serve the agenda of particular interest groups. This is a danger that an authentic interpretation of Paul's letters and their teaching must seek to avoid, through seeking to capture the spirit of the message and not relying on the text in isolation from the original context that gave it meaning.

An immense challenge for Christian ministers is how to appropriate New Testament teaching, such as that contained in the letters of the apostle Paul, to their own role of Christian teaching and pastoral care. Superficial reading and naïve transplanting of selected verses to a new situation is unsatisfactory for a number of reasons. To the educated and thinking minister, it must always raise questions as to whether the text is answering the questions he or she is asking, particularly when it does not seem relevant or appropriate to the pastoral problem being faced. At the same time, New Testament scholarship, which ought to be helpful to the pastoral minister, is increasingly technical and may often seem too academic and abstract to be relevant to the concrete pastoral situations faced in Christian ministry.

Baptism is precisely a situation in which these problems are frequently encountered. The Christian minister today is faced with real pastoral situations involving real people, to whom he or she must provide appropriate care and teaching in accordance with Christian doctrine and in keeping with ecclesiastical discipline. Christian denominations vary a great deal in their structures and in the level of discretion in interpreting church teaching accorded to the minister in his or her specific pastoral context. However prescriptive, or even rigid, the system may be, it will not provide for every possible pastoral eventuality, but it may guide the minister grappling with a pastoral issue, even if only by directing him or her to relevant instructions or to higher authority. Where no such ecclesiastical discipline or explicit pastoral guidelines are in force, Scripture may become a source not only for spiritual sustenance but also for practical guidance. Even where denominational polity and pastoral guidelines seek to prescribe a definitive interpretation of Scripture for all pastoral situations, the minister may well on occasion question whether the rules are applicable or appropriate, and seek to measure them against Scripture as the source from which they are ultimately derived.

Problems encountered by Christian ministers today, and also in previous generations, include whether or not they should baptize infants, particularly if the parents are unmarried or not active in the life of the Church. This raises questions as to the fundamental meaning and significance of Baptism, particularly in nominally Christian societies where the rite of the Church has become a social event, if not a cultural rite of passage. The relationship between the water rite and reception of the Holy Spirit has taxed generations of Christians and remains a matter of contention both within and between denominations. These issues may seem theoretical but they impact on all aspects of church life. As Baptism brings together the family and the Church in a rite in which reciprocal commitments are undertaken, it is important that common understanding, and consistency between teaching and practice, be reached. The teaching and guidance of the apostle Paul can be helpful, but only if pastoral ministers are able to relate their concrete situation with that to which the Pauline letters were addressed, appreciating both the similarities and the differences, and discerning where the spirit of the apostolic instruction directs them. The aim of this book is to help Christian ministers to do this, by making available to them the insights of scholarship in as accessible form as is compatible with the complexity of many of the issues.

Chapter 1 will consider the context in which Paul wrote, and compare it with circumstances in which the Church and Christian ministers are working today. It will raise some questions that will enable the pastor to compare his or her situation more fully with that to which Paul's letters were written. The role of Baptism in early Christian life can be understood only if we know how belonging to a community was conceived in the ancient world, what significance was attached to rites and ceremonies, and how spiritual forces were believed to be at work in the world. With this information, the texts in which Paul writes about Baptism can be read afresh, and insights reached that are relevant to the situation in which pastoral ministers are working today.

Chapter 2 will study key passages in Paul's letters. We have no systematic treatment of Baptism in any of the letters. The apostolic teaching on the subject would presumably have been delivered orally, in the course of mission preaching and teaching to new converts, not least at the occasions on which these converts were baptized. Baptismal teaching was therefore definitively transmitted while Paul and his companions were still present with the new Christian communities they had established, and so before any occasion for a letter to that particular church could have arisen. Paul's letters were a substitute for his physical presence in the community, written after he had moved on to establish churches elsewhere. The passages in the letters in which Paul draws upon the Christians' experience and understanding of Baptism in order to address other issues in their community life, presuppose some instruction as to the meaning and significance of the ritual. While the references are brief and sometimes even allusive, we can nonetheless derive some understanding of his teaching on Baptism from these texts.

Chapter 3 will look at the practice of Baptism in the early Church, as reflected in the Pauline tradition. Here we can be informed by the accounts of baptisms administered by Paul in the Acts of the Apostles as well as by references in his letters. We will not attempt at this stage to answer all the contemporary questions but merely to discover what we can of the ways those to whom the apostle Paul preached came to be converted and to receive Baptism. While some modern scholars are sceptical of the historical reliability of Acts, for our purposes it is unquestionably a useful source of information. Whatever questions may be raised about the historicity of particular incidents, the general pattern of conversion and incorporation into the community portrayed in Acts must have been credible and familiar to its original readers and hearers. Such accounts can therefore be taken as representative of the practice of the early Church in the Roman Empire, and are accordingly useful for our purposes.

Chapter 4 will draw together the insights of the previous three into Paul's teaching and the practice of Baptism in the churches he founded. It will at this stage become possible to identify ways this teaching can be made relevant to contemporary pastoral situations.

It is hoped that this book will provide pastoral ministers with the fruit of scholarship in an accessible and relevant form in the limited field of Paul's teaching on Baptism. It is hoped too that the approach of this work will encourage them to read the Bible in such a way that the contexts in which the biblical texts were written come alive for them, and they are able to draw appropriate analogies between the world of the text and their own contexts. Only if we see how the biblical documents addressed the world of their own day can they give life and practical guidance to the Church of our day.

I have provided my own translations from the original Greek for the texts discussed in Chapter 2. Readers may wish to compare these with the translations in the various English versions of the Bible in circulation, or indeed those in other languages with which they are familiar. However, not all Bibles in circulation are direct translations from the original languages. As well as paraphrases available in contemporary English, many of the translations into the vernacular languages of Africa were the work of people with no knowledge of ancient Greek and Hebrew, and who were therefore dependent on English, French or other translations into European languages from the original Greek and Hebrew. This is a problem that the United Bible Societies are seeking to rectify through new translations, but in the meantime we need to be aware that many Christians in Africa and elsewhere in the majority world have access to the Bible only in versions that are a translation of a translation, which can make discerning the original sense of some texts more difficult. Readers with a knowledge of the Greek language may wish to translate the texts for themselves, and compare their reading with that offered here. On the few occasions on which I offer a reading significantly at variance from the standard translations, I provide an explanation in endnotes, including a transliteration of the relevant words. Readers of Greek will be able to appreciate the reasons for my translations, while others will at least be able to understand the issues at stake.

Rather than providing a detailed bibliography of academic writings on the subject of Baptism at the end of this work, briefer, annotated, suggestions for further reading will be provided at appropriate points in the text. It is hoped that these will enable readers with the time and the access to libraries to study the issues further, to deepen their understanding of early Christian theology and their understanding of Scripture, and to enrich their pastoral practice.

Suggested further reading

Two useful popular books on Baptism dealing with contemporary issues in Western Christianity are Green, *Baptism* and Kuhrt, *Believing in Baptism*. Both authors are Anglican and evangelical. Both books are widely respected and valued, even if lacking depth and detail in their biblical scholarship.

Two recent books that locate Baptism theologically and pastorally in the context of Christian life are Radcliffe, *Take the Plunge* and Smith, *Christian Ritualizing and the Baptismal Process*. The latter reflects a North American Episcopalian perspective and is profoundly influenced by Fowler, *The Stages of Faith*, a book that has made a significant impact on contemporary pastoral theology in the northern hemisphere. Timothy Radcliffe is a prolific Roman Catholic author and former Master of the Order of Preachers who addresses Baptism in the context of Christian living in the face of secularism and fundamentalism.

Different positions on the practice of Baptism within Anglicanism are represented by Buchanan, Owen and Wright, *Reforming Infant Baptism* and Dalby, *Open Baptism*. While these books present issues of concern in Western Christianity in an accessible, if apologetic, format, readers are encouraged to continue their reading in works that begin their treatment with a study of the biblical texts.

An excellent treatment of Baptism from the Reformed tradition is Brownson, *The Promise of Baptism*. While written in critical reflection on the North American context, this book models integration of scholarship and ministry and has much to offer to Christians and in particular those in ministry in all traditions.

For long a standard work in English on early Christian Baptism is Beasley-Murray, *Baptism in the New Testament*. The author is committed to a Baptist position, but in a self-critical way, and the scholarship in the book is sound and even-handed, even if dated after 50 years. Another book written from a Baptist perspective, but with a broad and eirenic ecumenical vision, is Roy, *Baptism, Reconciliation, and Unity*.

A shorter work by an eminent continental European Protestant scholar is Cullmann, *Baptism in the New Testament*. A book of similar vintage, emanating from English Methodism, is Flemington, *The New Testament Doctrine of Baptism*. A more recent and highly acclaimed study emanating from the Scandinavian Lutheran tradition is Hartman, *'Into the Name of the Lord Jesus'*.

An important treatment of Baptism, specifically dealing with Paul and written by an eminent Roman Catholic scholar, is Schnackenburg, *Baptism in the Thought of St Paul*. Another major Catholic contribution is Walsh, *The Sacraments of Initiation*.

The most important book on Baptism emanating from the Eastern Orthodox tradition is Schmemann, *Of Water and the Spirit*.

A study emphasizing the importance of the Holy Spirit, and reflecting upon Pentecostalism and the charismatic revival in Western Christianity, is Dunn, *Baptism in the Holy Spirit*. A treatment of this issue, emanating from the charismatic movement in the Roman Catholic Church, is McDonnell and Montague, *Christian Initiation and Baptism in the Holy Spirit*.

A study that considers Paul's baptismal teaching in the context of covenantal identity in Judaism and early Christianity is Christiansen, *The Covenant in Judaism and Paul*. This work is particularly illuminating in that it locates Paul and early Christianity in the cultural context within which the initiatory rituals derived their meaning.

Two works addressing the question of the influence of contemporary Graeco-Roman mystery cults on Paul's baptismal teaching are Wagner, *Pauline Baptism and the Pagan Mysteries* and Wedderburn, *Baptism and Resurrection*. Also important in this area is Finn, *From Death to Rebirth*. These books may have a significance not envisaged by their authors in that Christian ministers in Africa and other parts of the non-Western world are constantly seeking to make the gospel meaningful in their own context. The evaluation of indigenous customs and their legitimacy in the lives of Christians is a constant concern for the Church in Africa, Asia and Latin America. It is also an issue with which the churches of Europe and North America ought to be concerned, as spiritual hunger in the West seems to have led many to an interest in the pre-Christian cults of our forebears as well as in the spiritual disciplines of Asian religions.

More comprehensive treatments of Paul's theology can be found in Dunn, *The Theology of Paul the Apostle*; Fitzmyer, *Pauline Theology* and Gorman, *Cruciformity*. Useful introductions to Paul include Horrell, *An Introduction to the Study of Paul* and Sanders, *Paul*.

Studies extending their scope into the second century and beyond, and that discuss catechumenate as well as Baptism, include Finn, *Early Christian Baptism and the Catechumenate* and the collection edited by Ferguson, *Conversion, Catechumenate, and Baptism in the Early Church*. Ferguson has subsequently published the magisterial *Baptism in the Early Church*; while clearly committed to the Baptist position, the scholarship is impressive. A useful treatment of Baptism from New Testament times to the modern period is Whitaker, *The Baptismal Liturgy*. The same author has collected many key texts in English translation in *Documents of the Baptismal Liturgy*. A more recent study is Johnson, *The Rites of Christian Initiation*.

A comprehensive treatment of Baptism, principally in the Western Church, is the two-volume work of Spinks in the Liturgy, Worship and Society Series: *Early and Medieval Rituals and Theologies of Baptism* and *Reformation and Modern Rituals and Theologies of Baptism*.

An important study on ways the early Church understood Scripture and gave expression to this understanding in its liturgies is Daniélou, *The Bible and the Liturgy*. See also Jones et al., *The Study of Liturgy*. Also important in seeking to bring scholarship of the ancient Church to bear on contemporary Christian practice is Kavanagh, *The Shape of Baptism*. An important and ecumenically influential treatment of Baptism from the Orthodox tradition is Schmemann, *Of Water and the Spirit*.

A great deal of work on Baptism has been stimulated by the ecumenical movement of the last century. The Faith and Order Group of the World Council of Churches published *Baptism, Eucharist and Ministry*, commonly known as the Lima Document, in 1982. The formal responses of various member churches, as well as of other ecclesiastical bodies, were compiled and published by the World Council of Churches in several volumes during the following years. A digest of these entitled *Baptism, Eucharist and Ministry 1982–1990*, with reflections on the process and on the responses received, was published, also by the World Council of Churches, in 1990. Subsequent World Council of Churches Faith and Order Papers on Baptism are Best and Heller (eds), *Becoming a Christian* and Best (ed.), *Baptism Today*. Another useful collection addressing contemporary issues is Root and Saarinen, *Baptism and the Unity of the Church*. An important book that reflects on this process and continuing ecumenical dialogues is Wood, *One Baptism*.

Notes

1 See in particular Cross, *1 Peter*. While much of the detail of the argument of Cross, and similar arguments by other scholars, is disputed, the importance of Baptism in giving expression to early Christian thought and experience, as reflected in the letter, is clear. See Kelly's discussion in *The Epistles of Peter and of Jude*, pp. 15–20 and also the treatments of Beasley-Murray, *Baptism in the New Testament*; Cullmann, *Baptism in the New Testament* and Dunn, *Baptism in the Holy Spirit*.

2 See Beasley-Murray, *Baptism in the New Testament*; Cullmann, *Baptism in the New Testament*; Dunn, *Baptism in the Holy Spirit*; Webb, *John the Baptizer and Prophet* and Taylor, *John the Baptist within Second Temple Judaism*.

3 See Brown, *The Gospel According to John*, pp. cxi–cxiv; Ng, *Water Symbolism in John* and Suggit, *Down to Earth and Up to Heaven*.

4 For the text of the *Didache* see editions of the *Apostolic Fathers*, all with English translations of the Greek, edited by Lightfoot, Lake or Ehrman. The most important commentary on the *Didache* currently available is that by Niederwimmer. Also important is Milavec, *The Didache*.

Paul in Context

Saul, later known as Paul, was a devout Jew whose convictions as a Pharisee led him into vigorous opposition to the early Christian movement. After a radical conversion experience, he became at least as vigorous an apostle of Christianity, particularly among the non-Jewish nations, conveniently and collectively known as gentiles (from the Greek *gentes*, nations). During two decades and more of evangelization, Paul established churches in several cities in provinces of the Roman Empire that now lie within the modern countries of Greece and Turkey. It was in his continuing pastoral oversight of these churches that Paul wrote most of the letters bearing his name, which now form part of the Christian New Testament.[1] The exceptions are Romans and Colossians, which are addressed to churches Paul had not himself founded. These two letters apparently represent Paul's first direct communication with the Christian communities in Rome and Colossae. Letters such as Galatians and 1 and 2 Corinthians are not Paul's first communication with the churches addressed, but supplement his previous teaching in the light of new circumstances that had arisen in those communities. In the case of Corinth, the letters follow up not merely Paul's mission preaching and initial teaching to his converts but also return visits Paul had made to Corinth and previous written and oral communications, alluded to in the canonical letters, but which we no longer have.

The Christians who first read letters such as Galatians or 1 Corinthians, or heard them read aloud in meetings of the church, would previously have heard Paul's mission preaching, and been converted through it; the exceptions, of course, would have been any converts made by the church subsequent to Paul's departure. We can nevertheless assume that recipients of Paul's letters had, either directly or indirectly through the agency of the church, previously received his initial teaching to his new converts, and its continuation for as long as Paul and his companions remained in that particular place. In some cities, such as Corinth, this may have been for a period of a year or more (Acts 18.1–18). In others, such as Thessalonica, Paul's mission was limited to a matter of weeks on account of local hostility (Acts 17.1–10). Even in the latter case, the recipients of these letters were not strangers to Paul but communities who had heard his oral preaching and teaching and been formed by them into a church, and had received directly from him the traditions concerning the gospel (cf. 1 Cor. 15.1–7), and instruction concerning Christian life. The letters continue an established and dynamic relationship between Paul and his churches, and therefore build on previous knowledge of Paul and his theology. As the recipients of the letters, members of these communities were familiar with the specific pastoral situations Paul is addressing, and he therefore does not need to describe them in detail. For our purposes it would of course have been very useful if Paul had done precisely this. We would then have been able to see more clearly how he applies Christian teaching to specific issues, and have gained some insight into precisely how doctrines and principles were brought to bear upon practical pastoral questions. As it is, however, we need to work with the material that is available to us: the letters, texts separated in time, space and culture from the contexts to which they were originally addressed. This gives us the responsibility for working out how we apply Christian doctrine as contained in the New Testament to the life of the Church today.

While the letters form part of a continuing pastoral relationship between Paul and the churches he had founded, for us today they are all that remains of his teaching. Nevertheless, the letters have acquired an authority for Christians of all time by virtue of their inclusion in the New Testament. They are also frequently cited, often referring to Paul simply as 'the apostle', by the church fathers of the second and subsequent centuries, as Christian doctrine was being debated and defined. If we are to begin to understand Paul's theology, and what it means for Christians living in the twenty-first century, we need first to understand so far as possible the situations to which the letters were originally addressed. Many specific details will always be beyond our grasp, but the process of attempted reconstruction can in itself be informative. The more we can bring alive the situations in which the first Christians lived, the more we can understand the teaching they received from Paul.

The churches Paul established were located in cities, many of them seaports and trading centres, linked by Mediterranean sailing routes and by the network of roads built by the Romans throughout their vast empire. The dominant culture in this area is known as Hellenism, the Greek system of beliefs, values and customs that had been superimposed on the other cultures of the region from the time of Alexander the Great (c.330 BC), and even earlier in those areas to which the Greek city states had extended their influence eastwards in competition with the Persian Empire. For people living in the areas we now call the Middle East, Hellenism was an imperial culture, akin to the European cultures that have been superimposed on African societies during the past centuries, and on South American cultures for much longer. By the time of Paul, Hellenism had been the dominant culture for a period much longer than that of European dominance in Africa in the nineteenth and twentieth centuries, and of approximately equal duration to the period of Roman rule in Britain during the first centuries of this era. In urban areas especially, Middle Eastern societies may have become more thoroughly Hellenized than many modern African and Asian societies have become Westernized.

Hellenization, like Westernization, did not mean that local cultures were completely eradicated or absorbed into the dominant culture; on the contrary, a coalescence of cultures gradually took place, so that distinctive local customs, languages, beliefs and values persisted within and alongside the dominant Hellenism. In cities, many of which had large and diverse immigrant communities, much more complex processes of cultural contact, including both assimilation and conflict, took place within the wider phenomenon of Hellenism. Some cultures and belief systems were more resistant than others to assimilation into the dominant culture, and this was particularly true of Judaism. The Jews' belief in the one true God distinguished them from other nations of the region, most of whom worshipped many deities and easily identified their own gods and goddesses with those of Greece and Rome. Jews, on the other hand, needed to negotiate their coexistence with their neighbours in Hellenistic societies. While some sought to demonstrate

3

an affinity to philosophical schools that articulated monotheistic ideas, the majority accommodated themselves to their surrounding societies as the circumstances permitted. While some Jews living in diaspora undoubtedly assimilated to Hellenistic cults and culture in ways that would have outraged their compatriots in Judaea, others found ways to preserve and promote Jewish identity, way of life and forms of worship in alien places. Not only were vibrant communities established in many places but these Jewish communities attracted adherents to their worship and way of life from among their gentile neighbours. Some undoubtedly converted fully to Judaism, the males among them undergoing circumcision as a sign of their incorporation into God's covenant with Abraham. But the majority would have remained on the periphery of the Jewish communities, adopting some beliefs and customs but retaining their inherited identity and commitments also. Gentiles such as these would have been among the first to hear the Christian gospel proclaimed. One of Paul's principal achievements was to find a way gentile Christians could remain within their inherited nations and cultures while accepting all that was essential to the gospel, including the Christian claim to Abraham's inheritance. His teaching on Baptism, as we shall see, was an important aspect of this.

The way human beings understand themselves is a product of their culture and environment. The modern Western world emphasizes the human being as an individual, a self-sufficient and autonomous entity with inalienable rights in society. We can easily recognize that this has influenced many contemporary understandings of Baptism, including such notions as 'believers' Baptism', which depend on a conception of personal conversion, a personal faith and a personal saviour; 'a personal relationship with God' as it is sometimes expressed, with 'personal' understood to mean 'individual'. It is in such individualistic cultural contexts that questions might be raised about the propriety of parents' entering their children into the life-long Christian commitment symbolized by Baptism. The society in which Paul lived perceived the human being in a very different way. 'Personal' did not mean 'individual'. The individual was not understood as autonomous and self-sufficient but as a dependent and integral part of a community, and in particular of the family or household into which he or she was born or was transferred through marriage, employment or sale as a slave. To be was to belong, to be integrated, to be identified as a member of a family or household and of the wider society of which the household was an integral social and economic unit. Anthropologists have termed this phenomenon dyadism.[2] Common identity and association were therefore much more important than individual identity and autonomy in all aspects of life, including activities that might be classified as 'religion' in modern societies. The African concept of *ubuntu* may well approximate the ancient sense of identity and belonging more closely than do modern Western individualistic notions of personhood.

Dyadism has considerable significance for understanding early Christian teaching about Baptism, including that of Paul. Individuals' self-understanding, and the ways they were perceived by others, were fundamentally different from modern individualist notions of identity. People were defined by membership of groups and not in terms of their own individual and particular characteristics or qualities. Characteristics perceived in people were regarded as having been derived from and as reflecting the group to which they belonged and from which they derived their identity. A Christian was therefore someone who belonged to a Christian group, a church. Belonging to a church meant accepting the doctrines and observing the customs of that particular group, and reflecting these in the wider society. The same would apply to membership of any other group. In other words, to be a Christian in the world of Paul was primarily a matter of belonging, and only secondarily and consequently of believing in the sense of giving intellectual assent to a particular set of doctrines. Believing, in fact, means far more in the biblical sense than in modern usage. The Greek verb *pisteuo*, commonly rendered into English as 'I believe', derives from the same root as the noun *pistis*, meaning 'faith'. In English, 'faith' has a wider semantic range than 'belief' and entails commitment as well as intellectual assent. This applies also, and more emphatically, to the Greek *pisteuo* and *pistis*. To believe in the biblical sense means not merely to acknowledge the truth of certain teachings but to embody them through belonging to the community that represents those teachings, and through living in accordance therewith. For the early Christians, faith was a matter of living out Christian doctrine, complying with a way of life defined by the Church, and not a matter of adopting certain opinions. This has significant implications for our understanding of Paul's teaching on Baptism, as we shall see.

The basic unit of society in the cities of the Graeco-Roman world was the family or household, *oikos* or *oikia* in Greek, *domus* in Latin. The notion of family is quite unlike the Western nuclear family or, for that matter, the African extended family. It is not defined by biological kinship at all but by the relationship of dependence and subordination between its members and the head or patron of the household. This personage was known as the *oikodespotes* in Greek or *paterfamilias* in Latin. As well as the biological family of the head, the household included any slaves, servants, clients and any other retainers directly or indirectly dependent upon the patron. Any business interests of the head were an activity of the household, which accordingly embraced all persons engaged in the business, whatever their status and role and however geographically distant from the residence of their patron they might be located.

A household did not necessarily occupy a single physical address, such as villas that have been excavated in places such as Pompeii, Corinth and Ephesus. Such homes could belong to only the most prosperous in society, and not all servile members, still less clients, would have lived on the premises. Many a household would have lived in their place of work, such as a shop or other small business premises. Others would have occupied tenements, which varied considerably in space and comfort. Many of the more prosperous households would have been dispersed between quarters in different centres, according to business and trading interests. Whatever the nature of their residence, the household was as pervasive as it was fundamental to social structure in the ancient world. This did not mean that every household was stable; on the contrary, economic pressures and political misfortune, as well as internal forces, could precipitate the fragmentation or dissolution of a household and the dispersal of its members. Displaced people might find refuge and security as a client, servant, or slave in another household, or become part of the destitute and potentially vagabond subcultures that inhabited the Graeco-Roman cities.

The real and perceived threats to its viability generated a measure of solidarity in the household, and the authority of the patron was legally enforceable. The household, like other social units in the ancient world, was a religious community that revered ancestral spirits as well as deities favoured by the patron. While there were restrictions on Jews' converting their slaves to their religion, household patrons nonetheless enjoyed plenary powers over the lives of members of the household. This authority would have been more remote and less easily enforced in larger and dispersed households. Nevertheless, belonging to the household in principle implied sharing the allegiance of the patron to the cults and deities he or she favoured, within and potentially without the household. Often a shrine to deities whose patronage was sought, as well as to the ancestors of the family, was located in the home. This meant that cultic observances, involving all members of the household, also took place in the house on a daily basis. Religious belief and practice were not matters of individual choice or conviction but were determined by membership of the household. 'It was ordinarily assumed that the subordinate members of a household, particularly the servile ones, would share the religion(s) of the master.'[3] Personal conviction was subordinate to the will of the all – powerful patron. Conformity, if not imposed by force, was brought about by group cohesion and solidarity. Legal power and group psychology combined to make religion a corporate act of the family or, perhaps more accurately, the personal allegiance of the head became the conviction of the members. Any who did not share intellectually the conviction could be compelled to practise outward conformity in the devotional and cultic life of the household.

'If we are to understand the biblical texts rightly, we must radically free ourselves from modern individualistic thinking.' So wrote Joachim Jeremias, one of the foremost New Testament scholars of the twentieth century, in 1960. More than half a century later we continue to grapple with what this means. Developments in scholarship, in particular application of the social sciences to ancient societies, have made possible a more adequate understanding of the world in which Paul lived, founded churches and wrote letters. It is important that those wishing to discover the teaching of the New

Testament make use of these insights, not least as they concern institutions such as the family. Jeremias continues:

> [I]n particular keep before our eyes the fact that the family represented by the father of the household was in old times much more strongly experienced as a unity than today. All important questions were decided by the father . . . and his decision was binding on all. In particular in its relation to God was the household a unity.[4]

These forces of cohesion and conformity operated when conversion took place as well as in situations of unbroken continuity. 'It was normal for the ancient mind to regard the faith of the father . . . as decisive, if a household broke away from the old religious community and embraced a new religion.'[5] This is reflected in the accounts of household conversion and Baptism in Acts, many but not all of which are the fruit of Paul's proclamation of the gospel. Paul also alludes to the Baptism of entire households in 1 Corinthians 1.16.

While household conversion and corporate integration into the community must be recognized as having been normative in the early Church, the situation was not as simple and uniform as Jeremias may be understood to suggest. Social relationships were much more complex than this, and there clearly were occasions on which the authority of the head of the household was less than absolute. This could be the case when the wife was of higher social status than the husband, or married on terms that enabled her to retain some control of the wealth she brought into the marriage and the household. A woman in such a position might be able to exercise some autonomy, and even to influence the way her children were reared, as may be the case where Paul addresses women in the church whose husbands are not Christian (cf. 1 Cor. 7.12–15). Here the authority of the head of the household had been moderated by conflicting social, economic or legal forces. We shall consider some specific instances in the course of this study.

While the solidarity of the household as a social unit is not to be underestimated, we also need to understand that members were not of equal status within it. The heirs of the householder would have enjoyed a particular standing. The preferred heirs would naturally have been the children of the householder and his wife. It was not unusual for the householder also to have children by other women of the household, such as slaves, but these children would not ordinarily have enjoyed the same status and privileges as those of the marriage, and they would not normally have stood to inherit the estate. However, Graeco-Roman householders were generally anxious not to see their estates divided or dissolved at their death, and their heirs lose status in society on account of reduced circumstances. Hence the tendency to have few children of the marriage, and for the male householder to divert his sexual energies and desires away from the marital bed. The risk, of course, was that there might be no male heir at all, if the marriage were childless or the only son were killed in war or succumbed to disease. It was accordingly quite commonplace for heirs to be adopted so as to ensure the continuation of the household. An heir could be chosen from close relations, such as a nephew, or could be a son-in-law or the son of a friend who had 'an heir and a spare' or, exceptionally, could be chosen from the children born to the householder out of wedlock. Roman law recognized a complete change in identity and legal status with adoption, and facilitated this process. An example that illustrates how widespread and accepted this custom was is that no Roman emperor until Titus (AD 79–81) was the legitimate biological son of his predecessor; Augustus, Tiberius, Gaius Caligula and Nero were all adopted heirs, and the remaining emperors all came to power through military coups. While status in the household could in principle be changed by legal means, we nevertheless need to recognize the privileged position of the family over against dependent members of the household, be they slaves, freed or freeborn, and of males over against females of otherwise comparable status in the household and in society.

The family was not the only unit but it was the foundational unit of society in urban Greece and Asia Minor. Other groups included trade guilds, burial societies and voluntary associations. There were also clubs for the various expatriate communities that gathered in the trading centres, and the cults of their deities, of which the Jewish synagogues are an example. All of these were likely to include cultic observances in their communal activities, and not only those established specifically to promote the cult of a particular deity. Corporate dining was another popular activity, which we need to understand as highly ritualized and as incorporating devotions to the patron deities of the group. None of these organizations would have been free from the system of patronage that governed civic life in any place. Early Christian groups need to be understood within this context, and the similarities and differences between early Christian life and worship and the activities of similar organizations recognized.

Another feature of ancient society, which differs considerably from modern Western societies, was its conception of and attitude to supernatural power. Spiritual beings were perceived to be present in and controlling all aspects of the natural order. These spiritual powers were regarded as capable of doing good or harm to human beings. Rather than being governed by moral principles, they were understood to be amenable to human persuasion in the exercise of their power.

Ritual was the means whereby supernatural power was invoked, in order that it might be directed to the protection and benefit of the one performing the rite or on whose behalf it was administered. Rituals are symbolic words and actions by which human beings seek to attain desired objectives through harnessing the power of the supernatural being to whom worship, sacrifice or prayer is offered. Ritual was institutionalized in the many cults that proliferated in the Graeco-Roman world. In addition to the domestic shrines already mentioned, temples and other shrines in public places were available for the performance of rituals, including the offering of sacrifices, to a specific deity or deities. Some cult centres, most notably that of Apollo at Delphi, were noted as places where the divine will could be discerned or the future foretold through the agency of cultic mediums or through analysis of such phenomena as the innards of sacrificial animals. Outside the cult centres, and without the assistance of their functionaries, divine power could be invoked through less formal rituals or by use of charms, commonly known as amulets, and oaths.

Different rituals were performed on different occasions through the year, to mark the seasons and to accompany or prepare for events of importance and to give thanks for success achieved or to seek remedy in the event of failure. Particular rites marked the stages in the human life cycle, accompanying such events as birth, puberty, marriage and death. These are collectively known as rites of passage, and have been the subject of extensive study, not least by anthropologists. As well as seeking divine protection over the transitional stages in life, which were widely perceived to be particularly hazardous, these rites gave expression to the culturally understood significance of the status attained by those who underwent them. As is well known, Jews circumcised boys when they were a week old, literally on the eighth day from their birth, to mark their membership of God's covenant with Abraham. While they became members of Israel and of the covenant by birth, it was nonetheless considered necessary that this be symbolized through circumcision. Other rites accompanied puberty and marriage, and funeral rites were performed at death to ensure the transition of the deceased from earthly life to the afterlife.

While Baptism undoubtedly became a rite of passage in later Christianity, whether at birth or at puberty or even at the point of death, this is not how the rite functioned or was understood during the earliest period. We cannot therefore simply equate Christian Baptism with Jewish circumcision in Paul's letters. Baptism functioned not as a rite of passage but as a conversion–incorporation rite, representing not the continuum in the established life cycle of a particular cultural group but rather the fundamental disruption in this cycle that saw some aspects of inherited identity repudiated and Christian identity conferred. '[C]onversion was embedded in richly articulated and complex ritual processes'[6] in the ancient world, and this was at least as true of incorporation into the early Christian communities as of any other transition in cultural identity and cultic practice. While conversion–incorporation rites can, and often do, imitate the outward form of rites of passage, as in the case of Jewish proselyte circumcision,[7] we need to appreciate the distinction between the ritual accompaniment to physical birth and the ritual expression of symbolic birth into a new identity and community. That this point is of crucial and often neglected importance in understanding New Testament teaching on Baptism will become clear in Chapter 2.

While we have emphasized that Baptism is to be understood as a conversion–incorporation rite, it is important that we also recognize that conversion is not to be understood simplistically as a matter of individual opinion or conviction, and the free and deliberate change in membership from one religious community to another that follows from this. We have already noted that religious affiliation was largely a matter of household membership rather than personal choice. Therefore most conversions to Christianity during the early years of the Church would have been involuntary and collective rather than individual and voluntary.

Recent studies in religious conversion by psychologists and sociologists have emphasized the collective and social process involved, in modern societies as well as in ancient. Becoming a member of a new community is the crucial change, and alterations to belief and behaviour are taught or acquired thereafter, so as to reinforce the change in identity that has been effected. Initiation rites represent and effect incorporation into the new community, and the change in identity is consolidated through continuing instruction in the beliefs and values of the community, and guidance in the adoption of a lifestyle that reflects those beliefs and values. Even where conversion is corporate and involuntary, therefore, the process serves to internalize the change that has been ritually effected.

Ritual was not understood as merely demonstrative action but as an effective means of harnessing and transmitting divine power for specified purposes. This may seem close to magic from a modern Western secular perspective, but in the ancient world magic was not a clandestine, or necessarily sinister, activity divorced from the mainstream of religious and cultic life. Nor was any religious or cultic activity meaningful apart from interaction between human and divine beings, and the invocation of the power of the latter for the benefit of the former. If we are to understand Paul's teaching on Baptism, we need to appreciate that the Holy Spirit was not believed to be some abstract and elusive concept, but the power of God invoked and transmitted in the ritual so that the one baptized became a member of the Church, embodied Christ's presence and power in the world, and became destined for eternal salvation. Christian Baptism evolved in a world in which physical substances were routinely used in symbolically significant actions to harness and direct divine power in order to attain specific objectives. We will discuss this point in detail further in the course of this study, but must recognize at the outset that Christian rituals cannot be understood apart from religious beliefs and practices in the world in which they originated.

The Judaism from which Christianity emerged was distinct in many ways among the cults of the Graeco-Roman world but cannot be understood in isolation from its religious and cultural environment. Insofar as it was the religious expression of a particular people, with ties to a traditional homeland and its cultic life centred on a particular temple, and with a diaspora that maintained stronger or weaker links therewith, Judaism was entirely similar to other national cults of the region. However, monotheism and the exclusive claims of the God of Israel as creator and ruler of the world meant that Judaism could not be so completely assimilated into the syncretistic and polytheistic patterns of cultic devotion prevalent in the Roman Empire. Nor could worship of the God of Israel be practised alongside participation in other cults without compromise. This does not imply that no such compromises were made, or that all ethnic Jews remained rigorously monotheistic worshippers of the God of Israel. The same was to be true of early Christians, as we will observe when studying some of the texts in the next chapter. Nevertheless, Jewish communities scattered throughout the Mediterranean world tended to maintain an exclusive and distinct identity, on which Graeco-Roman authors commented, usually with derision or suspicion. We should therefore conclude that Jews generally did not integrate as fully as did other expatriates, either with other immigrants or with the local populations, in the places where they lived. As a Jewish movement, Christianity shared many of the characteristics of other Jewish groups and was not generally recognized as a distinct, non-ethnic religious movement until the second century. This had considerable implications for the growth and spread of the Church, but we are concerned at present with the distinctive nature of Jewish cultic observances.

Monotheism and exclusivity, together with the Prophetic tradition that emphasized divine righteousness, meant that rituals tended not to be understood in as crudely mechanical a sense in Judaism as was often the case in Graeco-Roman paganism, with its plethora of lesser deities. God's sovereignty in the universe meant that God could not be manipulated through ritual or by other means, and that supernatural beings were subject to God's sovereignty in the exercise of their power. This did not in any way diminish the divine power perceived to be present and effective in Jewish and Christian ritual; on the contrary, the power transmitted through the ritual was regarded as more awesome in that it was beyond human control. The power of the Holy Spirit present in Christian Baptism meant that the rite was not merely the demonstrative action of human beings but an effective vehicle of sovereign divine power in the world.

The rite of Baptism involves the use of water to enact the transformation of the convert from being an outsider to being a member of the Church. Irrespective of any specific liturgical formula or associated rites that may have accompanied and expounded the meaning of the ritual, we need to take into account the symbolic significance of water in the ancient world.[8] The symbolic significance and ritual use of water, as of any other substance, derives from its natural use but gives sacred meaning to the natural properties and their cultural appropriation. Water is used in most societies primarily as a cleansing agent and as a source of nourishment for people, animals and plants, in particular livestock and food crops. The cultic significance ascribed to water in any society would naturally reflect its role in the economy and ecology. Most societies are very conscious of their dependence on water for life, particularly in areas as prone to drought and water shortages as are many parts of the Middle East. Where hard labour is required to obtain water and convey it in adequate quantities to the place where it is needed, as would have been the case before the invention of modern piping and pumping infrastructures, and where such plumbing as had been developed in the ancient cities did not extend to the homes and workplaces of the poor, the value of water would have been more fully appreciated than in places where its availability was taken for granted. In the ancient world the capacity for famine relief was limited and the consequences of drought could therefore be fatal for whole communities. The symbolic significance of water as a source of life is likely to be emphasized in such contexts. Rain-inducing rituals practised in some societies are a reflection of this, and water is also central to many fertility cults. Similarly, the ways water is used for cleansing purposes are likely to be reflected in its cultic use for ritual washing.

Modern people may be inclined to think of purity in terms of hygiene, as though this is an objective and scientifically based notion. Purity and impurity are in reality culturally determined concepts, and even the most rational and scientific beliefs and practices are shaped by conscious or subconscious presuppositions as to what constitutes purity and impurity. Water and other purifying agents are used within a culturally determined framework to effect purity where and when this is required. Ritual cleansing and purification with water of people and objects were widespread in the ancient world, in Judaism as well as in Graeco-Roman paganism, and the most basic of human ablutions was not without cultic overtones. In the early Church, water was therefore a culturally available symbol for invoking divine power to impart ritual purity and to enable life and growth.

As well as being significant in itself, ritual purity was in many ancient cults a prerequisite to worship. Washing all or part of the body before offering sacrifices or performing other rituals was widespread in Graeco-Roman paganism and in Judaism. The Greek epic the *Iliad*, traditionally ascribed to Homer and dated to approximately the ninth century BC, includes an account of a sacrifice to the god Apollo. Before the offering was placed on the altar, and before the priest recited the appropriate prayers, the participants all washed their hands (1.446–56). A similar observance in ancient Israel, attributed to King David, is reflected in Psalm 26.6: 'I wash my hands in innocence, and go around your altar, O LORD.' Detailed prescriptions for ritual washing in ancient Israel can be found in the Hebrew Bible or *Torah* (Hebrew for 'law'), most particularly in Leviticus 15 – 16. These have been interpreted and applied in Judaism throughout its history, including the time of Jesus and Paul. Ritual washing was an important part of the communal life of the Qumran community, as reflected in the Dead Sea Scrolls (written between the late second century BC and the destruction of Qumran in AD 68). The rabbinic traditions of interpretation of the biblical law were committed to writing from the second century AD onwards. The collections known as the *Mishnah* and *Tosephta* each have a tractate called *Mikvaoth* that deals with ritual washing. While these date from well after the time of Paul, they nevertheless illustrate the scrupulosity with which at least some Jews practised ritual purity. During the period in which the Christian Church was established, the homes of pious and prosperous Jews were often equipped with ritual baths known as *mikvaoth* (singular *mikveh*), in which men immersed themselves before offering their daily prayers. *Mikvaoth* were provided for public use in the vicinity of the temple in Jerusalem, and all worshippers were required to immerse themselves before entering the temple precincts. Particular provision was made for the ritual purification of priests serving in the temple. A ritual bath for this purpose is prescribed in Exodus 30.17–21, and such a facility was provided within the temple area (cf. Ecclus. 50.3; *Mishnah Middoth* 5.4; *Letter of Aristeas* 89–90; Josephus, *Jewish War* 5.165). Ritual cleansing as a preparatory observance also entered the Christian liturgy, where the priest washes his hands after preparing the altar for the Eucharist, before commencing the prayer of consecration. Many recite quietly the words of Psalm 26.6, cited above, while doing so. Ritual washing before prayer is also observed in Islam, and mosques are equipped with fountains for this purpose. While these cleansing rites are in no way initiatory and in this sense are unlike Baptism, they nonetheless illustrate just how integral to worship cleansing with water was in the ancient world. On the other hand, in that Christian life beyond the liturgy is often conceptualized as a 'living sacrifice' (Rom. 12.1), Baptism can in some sense be understood as preparing and purifying Christians for the lives of worship, witness and service that lie ahead of them.

Modern Western Christians tend to draw a distinction between 'outward rite' and 'spiritual reality' in Baptism, as in the other sacraments. But we need to recognize the close association between physical and moral or spiritual purity in the ancient mind, and that ritual reflects and reinforces this connection. Paul was fully aware that Baptism needed to be accompanied by transformation of the lives of those baptized but this does not mean that the Holy Spirit was not received in and through the rite of Baptism itself. As we shall see, modern distinctions between ritual and spiritual reality are a product of Western rationalism rather than being integral to the thought world of the first Christians. Modern biblical scholarship is a product largely of this rationalism, accompanied and perhaps sanctified by a Protestant suspicion of ritual, and is accordingly often blind to the conscious and subconscious function and power of ritual in ancient – and modern – societies.

In this chapter we have identified a number of aspects of the culture of the world in which the apostle Paul proclaimed the gospel and established communities of those converted through his preaching. These have concerned ways personhood was understood, and religious beliefs and practices functioned, in ancient society. The challenges posed to modern Western, highly secularized and individualized notions of Christian belief and practice are immediately apparent. The insights of sociology, anthropology and the history of religions into ancient culture are essential to reaching a sound understanding of the function and significance of rituals in early Christianity. As we proceed to study the texts in Paul's letters in which he refers to the rite of Baptism, we need to bear in mind how this and other cultic practices were understood in the world of Paul and his churches.

Suggested further reading

Malina, *The New Testament World*. Malina has pioneered the application of social scientific approaches, in particular cultural anthropology, to the study of early Christianity. His subsequent books include *Christian Origins and Cultural Anthropology* and several works on the Gospels and Revelation. Malina and Neyrey have jointly written *Portraits of Paul*. Neyrey has also published a collection entitled *Paul, in Other Words* and edited a useful collection entitled *The Social World of Luke–Acts*.

The notion of corporate personality in Israel in the Old Testament period was definitively articulated by Robinson in 1935. Robinson's two seminal lectures have been usefully published in *Corporate Personality in Ancient Israel*. Considerable refinement to the theory has been required. See especially Rogerson, *Anthropology and the Old Testament*.

Several important books on Judaism and the Jewish diaspora have appeared in recent years: Barclay, *Jews in the Mediterranean Diaspora*; Collins, *Between Athens and Jerusalem*; Harland, *Associations, Synagogues, and Congregations* and Trebilco, *Jewish Communities in Asia Minor*.

Meeks, *The First Urban Christians*. This book is an excellent description of life in the cities of the Graeco-Roman world and sheds a great deal of light on the context of the early Christian communities. The work is sociological and historical in its approach.

Gehring has emphasized the importance of the household in early Christianity in *House Church and Mission*. Adams has challenged aspects of his thesis in *The Earliest Christian Meeting Places*. While he illustrates a diversity of possible physical settings for early Christian worship, the pervasiveness of the household as a social, economic and legal entity is not to be overlooked.

Osiek and Balch have advanced scholarly understanding of the family in ancient society in *Families in the New Testament World*. They have also edited the collection that develops their project further, *Early Christian Families in Context*. Two important studies of the family, dealing specifically with the place of children in the early Church, are Bakke, *When Children became People* and Strange, *Children in the Early Church*.

Theissen, in *A Theory of Primitive Christian Religion*, explores ways religion functions in social life and includes a substantial treatment of ways rituals function to define identity and to give expression to belief and explain experience. Theissen's earlier books include *The Social Setting of Pauline Christianity*.

There have been many recent studies of Graeco-Roman religion. Particularly influential has been MacMullen, *Paganism in the Roman Empire*. A study that relates the religions of the Graeco-Roman world specifically to Christian origins is Klauck, *The Religious Context of Early Christianity*. The encounter between the early Church and Graeco-Roman religiosity is studied in the same author's *Magic and Paganism in Early Christianity*. Also useful are Dickie, *Magic and Magicians in the Greco-Roman World* and Price, *Religions of the Ancient Greeks*. The integral relationship of magic and religion is of crucial importance to understanding the issues of this study.

A treatment of ancient religious conceptions can be found in van der Leeuw, *Religion in Essence and Manifestation*. An important treatment of socially and culturally defined notions relating to purity and its consequences can be found in Douglas, *Purity and Danger*. The concept of purity in Judaism is discussed by Neusner in *The Idea of Purity in Ancient Judaism*. Jewish observances of the period are discussed very usefully by Sanders in *Judaism: Practice and Belief*.

On the social function of rituals and in particular initiation, see Bell, *Ritual Theory, Ritual Practice* and *Ritual: Perspectives and Dimensions*. Also important are Driver, *Liberating Rites*; la Fontaine, *Initiation*; van Gennep, *The Rites of Passage*; Mol, *Identity and the Sacred*; Smith, *To Take Place* and Turner, *The Ritual Process*.

The importance of awareness of the function and social power of rituals and symbolism in early Christianity is demonstrated by de Maris in *The New Testament in its Ritual World*. See also Dillistone, *Christianity and Symbolism* and *The Power of Symbols*. The symbolism associated with Baptism is discussed by Jensen in *Living Water* and *Baptismal Imagery in Early Christianity*. A book published too late for consideration in this volume is Uro, *Ritual and Christian Beginnings*.

An important book dealing with religious conversion in the New Testament is Gaventa, *From Darkness to Light*. Specifically on Paul, see Segal, *Paul the Convert*. A wider treatment of the phenomenon in the ancient world is Finn, *From Death to Rebirth*. See also Kreider, *The Change of Conversion and the Origin of Christendom*.

The most important recent book on religious conversion is that of Rambo, *Understanding Religious Conversion*. Several psychologists and sociologists have written often collaborative articles on the theoretical issues, as well as studies of particular groups and their recruitment and retention of adherents. Among the most important have been Snow and Machalek, 'The Convert as a Social Type' and 'The Sociology of Conversion'. The research of Snow and Machalek informed my 'The Social Nature of Conversion in the Early Christian World'.

Notes

1 Modern scholarship distinguishes between undisputed letters, those universally acknowledged as having been written by Paul, and disputed letters, which many scholars believe to have been written after Paul's death, using his name in order to invoke his authority. The undisputed letters are Romans, 1 and 2 Corinthians, Galatians, Philippians, 1 Thessalonians and Philemon. Disputed letters are Ephesians, Colossians, 2 Thessalonians, 1 and 2 Timothy and Titus. The practice of writing documents in the name of a revered figure of a previous generation is known as pseudepigraphy. This was

a common practice in the ancient world, where modern concepts of fraud, copyright, plagiarism and deception were not understood as they are today. These issues are discussed in commentaries on the individual letters and also in introductions to the New Testament, such as Brown, *An Introduction to the New Testament*; Collins, *Introduction to the New Testament*; Johnson, *The Writings of the New Testament*; Kee, *Understanding the New Testament*; Koester, *History and Literature of Early Christianity, I: Introduction to the New Testament* or Kümmel, *Introduction to the New Testament*.

2 For an explanation of this concept see Malina, *The New Testament World*, pp. 51–70. While Malina may overstate his case, the point he and others make is nonetheless important. For treatments of the family in ancient society see especially Osiek and Balch, *Families in the New Testament World* and Balch and Osiek (eds), *Early Christian Families in Context*.

3 Meeks, *The First Urban Christians*, p. 30.

4 Jeremias, *Infant Baptism in the First Four Centuries*, p. 22.

5 Jeremias, *Infant Baptism in the First Four Centuries*, p. 22.

6 Finn, *From Death to Rebirth*, p. 34.

7 Many gentiles associated in various ways with Jewish communities and participated in their worship without making the total commitment to, and identification with, the nation of Israel and its god, implied in becoming a proselyte. The majority, referred to as 'God-fearers' in Acts 13.26; 16.14; (17.4); 18.7, were much more loosely associated with the synagogues. We should be aware that the Greek terms behind the English translations in Acts are not uniform, and 'God-fearer' should therefore not be regarded as a technical term or official category akin to associate membership of the synagogue. Nevertheless the term represents a recognizable but diverse phenomenon, described clearly by Cohen in *The Beginnings of Jewishness*.

8 This is discussed in considerable detail, but accessibly, by Dillistone in *Christianity and Symbolism*, pp. 183–220.

2

Baptism in the Pauline Letters

The most important sources of Paul's teaching on Baptism are his letters to the Roman, Galatian and Corinthian churches. Romans, as noted previously, was not addressed to a church founded by Paul but nevertheless contains some of the most valuable insights into his thought, not least on Baptism. Galatians and the Corinthian letters, on the other hand, are addressed to churches founded by Paul and concern specific pastoral situations that had arisen in those churches subsequent to his mission. It is in the context of addressing these issues that Paul draws upon the Christians' experience of Baptism in order to direct their lives as a community and as individuals.

The letters to the Colossians and Ephesians, and those to Timothy and Titus, are widely considered to be deutero – Pauline or pseudepigraphical. By this we mean that, as has been argued by some scholars, these letters were written after Paul's death, and that his name is used in order to claim his authority and gain acceptance of the letters in the churches to which they were sent.[1] Attribution of the name of a famous person to a document written by another was a common practice in the ancient world and did not have the same connotations of fraud and deception that such a practice would have in modern societies; on the contrary, such documents were frequently written with the intention of honouring and enhancing the reputation of the person to whom authorship was ascribed. While we need to be aware of this issue, Colossians and Ephesians, and the letters to Timothy and Titus, nonetheless clearly originate from within the Pauline churches. Even if they were not written by Paul himself, they nevertheless reflect the way his teaching was interpreted and developed in new pastoral situations that arose after his death.

The apostle Paul was more than simply an individual. His name represents a broader movement within early Christianity, in which other men and women worked under Paul's leadership and after his example in the proclamation of the gospel and in pastoral oversight of the churches established through their mission. If we look at the opening words of the canonical letters we notice that most of these are a corporate enterprise rather than the writing of a single person. Paul is identified as the sole author only of Romans, Ephesians and the Pastoral Letters. Timothy is named as co-author of 2 Corinthians, Colossians and, with Silvanus, of the two letters to the Thessalonians. An otherwise unknown Sosthenes is identified as the co-author of 1 Corinthians, and unnamed brothers are mentioned alongside Paul in the opening of Galatians. It would therefore be a misconception to assume that every word in these letters was written or dictated by Paul himself. His companions may have drafted significant portions, if not entire letters, and would have been both experienced and accomplished in giving written expression to Paul's thought by the time of his death. To have continued acting in Paul's name while he was in captivity and after his death would therefore not have been a major departure for them; on the contrary, they would have claimed the guidance of the same Holy Spirit that had inspired Paul. We can therefore accept the disputed letters as part of the Pauline tradition, even if there are doubts as to precisely who wrote them and when. Our only hesitation is that we do not know precisely what stage in the development of the Pauline tradition these letters represent, whether they reflect the Church during the time of Paul's activity or possibly several decades later.

As well as the canonical letters there are other writings attributed to Paul or that purport to recount his life, but date from the second century and later. These include the second-century *Acts of Paul*, which includes the *Acts of Paul and Thecla*, the *Martyrdom of Paul*, the apocryphal third letter of Paul to the Corinthians and the fourth-century *Apocalypse of Paul*, as well as the apocryphal correspondence between Paul and the Stoic philosopher Seneca.[2] Not only are these documents much later than Paul, but they have never been accepted as part of the New Testament and therefore do not have any authority for regulating Christian doctrine, life and ministry in the present day. Nor do they provide any reliable insight into the first-century communities established through Paul's preaching and into which converts to the Christian gospel were baptized. Therefore while these documents testify to Paul's continued importance in the Church of the second and subsequent centuries, they are a reliable source neither of historical information nor of authoritative teaching. They will therefore not require further attention in this study. We must nevertheless recognize that the stories contained in these documents would have informed the interpretation of Paul's letters in churches in which those stories were transmitted, irrespective of whether the documents were known or received as Scripture.

As is well known to readers of the New Testament, the Acts of the Apostles devotes considerable attention to Paul. Over half the book deals with Paul's conversion and subsequent missionary activities. Luke, identified by tradition as the author of Acts, appears to have been, at least for a time, a companion of Paul (Col. 4.14; 2 Tim. 4.11; Philem. 24).[3] At first sight this book should therefore prove a rich source of information to complement the teaching contained in Paul's letters. However, scholars have long questioned the reliability of Acts as a source of historical information, especially on Paul. It is generally thought to have been written some time after Paul's life and ministry, and therefore to be a secondary rather than a primary source. Luke is, furthermore, recognized as having his own particular theology, closely related but nonetheless distinct from that of Paul. The material in Acts is of a rather different type from that in the letters, consisting largely of narrative and speeches. The speeches must be regarded as the attribution, by the author to the speaker in the narrative, of words appropriate to the occasion. While reflecting in a concise form what the author of Acts believes the character would have said, the speeches cannot with confidence be used to reconstruct the theology of the historical figures depicted. The letters therefore bring us closer to Paul's actual words, and there can be no disputing they are the primary source of his teaching. On the other hand, they provide no narrative accounts of the events through which people were converted and incorporated into the Church through Baptism. To understand the processes whereby the gospel was proclaimed, people were converted and churches of baptized converts established, we are accordingly dependent upon the narrative accounts in Acts.[4] In conformity with the conventions of his day, Luke composed the speeches that he attributes to his major characters, including Paul. Although in doing so he may draw on oral traditions that reflect memories of Paul's actual teaching, the speeches in Acts cannot be regarded as the actual words spoken by Paul on the occasions related. We have to be cautious, therefore, in attributing the thoughts expressed in these speeches to Paul, and we cannot use them as the basis for reconstructing his theology. Acts therefore cannot be regarded as an entirely reliable source for Paul's teaching, but it can be used to supplement and clarify information that derives from his letters. Acts reflects the same cultural assumptions and much the same experience of early Christian life as does Paul himself. We can assume that Luke was familiar with the community life of the early Christian churches, such as those established by Paul. He and many of his readers would have known something of the ways people were converted to Christianity, and how they were incorporated into the Church through Baptism, during the course of the early Christian missions such as those led by Paul.

Notwithstanding our reservations about the depiction of Paul's mission preaching in Acts, we can learn a great deal about early Christian baptismal practice from the Acts narratives. Even if there is doubt about the historicity of the specific incidents recorded, the stories nonetheless reflect practices and developing traditions that would have needed to be consistent with the knowledge and experience of the intended readers and hearers. Luke in his reconstruction of the events would have drawn upon early Christian customs as well as any specific information he may have had about particular events. Even if he does not record specific events on the basis of reliable historical information, he is able to surmise what is most likely to have happened on the basis of knowledge of analogous events and of the diversity of early Christian practice.

Before we turn to specific texts we need to give some thought to the nature and intention of the letters. We have already noted that most are addressed to churches Paul had founded and over which he exercised continuing pastoral oversight. Others, such as Romans and Colossians, seek to bring Paul's influence to bear upon other churches, even if we cannot be sure what the precise intentions are. Paul's 'letters are occasional, but not casual . . . aimed at particular situations in particular times and places . . . but also authoritative'.[5]

Although Paul's letters were addressed to particular churches or groups of churches, and offered teaching and guidance concerning particular circumstances within those churches, the fundamental teaching included in them applied throughout the Pauline churches and, in Paul's view, throughout Christianity. The contents of the letters need to be read in context but the universal applicability of the basic doctrines also needs to be appreciated.

The rite of Baptism is nowhere described, however briefly, in Paul's letters. The recipients had been baptized; they had direct experience of the rite and required no such description to recognize allusions and appreciate the inferences Paul drew from their experience of ritual incorporation into the Church. Baptism is mentioned or alluded to on several occasions in the letters. These occurrences do not provide a complete description of the rite but allude rather to those aspects of the ritual and its interpretation relevant to Paul's purpose in writing. Because of the contextual orientation of each statement, a fully comprehensive reconstruction of Paul's teaching on Baptism is not possible. Paul addressed particular situations and mentioned those aspects of his baptismal theology that were relevant to those situations or useful for illustrating the point he was making. Those aspects that were not relevant to any of the problems dealt with in his extant letters have not been preserved. All that can be accomplished, therefore, is a partial reconstruction of Paul's teaching, based on the relevant allusions in his extant letters and taking into account the context into which he is writing.

Galatians 3.26–29

Galatians is addressed collectively to a group of churches in central Anatolia, now part of Turkey, then known as Galatia. Scholars differ as to whether Galatia designates the Roman province of that name or a more loosely defined, overlapping but not coterminous geographical region. The details of this debate need not concern us, except to note that there is some dispute as to whether the churches of Derbe, Lystra and Iconium, whose evangelization is reported in Acts 13–14, are among those addressed. These cities would have been more thoroughly Hellenized than the regions to the north, in which the Gallic immigrants who gave their name to the Roman province predominated. The historical background and geographical location of the addressees have implications for our understanding of Paul's thought in general but not his teaching on Baptism in particular.[6] It is of significance, though, that Paul evangelized Iconium, Lystra and Derbe as the partner of Barnabas in a mission sponsored by the church of Antioch in Syria (Acts 13.1–4; 14.26). This community was to be of considerable significance in the growth of Christianity during the first century and beyond. Not only did the church of Antioch initiate a major movement of Christian missionary expansion but it was among the first to admit gentiles to its membership (Acts 11.19–26), and to grapple with the social and cultural, as well as theological, issues this development brought into focus. The practicalities of their community life and worship confronted the early Church with fundamental theological as well as pastoral and missiological questions, in addressing which Paul played a prominent role, reflected both in Galatians and in Acts. In other words, the church of Antioch played a crucial role in the inculturation of the Christian gospel outside of Jewish Palestine.[7]

While the basis of coexistence of Jew and gentile in the church of Antioch is disputed in recent scholarship, it is clear that the church was in some way able to function inclusively, without Jewish cultural observances becoming an insuperable obstacle to Christian fellowship.[8] While it may seem self-evident to the modern Christian that a common identity in Christ implies common worship, mutual respect and fellowship, this would not have been so apparent in the first century. We need to recognize, furthermore, that much of Christian history, until the present day, has reflected a failure to recognize precisely this principle. Jewish cultural observances, such as dietary laws, whatever their origins in the history of ancient Israel, served in the Graeco-Roman diaspora precisely to maintain the distinctiveness of Jewish identity in pagan society, and separation from their gentile neighbours. When those neighbours became Christian, or indeed when some associated with the synagogue or even became Jews, the social boundaries were challenged and ways of coexistence needed to be negotiated. It is vitally important for our understanding of the issues, and for appreciating how and why some of the most revered figures in the early Church disagreed so strongly, that we recognize just how new the situation was with which they were dealing. It is precisely in that they dealt with this issue so forcefully that Paul and others not merely laid the foundations for the Church of today but continue to challenge Christians to live according to their faith.

Some time after the events recorded in Acts 13–14, Barnabas and Paul had been constrained to defend their proclamation of the gospel to gentiles, without requiring that they observe the law of Moses in full, before the apostles in Jerusalem (Gal. 2.1–10; Acts 15). While they were successful in this, the practical implementation of the agreement reached posed further difficulties, and the resultant controversy in Antioch brought Paul into confrontation with Peter and Barnabas and indirectly with James the brother of Jesus and leader of the church in Jerusalem (Gal. 2.11–14). Most scholars believe that Paul lost standing and influence in Antioch through this incident, and in any event the question of coexistence between Jews and gentiles in the Church needed to be further clarified.[9] This was one of the most vexed questions that the first Christian generation faced, the solution to which was neither as obvious nor as inevitable as it may seem with centuries of hindsight.

The turbulence in the church of Antioch, and especially the rift between Barnabas and Paul, created something of a vacuum in pastoral oversight of the new churches they had founded. It seems clear from allusions in Galatians (3.1; 6.12) that Paul was not alone in asserting pastoral authority over the Galatian churches. We are not told precisely who else was active in this but it is clear both that they sought to impose a way of life quite different from that which had been modelled by Barnabas and Paul, and that they were successful in presenting themselves as authoritative figures to the young churches. A great deal of caution is needed in reconstructing their theology and their pastoral guidance on the basis of allusions in Paul's letter; 'mirror-readings' are not always reliable and are inevitably influenced by our own perspectives. It does seem clear, however, that they sought to impose a more thoroughly Jewish identity and lifestyle on the gentile Christians, and that the (male) Galatian Christians were being encouraged to undergo circumcision.

They may have suggested that, in waiving the requirement of circumcision and observance of the law of Moses, in other words of
proselytizing to Judaism, Barnabas and Paul had converted the
Galatians into an inferior and incomplete form of Christianity. If
the Galatians were to take the further step of circumcision, with or
without adopting a Jewish way of life in other respects, they would
complete their Christian commitment and identity, and accordingly
receive greater salvific benefits.

However it was that Paul came to learn of these developments,
his response was to write the letter to the Galatians, urging these
Christians to continue in the form of Christianity he had taught
them. Their Baptism had brought them all the benefits of Jesus'
death and resurrection; they would gain no further benefits through
undergoing circumcision and they would stand to lose the benefits
they had already obtained, because with circumcision would come
the obligation to observe the law of Moses in full, and they would
be judged accordingly (3.1–5; 5.2–11).

While we cannot locate the Galatian Christians with any geographical precision, we know they were communities of converts who had recently been brought to the faith through Paul's
teaching (cf. Gal. 3.1). They would have undergone Baptism as
they entered the new churches and begun their Christian lives.
Paul reminds them of this as he seeks to assert his authority and
to correct the Galatian Christians' deviation from the way of
life he had taught them during his mission. It is important that
we recognize that in Galatians 3.15–25 and 4.1–7, the context
within which the passage that mentions Baptism is located, Paul
is employing the metaphor of the household as a figure of the
Church. We have noted how fundamental the household was to
ancient society, and some of the ways it operated. Paul suggests
that the Church is a household and God is the householder. The
promises of God are compared to the will of the householder;
this of course does not imply that Paul expects God to die but he
nonetheless compares God's promises to a bequest. The laws of
inheritance, as they applied during the minority of the heir, illustrate the role of the law of Moses in God's saving purposes. The
coming of Christ has enabled the heirs to attain their majority
and come into full possession of their inheritance. The status of

heirs in God's household is fundamental to the point Paul illustrates through reference to Baptism:

> [26] For you are all children[10] of God through faith[11] in Christ Jesus,[12] [27] for as much as[13] you have been baptized into Christ you have put on Christ. [28] There is neither Jew nor gentile,[14] neither slave nor free, no male and female, for you are all one in Christ Jesus. [29] If you are of Christ, you are Abraham's seed, and heirs according to the promise.

Many scholars believe that here Paul is quoting from an early Christian creedal statement or, perhaps more likely, from catechesis addressed to candidates after Baptism, expounding the significance of the rite they have undergone. If this is the case it is significant for three reasons. First, it is earlier even than Paul's letter. Second, it reflects a wider segment of early Christian thinking than Paul himself. Third, such a creedal formula may well have formed part of an ancient Christian baptismal liturgy and therefore reflect directly how Baptism was understood during the earliest years of the Christian Church. For these reasons this passage has been important not only for reconstructing early Christian teaching on social relationships but also for applying these values to the life of the Church today.[15]

We have good reason to believe that this formulary may have originated in the church of Antioch, the first recorded Christian community to include both Jews and gentiles and the first to be known as 'Christian' (Acts 11.20, 26). The contrasts of social opposites in verse 28 reflect the social structure of the Graeco-Roman world as it would have been perceived by a Jew conscious of Israel's election and separation from other nations. For Jews committed to the uniqueness of their nation and its covenant relationship with God, the distinction between themselves and other nations was the cardinal criterion of identity. For Paul and Christians like him committed to a Christian Church that included people from both sides of this ethnic and social divide, forging a common identity in Christ was essential to their programme. This is an important aspect of Paul's agenda in Galatians and in the controversies that lie behind it. The distinctions of social class, between slave and free, and of gender, between male and female, may seem less prominent in Paul's letters or not to be addressed as rigorously, but they are vitally important for the Church today.

For Paul and the Christians who professed the formulary he quotes, Baptism creates a new identity for Christians, one that bridges or abolishes the distinctions that separate them in society outside the Church. Through Baptism they become children of God, in other words members of the family in a household in which God is father and patron. This reflects the process of adoption, whereby an heir receives through a ritualized legal transaction an identity and status that have precisely the same force as though inherited through birth. This is particularly significant given the contrast Paul posits in the household of God between slaves on the one hand and children who are heirs on the other in the passage that follows this text (4.1–7), and in the convoluted contrast between the descendants of Isaac and of Ishmael a little further in the letter (4.21–31). While Paul does not develop the point, neither he nor the Galatian Christians would have been unaware that inheritance provisions almost invariably favoured male over female heirs. The status of Christians as children of God transcends their former identities, derived from their ethnic origins, social class and gender. This status and identity as children of God is of course what God intends in creation, as the broader context of this passage makes clear. The children of God are redeemed from slavery to sin, a state contrary to God's intention. By implication, therefore, the social divisions abolished in Baptism are the product of sin and contrary to the created order as God envisaged it (Gen 1.27). The biological distinctions inherent in creation may remain unaltered but the ways they impact on relationships are transformed 'in Christ'.

If Baptism has accomplished for Christians their adoption as children and heirs of God, then it is an immensely powerful ritual. Members of other nations who converted to Judaism during this period underwent, in the case of men and boys, circumcision. While this conferred membership of Israel, and the obligation to live according to the law of Moses, proselytes were considered inferior to Jews by birth. Their status was more akin to slaves who had been manumitted, but remained subordinate and dependent upon their former owners and forever tarnished by their former servile status. Their freedom was a chimera and they remained inferior members of the household of God. Their children and grandchildren, born into Israel, might enjoy the full status of children of God to which they could not aspire.[16] Baptism into Christ is therefore a more powerful ritual than circumcision into Judaism, bringing greater and more immediate benefits. Christians who chose to undergo the inferior rite of circumcision would gain nothing but thereby lose their freedom (4.21—5.15).

Those who are baptized are described as having 'put on Christ'. This is suggestive of clothing, as if with a garment, as a sign of spiritual transformation. This suggests that converts were stripped of their clothing in anticipation of the baptismal rite and dressed again on emerging from the water. Practical measures that would have accompanied bathing could quite naturally acquire a symbolic significance in a ritual context. The implication here is clearly that the clothing donned after Baptism is different from that worn before, and reflects something of the transformation undergone in the rite. In Graeco-Roman society, as in many others, clothing was not a matter of personal sartorial taste but rather an important indicator of social identity and rank. Their new identity, which Christians acquire at Baptism, abrogates the distinctions of race, social standing and gender that their clothing would normally indicate and emphasize, thereby identifying them in terms of their status in society. If Christ is symbolically the garment with which Christians are clothed at Baptism, that garment represents also the common identity they acquire in and through the rite. The Christian community has become the group in terms of which its members derive their identity. Their common identity in Christ, illustrated by the image of clothing in Christ, indicates that the Christians' public image derives from Christ. It is as members of the Church that they should be recognized both among themselves and in the world, irrespective of what social distinctions defined their identity before conversion.

The rite of Baptism signifies the repudiation of one identity and the acquisition of another. The new identity represented by the clothing indicates permanence. Putting on Christ is, so to speak, not only about getting dressed but also about remaining clothed in Christ. Christ is the symbol of the new identity of the Christians in the unity of the Church. 'Christ, in whom the baptized lives, is . . .

31

his new "unity garment" . . . that makes the distinguishing signs of earlier existence meaningless'.[17]

As well as signifying a new identity, the image of clothing symbolizes the new role Christians play in the world. Those who 'put on Christ' represent Christ in the world just as actors embody and represent those whose parts they play in the theatre.[18] The image, even if partly inspired by the theatre, does not imply that the role assumed by Christians in Baptism can be undertaken and discarded at will, or that it applies in a way analogous to a role performed on stage, so that once the gathering of the church has concluded, Christian identity is discarded. Paul does not suggest that Christians adopt one role in a particular context, their life as a church, but resume their previous social roles once outside the gathering of the Christian community. They cannot avoid or repudiate altogether their inherited or acquired social identities and roles, the relationships and obligations that accompany these or the possible compromises that conflicting identities may imply. Neither can they relinquish their Christian identity and role when outside the fellowship of the Church. Once a new identity 'in Christ' has been assumed, the role of representing Christ in the world is constant and lifelong.

Paul's argument can therefore be summarized as: those who place their faith in the one true gospel become children of God, are baptized, receive a new identity and role and undergo a radical spiritual transformation that continues throughout their lives. The Christian community becomes the source of their identity as a family under God's fatherhood, and distinctions that formerly separated them, and continue to separate people outside the Church, cease to have any significance. All Christians are united in Christ, and 'in Christ' form a single new entity, the Church. Being 'one in Christ' implies not only a common identity as members of the body representing Christ in and to the world in their daily lives. It implies also that the distinctions that divide society are eliminated in the life of the Church.

However clearly Paul and other early Christians who used this formulary may have stated the principle, this does not mean that previous identities derived from ethnic and geographical origins, gender and social status could or would simply have been discarded on conversion. The first Christians, like Christians today, continued to be part of wider networks of relationships, with the obligations and identities these entailed. While in principle Christian identity may have transcended and superseded all other criteria of identity, in reality Christians have had to struggle to reconcile their new identity with circumstances and roles in society which they could not control or abolish.[19]

While for Paul and the Christians of his day the creation of a common identity between Jewish and gentile Christians was the highest priority, for Christians today overcoming discriminatory divisions and attitudes based on social class and gender prejudice are no less a priority than addressing the legacy of racism in many churches. The Baptism that unites Christians and defines their common identity needs also to be the basis on which they relate to each other.

Suggested further reading

Much of the argument in this section is more fully developed in my article 'Liturgy and Identity'.

For more detailed exegesis of the text, in the wider context of the letter, readers may wish to consult the commentaries on Galatians of Betz, Bruce, Dunn, Jervis, Longenecker and Martyn. Of these, Dunn and Jervis are more accessible to the non-specialist reader.

Two important studies of Galatians, which can shed useful light on the issues surrounding the text in which Baptism is mentioned, are Barclay, *Obeying the Truth* and Longenecker, *The Triumph of Abraham's God*.

1 Corinthians 1.13–17

Corinth was a major city in the Roman province of Achaia, in what is now Greece. The Isthmus of Corinth, linking the Peloponnesus to the mainland, was the obvious location for a city of strategic and mercantile importance. Corinth had natural sea harbours both at Lechaeum on the Corinthian Gulf to the west (facing Italy) and at Cenchreae on the Saronic Gulf to the east (facing Asia). Corinth was during the first century a major trading centre to which immigrants were drawn from many nations. As well as Roman colonists and native Greeks, there were certainly Jews among the many ethnic groups that populated Corinth at this time.

A cosmopolitan trading port on the Mediterranean would have been a natural and potentially fruitful centre for Christian mission. When Paul arrived in Corinth after a memorable but not particularly successful mission in Athens (Acts 17.16–18.1), he met Aquila and Priscilla, a Jewish couple from Rome who became important partners in his missionary enterprise (Acts 18.1–3; cf. Rom. 16.3). Working in their business enabled Paul to maintain himself without drawing support either from his converts or from any sending church. It was important that Paul, having lost his base in Antioch, should find the means to sustain his independent missionary movement. In a mercantile centre such as Corinth, any financial dependence on his converts would inevitably have drawn Paul into the complicated web of rival patrons with competing business and political interests, vying for status and influence in the city, and in the church. It is clear from 2 Corinthians that Paul's financial independence was to become controversial, partly because he was perceived to have degraded himself by engaging in manual labour and partly because he was felt to have rejected the support of local Christian benefactors while receiving donations from Philippi. While working to sustain himself and his mission may not initially have been Paul's principled position, but rather a pragmatic measure, his involvement in Aquila and Priscilla's business enabled him to remain aloof from the rivalries that emerged as his mission attracted increasing numbers of prominent householders.

Assisted by Silas and Timothy, Paul began his mission in Corinth at Sabbath worship in the Jewish synagogue (Acts 18.4–10). He made a significant number of converts, and, following controversy, subsequently ceased attending the synagogue and gathered his community of converts in adjacent premises. Paul remained for up to two years in Corinth (Acts 18.11, 18), a substantially longer period than surviving records suggest he spent in any other city during the course of his missions. In the case of his mission to Thessalonica, by way of contrast, Paul was driven out by opposition within little over three weeks of establishing the church (Acts 17.2, 10). The letters Paul wrote to the church in Corinth are subsequent to his mission in the city, and address conditions in the community that had been brought to Paul's attention through rumours, messages and at least one letter from the church addressing specific questions to him (1 Cor. 7.1).

The Corinthian letters form the most extensive body of correspondence from Paul, or any other Christian leader of the first century, to any single church. They are therefore a particularly important source of information on early Christian life, and we are able to relate Paul's teaching to concrete circumstances in the Corinthian church to a greater extent than we are with any other community he founded. Despite the relative wealth of the Corinthian letters as a source of information on Paul and the church in Corinth, we need to be aware that our knowledge remains incomplete. 1 Corinthians 5.9 refers to a previous letter of Paul to the Corinthian church that is no longer extant and whose contents we can only surmise from this brief allusion in which Paul seeks to correct a misinterpretation of that letter.[20] 1 Corinthians 7.1 refers to a letter from the Corinthian church to Paul, the contents of which we can reconstruct only on the basis of Paul's response in the following chapters. 2 Corinthians probably originally consisted of more than one letter, with one possible exception all subsequent to 1 Corinthians.[21]

In 1 Corinthians Paul is responding not only to the enquiries sent to him in a letter from the church but also to reports he has received from at least one other source about divisions in the community (1.10–12). It is in the context of addressing the latter issue that he makes his first reference to Baptism.

[13] Has Christ been divided?[22] Was Paul crucified for you? Or were you baptized in the name of Paul? [14] I give thanks that I baptized none of you except Crispus and Gaius, [15] lest anyone should say you were baptized in my name. [16] I also baptized the household of Stephanas, but do not know whether I baptized anyone else. [17] For Christ did not send me to baptize, but to proclaim the gospel.

Paul is calling for unity in the Corinthian church. The number and nature of the factions has been a topic of considerable scholarly debate, the details of which are of marginal significance to the principle Paul is asserting. He seeks to demonstrate that discord in the community is incompatible with the gospel and that therefore no group could claim legitimacy in such a situation. There is one gospel and one Church, and the rite of Baptism is the one rite of incorporation into the single body of Christ (to anticipate 1 Cor. 12.13).

To Paul the existence of factions that profess allegiance to leading personalities in the Church, as well as to Christ, implies that Christ is divisible, which is fundamentally contrary to the gospel. The profession of such loyalty to leading figures in the Church, as well as dividing Christ and the Church, implies that that person and not Christ is central to the faith of those professing such allegiances. It could also imply that the power transmitted in the ritual was that of the person administering Baptism and not the power of God. This would in effect be to imply that Paul, or for that matter Peter or Apollos, and not Jesus, had been the one crucified. This would be a fundamental denial of the gospel. Paul is not suggesting that any individual or group is consciously supplanting Christ as the object of their faith and devotion, but he is asserting that this is the implication of their behaviour.

Baptism serves to illustrate Paul's point. The Corinthian Christians knew that they had been baptized 'in the name of Jesus', whoever may have administered the rite. This implies that the power associated with 'the name of Jesus' was invoked in the rite and was the agent of transformation effected in it; the person who administered the rite and invoked 'the name of Jesus' was merely the instrument of this process. Jesus Christ was the one who had been crucified and whose resurrection was the basis of the Corinthians' faith (1 Cor. 15). To allow allegiance to Paul or to some other prominent figure to transcend allegiance to Christ was effectively to transfer to that person everything Christians were to believe and profess about Jesus. In terms of the gospel the crucifixion and resurrection of Jesus is unique and the only means to salvation. Baptism is the rite by which Christians avail themselves of this saving work of Christ and acquire a new identity as members of the Church. This is an identity common to all Christians, irrespective of whose mission preaching had brought them to faith and regardless of who had incorporated them into the Church through Baptism.

Baptism demonstrates the inherent unity of the Church in allegiance to Christ. Although he is dealing here with the specific situation in the local church in Corinth, it is clear from the question, 'Has Christ been divided?' that the whole Church, not only the local congregation, is inherently one. The question also implies that the unity of the entire Church is threatened by factionalism in Corinth. Baptism is therefore a symbol of the unity of the Church as a universal body in its allegiance to Christ. The rhetorical question of course requires only one possible answer. Any behaviour that divides the Church denies its very nature as the body of Christ.

We need to remember that Paul lived and wrote long before the denominational divisions came about that Christians today almost take for granted. While the Church did not have any institutional structures or organic unity in Paul's day, and *ekklesia* almost invariably refers to the local congregation, there was nevertheless a clear sense of common Christian identity. The conflicts in which Paul was at times engaged with other Christian leaders can be understood only on the basis of their common faith and sense of belonging to the same community, however geographically dispersed that community was. Whatever the specifics of their various positions on the issues that divided them, it was the same gospel and the same Church with which they were concerned and whose doctrine and discipline they sought to define. If there had not been this sense of common identity there would have been no basis for conflict. The challenge to the churches today is to recover the vision of fundamental unity and to realize it. The recognition that there is one Baptism, common to all Christians, and not different baptisms of different denominations, has been an important step in that direction in recent decades.[23] Nevertheless, the institutionalized division of Christ's body remains quite contrary to Paul's understanding of the Church and that of other Christian leaders of his day.

The problem of dominant personalities becoming cause for division in the Church is evidently not a new one. But in the case of first-century Corinth there is no evidence of rivalry between the three figures mentioned, only between Christians who professed allegiance to them and perhaps adhered to their specific interpretations of the gospel. Paul nevertheless clearly feels responsible for any misplaced allegiance to himself, or at least for ensuring that this aberration is brought to an end. Paul condemns any allegiance to himself that causes division in the Church, despite his having been the founding apostle of the church in Corinth (cf. 1 Cor. 3.5–15), who could perhaps claim some degree of loyalty from his converts. The quest for Christian unity in the Church today cannot be furthered if Christian leaders allow loyalty to themselves to undermine the allegiance all Christians owe to Christ and to Christ alone.

Paul's statement that he is thankful that he did not personally baptize many of the Corinthian Christians, and that 'Christ did not send me to baptize, but to proclaim the gospel', has often been construed to mean that Paul disregarded Baptism as little more than an irrelevant ceremony. The statement belongs to a particular rhetorical context and exaggerates Paul's position, or even wilfully parodies it for effect, in order to persuade the recipients of the letter of the error in their attitude. The interpretation that takes this statement at its face value, ignoring Paul's use of contemporary literary and rhetorical conventions, reflects modern Protestant anti-sacramentalism and attributes this essentially modern, Western, attitude to Paul. The contrast between word and sacrament, which elevates the former and denigrates the latter, belongs to a cultural and religious context entirely alien from the world of the early Church. Paul and the Christians he addressed in his letters lived in a world in which supernatural power was believed to be present and effective in ritual. Baptism for Paul and the first Christians was not merely illustrative or evocative; the power of God was at work in the rite, and its continuing spiritual significance could not be separated from the symbolic action. In the modern world such an understanding of ritual and the operation of divine power in the world may encounter objections on rational or empiricist grounds, but such ideas were entirely at home in the world to which Paul proclaimed the gospel, and we cannot suppose that he was entirely immune to such thinking. What is important to Paul is that Christians recognize that it is the power of God that is transmitted in Baptism and not any supernatural power vested in the person who administers the rite. Baptism was far from unimportant to Paul. Administration of the rite was simply not his primary function in the proclamation of the gospel and establishment of the church in any place.

The practicalities of Baptism could have been another factor in Paul's having usually delegated this function to others. Water would not have been readily available in all locations, and Baptism would often have had to be administered in a different venue from that in which the gospel was proclaimed or where the church gathered for worship. Even in houses with their own baths or wells, considerations of propriety may have required that Baptism take place away from the gathered congregation. While we should not suppose that elaborate rituals, such as recorded in later centuries, had already been developed, we should assume that cultural sensitivities surrounding nudity would have influenced the modalities of Baptism, determining who may have been present to witness or administer the rite.[24] In the Acts account of the Baptism of Cornelius and his household, Peter gives instructions that those newly converted through his preaching be baptized (10.48). Peter does not, by implication, administer the rite but delegates it to others. Writing a century after Paul, Justin Martyr describes candidates being taken to a place where water is available, and after Baptism being brought back to where the church had assembled, where they are greeted and prayed for before the Eucharist is celebrated.[25] There is no indication that the 'one who presides' baptizes, or even that he accompanies the party to the place of Baptism, but he nevertheless exercises an oversight over the entire ritual process. Such a pattern continued to be reflected in later and more elaborate baptismal liturgies in subsequent centuries.[26] We do not need to be able to trace a direct connection between Peter or Paul and Justin to suppose that a similar custom may have been quite widespread during the period before the Church was able to acquire or construct its own buildings, adapted to its liturgical requirements.

Paul's relief at not having administered Baptism to most of his converts, if more than a rhetorical gesture, is retrospective. As others had administered the rite to those converted through his mission preaching, one potential area of misunderstanding had been excluded: Baptism by Paul could not be equated with Baptism in Paul's name. The fact that the leader of the mission had not personally administered Baptism to all the converts demonstrates that the ritual functionary, not the rite itself, is irrelevant. Paul is thankful that Baptism, which for him was a vivid symbol of the unity of the Church, had not become, on account of his having administered the rite, the source of dissension or misunderstanding in the community; on the contrary, he was able to appeal to the Corinthian Christians' experience of Baptism to demonstrate the essential unity of the Church, which it was their duty to uphold. During Paul's mission to Corinth, Baptism 'in the name of Jesus' had been administered in such a way that it could not possibly be interpreted as Baptism in Paul's name.

Paul states that he sees his mission primarily as preaching, not because he deprecates the meaning and significance of Baptism but because it was proclamation of the gospel that was his primary, and perhaps distinctive, function. Preaching was a prerequisite to conversion and therefore to Baptism, and the function primarily of the leader of the missionary team. Baptism was a function that belonged to no particular minister and could naturally be delegated to Paul's companions and in due course to the leaders of the churches they established. Furthermore, it was the content of the preaching, and not the rite of incorporation, that was the source of disunity in Corinth. While Baptism was, so far as we are aware, common to all strands in early Christianity, preaching and teaching were diverse and potentially divisive. The Corinthians are to recognize and respect Paul's preaching ministry, even though it distinguishes him from other preachers of the gospel. Beyond the diversity of Christian preaching is the unity symbolized by Baptism 'in the name of Jesus'.

1 Corinthians 6.11

Baptism is mentioned only allusively in this verse, but Paul is quite clearly referring to the rite and to the conversion and transformation in human lives enacted in it. He is dealing in this passage with the conduct of certain members of the church. He has declared that the unrighteous will not attain salvation, and listed a number of vices of which some of the Corinthian Christians had been guilty before their conversion. Then follows this allusion to Baptism:

> But you (came to be) washed,[27] you were sanctified, you were justified in the name of the Lord Jesus Christ, and by the Spirit of our God.

The symbol of washing is a clear allusion to Baptism. Not only does the context refer quite explicitly to the formerly pagan Corinthians' conversion to the gospel but the reference to washing and the formula 'in the name of the Lord Jesus Christ' are deeply suggestive of the ritual that accompanied or realized their conversion. The role of the Holy Spirit in the transformation effected at conversion further indicates the rite of Baptism, as becomes clear in the light of Paul's subsequent treatment of the Spirit in 1 Corinthians 12.

Conversion had brought about a fundamental change in the conduct of these people. They had been washed, the waters of Baptism being symbolic of purification from their former vices and the effects these had had on their lives. Purification through ritual washing in water was a well-known and regular Jewish observance and was known in other cults of the period. Moreover the natural symbolism lent itself to application in other contexts. The Corinthians had been sanctified, Baptism being the rite of sanctification in which the convert is made holy. They had been justified, brought into a right relationship with God, and made righteous, all in the name of Christ, and through the Spirit of God, the divine power transmitted in Baptism through which the transformation is effected.

Paul is reminding the Corinthians that their conversion had changed their way of life, and warning them of the dire consequences of continuing in or reverting to their old ways. Baptism symbolizes their break with the past and the beginning of the new life of purity and sanctity, and therefore has definite moral and ethical implications. Their new identity in Christ defines the way Christians are to conduct their lives. Paul is appealing to those who had relapsed into immorality to conduct themselves in a manner compatible with their faith, reminding them that they had been purified, sanctified and justified at their conversion and that the immorality of the past is no longer part of their lives.

Baptism is a rite of cleansing and sanctification, which symbolizes a radical transformation in the life of the convert. The power transmitted in the rite brings about spiritual changes in the one baptized, and he or she is obliged to live according to the ethical demands of the new life, empowered by the Spirit imparted in the rite. Reversion to the morality of the old life does not invalidate the Baptism undergone but it does cause its benefits to be forfeited.

Baptism therefore requires the adherence to moral standards in the life of the Christian.

This passage reminds us of the continuing process of adjusting the convert's way of life into conformity with the gospel. Conversion needs to be sustained as the neophyte is formed in the faith through integration and orientation into the community of the Church, adopting its beliefs and values and adapting his or her behaviour accordingly. Even if most Christians today are not converts but were born to Christian parents and therefore cannot speak of the transformation in their lives that accompanies religious conversion, they are nonetheless baptized and their lives need to be formed in conformity with the gospel and with the identity they have acquired in and through Baptism. The way of life Paul enjoins upon Christians is no less an obligation of those born into Christian families and into the Church than it is of those converted to the gospel.

1 Corinthians 10.1–5

This passage forms part of Paul's argument in 1 Corinthians 8–10, in which he addresses the question whether Christians might partake of the meat of animals that had been offered in sacrifice in the pagan temples. This would include not only attendance at sacrificial rites in the temples and participation in the cultic meals held within the temple precincts, but also eating meat from this source that was sold in the markets.[28] An overt prohibition of such behaviour would have antagonized those relatively wealthy and powerful members upon whose patronage the church depended. Such men needed to be seen at civic ceremonies and to attend dinners at which other rich and powerful men were present, in order to sustain and if possible increase their prestige and prosperity. In chapter 8 Paul therefore addresses the issue with considerable circumspection, conceding arguments about the weaker consciences of those who supposedly have less knowledge and more scruples. In chapter 9 he reminds the Corinthians of the rights and freedoms he has waived, by implication at considerable cost to himself, in order to proclaim the gospel more effectively; an example the Corinthian Christians ought to be willing to follow. In returning to the question of idolatry and the consumption of meat from animals offered in sacrifice in the Corinthian temples, Paul reflects on the exodus experience of Israel and the Christian rites of Baptism and the Eucharist. Baptism and the Eucharist are not directly discussed or explicitly mentioned at this point, although Paul turns to the corporate worship of the Church, including the Eucharist (10.15–22), once he has addressed the issue of idolatry (10.1–14). The metaphor of Israel passing through the Red Sea after leaving Egypt, under the protection and guidance of the cloud that represents God's presence and power (Exodus 14), and allusions to their being fed with manna in the wilderness and drinking water from the rock, are quite clearly intended to evoke the Christian rituals known to the Corinthians. The identification of the rock with Jesus, and the attribution to it of mobility during Israel's wandering through the Sinai desert, reflect Jewish messianic motifs of the period. The notion of baptism into Moses is clearly intended as a type of the Baptism undergone by the Corinthian Christians.

[1] I do not want you to be ignorant, brothers [and sisters],[29] that our forebears[30] were all under the cloud, and passed through the sea, [2] and were all baptized into Moses in the cloud and in the sea, [3] and all ate the same spiritual food [4] and all drank the same spiritual drink; for they drank of the spiritual rock which followed them, and Christ was the rock. [5] But God was not pleased with the majority of them, and they were scattered in the desert.

Despite the sequence of events in which God's power is manifested in the Exodus narrative, effecting the deliverance of Israel from slavery in Egypt and from the perils of travel through the desert, all but two, Joshua and Caleb, of those who followed Moses out of Egypt perished in the wilderness on account of their idolatry and moral failings. It is of immediate interest that despite the gentile origins of the majority of the Corinthian Christians, Paul identifies the Israelites who followed Moses out of Egypt as their forebears. Not only had they similarly been delivered by God from peril and servitude but there is a spiritual connection between them that Paul uses to illustrate the dangers that beset those who have been saved. We can compare this with the idea Paul develops in Galatians 3 –4 and Romans 4 that Abraham is the spiritual ancestor of all Christians, irrespective of their ethnic origins. God's promises to Abraham are fulfilled in Christ, the 'seed of Abraham' (Gal. 3.16), and therefore all Christians are descended from Abraham in a spiritual sense (Gal. 3.29). While Abraham is mentioned in the Corinthian correspondence only in 2 Corinthians 11.22, we can be certain he would have featured in Paul's mission preaching and catechesis, as essential to relating gentile Christians to Israel and to the fulfilment of God's promises regarding the salvation of the nations. Here, however, Moses rather than Abraham is the significant figure from the Hebrew tradition. There is a sense in which Moses fulfils within Judaism a role analogous but not equivalent to that of Jesus for Christians, and there are traditions of this period in which Moses is interpreted as a quasi-redeemer figure.[31] Nevertheless, given the contrast Paul posits in Galatians between Abraham as the recipient of God's inclusive promises and Moses as the mediator of the law imposed on Israel alone, it is significant that Paul should here associate Israel at the time of Moses with the spiritual ancestry of the gentile Christians of Corinth.[32]

There is possible though very uncertain evidence of Jewish traditions of this period that interpreted the passing of Israel through the Red Sea at the exodus as analogous to proselyte baptism; that is, the initial and perhaps initiatory ritual washing undergone by converts to Judaism, which is not unambiguously attested at this time.[33] The 'baptism' undergone by Israel at the Red Sea before receiving the law at Sinai would be a type of the purificatory rite preceding the entry of gentiles into the covenant community. In the Exodus narrative the Israelites who left Egypt with Moses were already members of the covenant by birth. Whatever new forms the covenant took at Sinai, membership was still defined essentially by descent from the patriarchs Abraham, Isaac and Jacob. Gentile Christians enter the community formed by God's covenant with Abraham, which Paul understands to mean the Church,[34] through Baptism 'in the name of Jesus Christ'. At this point there is some analogy with Jewish proselyte baptism and, symbolically, with the exodus from Egypt of the historical Israel. Similarly, the manna from heaven (Exod. 16.12–36; cf. Ps. 78.24–25) and the water from the rock (Exod. 17.1–7;

Num. 20.2–13), which sustain the natural lives of the Israelites in the wilderness, are interpreted to prefigure the Eucharist; the identification of Jesus with the rock makes this clear.

It is interesting that Paul should have chosen to describe the 'baptism' of Israel through their passing through the Red Sea as baptism 'into Moses'. While in some forms of Judaism of this period, Moses was interpreted as a quasi-redeemer figure, nowhere does his role approximate that of the Christian understanding of Jesus in his death on the cross.[35] Paul may nonetheless be contrasting the covenant associated with Moses with that brought about through the death and resurrection of Jesus. Nevertheless, to describe the ritual of entry into the former as 'baptism into Moses' would be as much of an aberration as the notion of Baptism 'in the name of Paul', which Paul employs to parody the excessive and inappropriate loyalty of his own adherents in 1 Corinthians 1.13–17. Rather, baptism into Moses should be understood metonymously, as indicating entry into the covenant associated with Moses.

The main point Paul is making, however, is that the supernatural experiences of ancient Israel at the Red Sea and in the Sinai desert did not guarantee their godliness, freedom from temptation and moral rectitude, or exempt them from the requirements of obeying God. Nor did passing through the Red Sea guarantee their ultimate entry into the promised land; on the contrary, Paul alludes to the notorious incident of the golden calf, constructed as an idol while Moses was with God on Mount Sinai, receiving the Commandments (Exodus 32). The archetypal apostasy of Israel, which incurred God's judgement on that generation, serves as a warning to the Corinthian Christians not to lapse into idolatry. Receiving Baptism and partaking in the Eucharist do not guarantee salvation. This is not a denial of the power invoked in the ritual but an assertion that having received Baptism is of no avail unless the Christian conducts him or herself in a manner acceptable to God. Just as the liberation of Israel from Egypt, so for Christians, Baptism marks a new beginning in their life with God, one that brings with it freedom from slavery but also new obligations and subjection to God's judgement. Paul is emphasizing that God remains sovereign over the power invoked in the ritual and that it will be operative for the salvation of those baptized only if they live according to their

Baptism. In other words, the power of God cannot be manipulated through Baptism to guarantee unconditional salvation. The lives of the baptized must conform to the will of God if the salvation attained through Baptism is to be realized. If not, the consequence will be God's judgement and condemnation.

The relationship between the rite and its spiritual effects has continued to vex Christians. While many modern Christians are so concerned to avoid superstition and magic that they minimize the connection, converts from Graeco-Roman paganism may too easily have assumed that the spiritual effects of the rite were guaranteed simply through its administration. Fundamentally this reflects on their understanding of God and of the ways God's power is operative in the world. Paul clearly did recognize the Holy Spirit at work in the rite of Christian Baptism, but not in a way that could be manipulated to guarantee its benefits irrespective of how converts live out the consequences of the rite in their lives. As with the previous text, Paul recognizes or at least reflects what modern scholars would call the sociological and psychological need for conversion to be sustained through integration in the community, imbibing its values and adopting its way of living.

1 Corinthians 12.13

A major problem in Corinth was how the gifts of the Holy Spirit were understood and used within the community. This issue runs through the range of questions Paul addresses in chapters 12–14 of 1 Corinthians. Paul has already made it clear that reception of the Spirit does not bring any exemption from moral responsibility. In this section he is concerned to explain the fundamental unity of the Spirit and the diversity of the gifts manifested in the power of the one Spirit. It is clear that some gifts were regarded as something of a status symbol and were being used to enhance the image and influence of the person rather than to build up the Church. Paul responds by stating that the gifts are given to the Church but entrusted to individuals to be used for the benefit of the community. The Church is, as it were, a body, an organic unit comprising a variety of complementary and interdependent parts. This is an image that all the Corinthian Christians, irrespective of their detailed knowledge of anatomy and intellectual and cultural background, could be expected to understand. The analogy between human communities and the 'body politic' was well established, as well as the notions of corporate identity rooted in the Hebrew tradition and other mythologies of the period.[36] All gifts, however spectacular or mundane their manifestation, are bestowed by the same Spirit, and all are needed in the life of the Church. The use of the gifts should never disrupt good order in the community and its worship. It is in this context that Paul makes reference to Baptism.

> For indeed we were all baptized by[37] one Spirit into one body, whether Jew or gentile,[38] whether slave or free. And we were all given of the one Spirit to drink.

Paul is seeking to rectify the misunderstanding of the nature and function of the gifts of the Spirit. He has emphasized that all the diverse gifts entrusted to the various members of the community are manifestations of one and the same Spirit for varieties of service to the one Lord, and are therefore complementary and not a cause for rivalry or envy in the community. The gifts are apportioned in the community for the benefit of the Church as a whole and not for the glorification of the individual who manifests the particular gift. The various gifts are varieties of manifestations of the power of the same Holy Spirit, operating in various people, not according to their virtue or status but according to the will of God and the needs of the community. The gifts are therefore not a status symbol for the individual but are given to the Church, even though a particular gift is conferred on the individual. The analogy of the physical body illustrates this point. Each gift has its place in the life of the community, just as each organ has its essential function in the physical body, without which the entire body is unable to function adequately.

The working of the Spirit in the Church is therefore the sum total of its various manifestations, operating through the various members of the community. They were all 'baptized by one Spirit' whose power is continuously manifested in various ways in their lives. Despite the diversity and apparent inequality in the gifts of the Spirit, there is nevertheless only the one Spirit, the sole agent of Baptism whose power is transmitted to the Christian through the rite.[39] The gifts are given to the Church, which cannot here be limited entirely to the local community but must include all Christians baptized by the one Spirit. Spiritual gifts are conferred upon, manifested in and exercised by individual baptized Christians. There is therefore intrinsic unity and complementarity in the diversity of the charismatic gifts, and so the Church is united in its diversity because the varieties of charismatic gifts are manifestations of the power of the Spirit of God, which all Christians have received through Baptism.

Baptism by the one Spirit further implies that all baptized Christians have received the Holy Spirit and are thereby empowered for their role in the life and work of the Church. The presence of the Spirit inhabiting the Christian must be understood as permanent from the moment of Baptism and not as transient or sporadic, present only when particular gifts are publicly exercised or manifested. Whereas at the nearby sanctuary of Apollo at Delphi, priestesses would pronounce oracles while in a temporary state of altered consciousness or ecstasy, the Christian is permanently inspired. The list of gifts and of functions in the discharge of which the Spirit is active, which Paul catalogues in verses 4–11 and 28–30, are essentially about service in and to the community and not about independent activity of any kind. The only exception might be apostleship and in particular Paul's conception of it, but even this is integrally bound up with the lives of the communities established through apostolic ministry.

While Paul emphasizes the essential unity of the spiritual gifts, he nonetheless acquiesces in the prevailing understanding that the body functions most effectively when the parts are in harmony, and that this harmony is maintained by the hierarchy of its parts. The concept of laity as passive recipients of a ministry exercised by an elite group is nevertheless quite contrary to Paul's understanding of the Church and of the Holy Spirit, and therefore of Baptism. It is precisely because all Christians are in principle engaged in the ministry of the Church, in the power of the Holy Spirit, that Paul is concerned to preserve authority and unity of purpose in the midst of diversity of charismatic manifestations, and of considerable potential for conflict and competition within the community.

Baptism symbolizes not only unity in the diverse manifestations of the Spirit in the community but also unity in the diverse ethnic and social origins of its members. The distinction between 'Jew' and 'gentile' or 'Greek' may refer not so much to the gulf many Jews defined between themselves and the people of other nations as to competing and at least potentially conflicting bases of claims to authority and attainment in the intellectual and spiritual heritages of Israel and of Greece. Distinctions of social status, exemplified in that between slave and free, are also abrogated in the unity of the Church.[40] The one Spirit operates in all Christians from the point of their conversion and incorporation, forging unity and common identity in place of the distinctions that divide the wider society. Baptism therefore symbolizes and realizes unity in diversity in the Church, both in diversity of origin and in diversity of charismatic activity.

We have seen that in 1 Corinthians Paul uses Baptism to illustrate two essential points. The first is the intrinsic unity of the Church, of which the one Baptism is a powerful and graphic symbol: one Lord, one Spirit, one Church, one Baptism. The Holy Spirit does not confer a private gift of power upon any individual; the gifts are given to the Church and manifested in individuals to enable them to play their complementary roles in the life of the community. Second, Baptism has moral consequences for the lives of believers. However real the power of the Holy Spirit at work in their conversion and transmitted in the baptismal rite, salvation will not be effected unless those baptized continue to live in the power of the Spirit and according to the will of God.

The two serious misunderstandings of Baptism that Paul addresses remain problems for the Church today. Divisions and rivalries continue to beset Christian communities, and claims to the inspiration of the Holy Spirit are frequently used to justify divisive and egotistical behaviour disruptive of the unity of the body. There have, from time to time since early in the history of the Church, been movements that have misinterpreted Paul's doctrine of justification by faith, posited a complete separation of soul and body and misconstrued Baptism as a guarantee of salvation, irrespective of the way of life that followed incorporation into the Church. Such attitudes to Baptism border on the superstitious and presume upon the grace of God in ways that Paul warned against very clearly.

There have nevertheless been Christian movements that have been oblivious to the moral imperatives of the faith or have simply denied that the physical body, and the deeds it performs, are relevant to the salvation of the soul. This leads to and is used to justify licentious behaviour, often but by no means always of a sexual nature: Paul is at least as outspoken about disregard for the poor in the Corinthian church as he is about matters of sexual propriety. What he teaches about Baptism, the gifts of the Spirit and the unity of the body of Christ pertains directly to this. An informed, comprehensive and balanced, understanding of Paul's teaching on Baptism can help address these issues in the life of the Church today.

Suggested further reading

For exegesis of the texts in their broader contexts, readers may wish to consult the commentaries on 1 Corinthians of Barrett, Collins, Conzelmann, Fee, Fitzmyer, Hays, Horsley, Soards and Thiselton. Of these, Barrett, Hays and Soards are more accessible to the non-specialist reader.

Important recent books on the early church in Corinth that illustrate the complexity of the issues with which Paul is confronted in establishing normative Christian behaviour in an overwhelmingly pagan environment include Chow, *Patronage and Power*; Horrell, *The Social Ethos of the Corinthian Correspondence* and Winter, *After Paul left Corinth*. A more narrowly defined work but directly relevant to this study is Chester, *Conversion at Corinth*.

There have been several important books on the image of the Church as the body of Christ and on aspects of what this means, including Martin, *The Corinthian Body*; Lee, *Paul, the Stoics, and the Body of Christ* and Kim, *Christ's Body in Corinth*.

2 Corinthians 1.21–22

2 Corinthians is a complex document that many scholars believe may have been compiled from excerpts or fragments of two or more letters Paul wrote to the Corinthian church during the years

following his writing of 1 Corinthians. While perhaps a majority of scholars would argue that 2 Corinthians is a composite letter, there is some variety of opinion as to the number of documents incorporated and the order in which they were written.[41] What is generally agreed is that 2 Corinthians, or the letters incorporated into it, reflect a difficult period in Paul's relationship with the Corinthian church following the writing of 1 Corinthians. In addition to the conflicts and controversies apparent in the earlier letter, Paul's authority had come to be challenged by rival claimants to apostleship. Quite who these were is far from certain but they clearly challenged Paul's apostolic credentials. Tensions had been further exacerbated by Paul's having changed his travel plans, so that an anticipated visit to Corinth had been deferred.[42] It is in this context of seeking to restore a relationship that had become strained that Paul makes a passing allusion to Christian Baptism.

> [21] For it is God who strengthens us with you in Christ, and has anointed us, [22] and has sealed us and given us the Spirit in our hearts as an assurance.

In a single sentence Paul brings together a sequence of integrally related concepts, drawing upon not only the Christian experience of Baptism but also legal and commercial conventions of the period.

Paul's relationship with the Corinthian Christians is God-given and rooted in their Baptism. While Baptism may not be explicitly mentioned, in that no word rendered 'baptize' or 'Baptism' is used, the expression 'in Christ' alludes to the state of being that Christians enter through Baptism. The reference to the Christians' having been 'anointed' by God, similarly, is not merely a pun on the word *christos*, 'anointed one', but reflects directly the outpouring of the Holy Spirit at Baptism and the relationship the baptized come to share with Jesus, the one God had definitively anointed, so that he is known as 'Christ', the anointed one. This does not in itself imply that Christians were at this date anointed with oil during the course of the Baptism rite. However, olive oil was used as a cleansing agent and as a massage lotion when bathing, and was therefore a natural symbol readily available for ritual use in Christian Baptism. Given the prominence of the imagery of anointing in the interpretation of Jesus' significance, and its antecedents in the inauguration of priests, kings and prophets in ancient Israel (Exod. 40.12–15; 1 Sam. 10.1; 16.13; 1 Kings 19.15–16; Pss. 89.20; 132.2; Isa. 11.2; 42.1; 44.3; 61.1), as well as its use in washing, it is entirely likely that oil was introduced to Christian baptismal rites long before the earliest explicit accounts of this, which date from towards the end of the second Christian century.[43] While these texts allude to anointing at Baptism as an established and uncontroversial custom and not as an innovation, we can nonetheless not be certain that the practice was already part of the baptismal rite in Corinth by the middle of the first Christian century.

Paul refers further to the Christians having been 'sealed'. Imprinting an image in molten wax or making a mark on an object by other means served to indicate identity and ownership or the authority behind an official document. Livestock were often marked by branding with a recognizable symbol, and this could be extended to slaves, particularly escaped slaves who had been recaptured. Tattooing was another means of making an indelible mark on a person, and was used to mark slaves and soldiers. While used as a sign of allegiance in some cults of the period, tattooing was prohibited in the law of Moses (Lev. 19.28) and in Judaism was regarded as violating the body made in God's image. While there may well have been dissent from this interpretation in some Jewish movements of Paul's day, it is unlikely that he or other early Christians formed in Pharisaic and similar traditions of interpretation of Scripture would have advocated such a custom. While the branding or tattooing of Christian symbols on the body, in particular the cross, is attested or at least alleged by the end of the second century,[44] and was later to become customary among, inter alia, Coptic Christians, it is highly unlikely that this is what Paul envisages by having been 'sealed' by God.

In Romans 4.13, written probably not long after this letter, Paul describes the circumcision of Abraham as a 'seal', a visible sign that represents and endorses the righteousness he had previously received by faith.[45] As we have noted already, there was at this time no correlation between the circumcision of male Jewish babies and Christian Baptism. However, Abraham is the archetypal proselyte, and proselyte circumcision is indeed analogous to the Baptism of Christian converts. It is therefore entirely likely that Paul is referring to their Baptism in describing the Corinthian Christians as having been 'sealed' by God. Following Baptism, no permanent physical or visible mark remains on the body, which leaves the question of whether Paul is alluding to a particular symbolic act that formed part of the baptismal ritual or to an invisible but fundamental consequence of the rite as a whole. We have noted above that in Galatians 3.26–29, clothing is a visible symbol of the identity received at Baptism. A seal corresponding to Jewish proselyte circumcision would be an invisible yet in a mystical sense indelible mark imposed on the body, permanently representing the transformation that Baptism had effected.

We have noted that the earliest unequivocal evidence of anointing with oil at Baptism, whether before or after immersion in water, is not attested until the end of the second century. The earliest attestation of imposition of the sign of the cross at Baptism dates from much the same period and, indeed, from some of the same writings.[46] Recent scholarship has shown that the cross was used as a Christian symbol at a much earlier date than previously thought, and a strong case has been made for its attestation by the third quarter of the first Christian century.[47] This requires that references to the marking or signing of Christians in the New Testament be reconsidered.

In Ezekiel 9 a vision is recounted in which the righteous of Jerusalem are marked, with ink by a scribe, on their foreheads. The purpose of this marking is to set the righteous apart from the general populace so that the former might be spared when the latter perish in the destruction God was about to bring on the city. The Hebrew word for 'mark' (Ezek. 9.4, 6) is *tav*, which is also the name of the final letter in the alphabet (ת). The pun is intended, indicating that the mark took the form of the letter. This mark was interpreted as a sign of eschatological deliverance in Judaism of the Second Temple period and would have been available for Christian appropriation and reinterpretation from an early date.[48] In ancient Hebrew (Paleo-Hebraic or Phoenician) calligraphy, the *tav* was cruciform (✗ or ✝), and therefore resembled the Greek *chi* ('χ'). *Chi* is the first letter of *christos*, 'the anointed one' or 'messiah', which for Paul is as much a name as a title of Jesus. A cruciform mark that was already understood as a sign of eschatological deliverance invited Christian reinterpretation, and the transformation of the cross from an instrument of criminal execution to a symbol of triumph and deliverance. This is of course a process to which Paul's theology bears powerful testimony. The question is whether Paul gave his theology of the cross ritual expression in Baptism and whether this symbolic action could be described as a 'mark' or 'seal'.

Paul describes himself as bearing 'the marks of Jesus' on his body (Gal. 6.17), almost certainly referring to the scars of torture and specifically flogging (cf. 2 Cor. 11.24–25) he had endured in the course of his missions. The marks of Jesus distinguish Paul both from the Galatian Christians and from his rivals in apostolic authority in those communities, to whom he imputes a concern to avoid persecution (Gal. 6.12). He is therefore not referring to any covenantal symbol, physical or otherwise. Nevertheless, Paul implies a connection between his scars and the wounds sustained by Jesus at his crucifixion, and in Romans 6.3–4, written shortly after his correspondence with the church in Corinth, he makes a ritual connection between the Christian and the death of Jesus in Baptism, which we will consider in greater detail in the following section.

That Paul could quite graphically describe the scars on his body as 'the marks of Jesus' does not imply that his reference to Christians having been 'sealed' had no ritual counterpart. An allusion to the crucifixion of Jesus in the Baptism rite could quite naturally have been accompanied by describing the cross, visibly or otherwise, on the body, and specifically on the forehead, following the pattern set by Ezekiel and continued in the tradition.

God is described also as having 'given' the Corinthian Christians 'his Spirit', an empowerment that Paul has, in his earlier correspondence with this church, linked inextricably to Baptism (1 Cor. 12.13), as we have discussed above. This reinforces the baptismal resonances of this passage and underscores just how fundamental to Christian life and identity Baptism is for Paul. The gift of the Spirit is described as a pledge or 'assurance', the guarantee that God would complete the saving work begun in Baptism and bring to fulfilment the resurrection anticipated in Christian life 'in Christ'. The life of the body of Christ that has been disrupted by the tensions within the Corinthian church, and between the church and Paul, will be restored; the gifts and assurances God has bestowed will be fully realized, both in Paul's immediate purpose in the letter and in the eschatological consummation of God's saving work in Jesus.

While this passage may be deemed to add little if anything to our certain knowledge of Baptism as understood and practised in the churches established by Paul, it does illuminate a complex interaction of natural and traditional symbols relating to early Christian baptism. It is at the very least suggestive of a rite that may have been less simple than is often assumed, and illustrates the potential for ritual accumulation as words and metaphors lent themselves to symbolic enaction. This raises questions that will be considered in greater detail in the next chapter.

Suggested further reading

For exegesis of this text within its epistolary context, readers may wish to consult the recent commentaries on 2 Corinthians of Barrett, Collins, Furnish, Lambrecht, Martin, Scott and Thrall. Of these, Barrett, Collins and Scott are more accessible to the non-specialist reader.

Two further important works are Horrell, *The Social Ethos of the Corinthian Correspondence* and Winter, *After Paul left Corinth*.

Romans 6.3–5

The letter to the Romans was not written to a church Paul had founded, but served as his introductory overture to the Christian community already established in Rome. It is also the longest of Paul's letters and explains his teaching on key issues with perhaps greater care and clarity, and considerably less polemic, than is sometimes the case with his other letters. Some scholars have argued that Romans is a general, even definitive, statement of Paul's theology, written without regard for the specific pastoral circumstances that may have pertained in the Roman church, and with which Paul is unlikely to have been familiar. The letter has sometimes been described as Paul's 'last will and testament', and in his preface to Romans the reformer Martin Luther described it as the 'most important' document in the New Testament.

It is certainly true that Paul was not the founding apostle of the church in Rome and therefore could not claim the same pastoral authority he asserted in his dealings with churches such as those in Corinth and Galatia. This does not mean that Paul was entirely unaware of circumstances in the Roman church. Romans 16.3–16 indicates that he was acquainted with several of the Roman Christians, from whom he would almost certainly at some stage have learned something about the church in Rome. Paul may therefore have presented his theology so as to address issues he knew to be of concern to the Roman Christians and on which he perhaps perceived a need to clarify his position. The letter was written in anticipation of his arrival in Rome in person (Rom. 1.11–15; 15.22–33). He intended to exercise some form of ministry in Rome before continuing his missionary endeavours further west (Rom. 15.23–24). In that Paul clearly did not believe his ministry was about to be brought to an end, it would therefore not be accurate or helpful to describe Romans as Paul's last will and testament. It nevertheless remains a particularly important statement of his theology, reflecting his mature thought, expressed with care and awareness of his pastoral and missionary objectives.

A major purpose in Paul's letter to the Roman Christians was to prepare the ground for the visit to Rome he was planning. If the church in Rome was to be hospitable and receptive towards him, Paul needed to remove any suspicion or hostility there may have been on account of his reputation. His refusal to impose observance of the Jewish ritual laws on gentile converts to Christianity had brought him into conflict with other Christians who saw the law of Moses as normative for all Christians, irrespective of whether they had been born into Israel.[49] This created an impression, which persisted for centuries in Jewish and Christian-Jewish circles, that Paul had betrayed his Jewish heritage and encouraged a culture of moral licentiousness among those he converted to the Christian gospel: in placing their faith in Christ's saving death, rather than in observing the law of Moses, Christians could conduct themselves as they pleased and be nonetheless assured of salvation. We have seen that this may indeed have been a problem in the Corinthian church, and it is one that has occurred repeatedly throughout Christian history.

In the letter to the Romans Paul is responding to such a misconception of his theology and seeking to explain his position in ways the Roman Christians would find both acceptable and persuasive.

Paul draws on the rite of Baptism and the imagery associated with it to clarify his theology. His interpretation of Abraham, the archetypal proselyte and ancestor of Israel, of the covenant God formed with Abraham and of the saving death of Jesus, and his explanation of the role of the law of Moses in God's saving plan, lead into the passage in which Baptism reinforces the moral obligations of Christians. Paul's baptismal theology is not articulated as a subject in its own right but this is nonetheless arguably the text from which we can derive some of our most valuable and vivid insights into his teaching. It is significant that Paul assumes that the Roman Christians would share his understanding of Baptism, at least to the extent that they could be expected to identify with his line of argument. This suggests that the substance of Paul's teaching on this particular point is representative of a broader spectrum within the early Christian movement of his period. At the very least the mystical interpretation of Baptism in this passage, even if not integral to prevailing Christian thought in the Roman church, is assumed to be uncontentious among those to whom Paul addressed the letter. In other words, the interpretation of the rite of Baptism Paul offers in this passage presupposes some common ground between him and his addressees as to the essential nature and significance of Christian Baptism. This indicates a shared understanding of Baptism in the churches of the Mediterranean world during the middle decades of the first Christian century.

[3] Do you not know that as much as[50] we were baptized into Christ Jesus we were baptized into his death? [4] We were buried[51] with him through baptism into death, so that, as Christ was raised from the dead[52] through the glory of the Father, so also we might walk in newness of life. [5] For if we have become united to the likeness of his death, then we will be [united] also [to the likeness] of his resurrection.

Paul is countering any suspicion there may have been in the Roman church that his proclamation of the gospel, without requiring observance of the Jewish law, permitted or encouraged immoral behaviour. He employs his understanding of Baptism to demonstrate just how such conduct is, in fact, totally incompatible with the gospel he preaches. He poses the question rhetorically, expressing in the crudest fashion possible the extreme antinomian doctrine that Christians are free from all moral imperatives: 'Shall we continue in sin that grace may abound?' (Rom. 6.1). The logic Paul imputes to his, in this case hypothetical, opponent, known by some literary critics as an interlocutor, is: if (a) salvation is acquired through the grace of God and not through observance of the law of Moses or any other code that distinguishes right from wrong, and (b) the greater the sin, the more abundant the grace required to negate that sin and bestow salvation, then (c) the way to obtain maximum benefit from the grace of God is to commit sin as much as possible. Expressed less articulately and more amorally, antinomianism implies the irrelevance of moral behaviour and encourages total disregard for any standard of ethical conduct, in the assurance that grace will prevail unconditionally.

Paul rejects the antinomian ethic on the ground that conversion to Christianity involves 'death' to sin. Sin is to be understood as the power, deriving from Satan, that causes people to do wrong; it is not simply a category of behaviour but a spiritual force that influences human behaviour. It is therefore inconceivable that a Christian should condone, still less actively encourage, sinfulness or the wilful submission to the power of sin. In the preceding chapters of Romans, Paul has reaffirmed his doctrine of salvation procured through the grace of God alone and obtained through faith, apart from works of the law of Moses. While scholars continue to debate precisely how Paul understood the law of Moses and what continuing value he attached to it, it is clear that he did not reject its moral precepts. In common with other Jewish teachers of his day, Paul recognized that salvation could not be earned through observance of the law, but this did not mean that the law was of no value.[53]

Paul proceeds to demonstrate the incompatibility of the Christian life with amoral attitudes by expounding the ethical significance of Baptism. Baptism in the name of Jesus is Baptism 'into the death' of Jesus Christ. The rite of Christian Baptism, administered at some point in the past, continues to govern the life of the Christian in the present.[54] Scholars differ as to precisely how the crucifixion of Jesus and the Baptism of the Christian relate, or how the symbolic death undergone by Christians in the rite of Baptism can be equated with the death of Jesus on the cross. Some argue for a mystical identification, whereby the symbolic death undergone by the person baptized is identified with the death of Christ and therefore avails the benefits of Christ's death for the Christian.[55] A less absolute identification is also argued, in terms of which the death of Christ on the cross is 'actualized in Baptism' for the one baptized.[56] Alternatively, it is argued that baptism is identification with Christ in his death and resurrection, and death to sin in an ethical sense.[57] The differences between these interpretations concern the degree of mystical identification implied, but all agree that the salvific significance of Christ's death becomes realized, ethically, symbolically and spiritually, in the life of the person baptized. The analogy between Baptism and death is both more ancient and more widespread than Paul: the Gospel traditions record Jesus' having referred to his impending death as 'the baptism with which I am baptized' (Mark 10.38–39; Luke 12.50). More important to Paul than precision on a point of theological speculation, however, is the effect of 'death' and 'burial' with Christ in Baptism for the life of the Christian.

The imagery employed in this passage may seem uniquely vivid, at least to modern Western readers for whom interment of the dead in a hole in the ground (shaft grave), filled in with earth over the coffin, has been traditional and was normative until cremation was introduced during the twentieth century. A tank of similar proportions to a shaft grave, filled with water in which converts could be submerged, might allow a vivid analogy between Baptism and interment of the dead. This image has been so vivid and seemed so obvious that it has been one of the arguments, among Baptists and Pentecostals in particular, that submersion in water is essential to Christian Baptism. However, the imagery was by no means as obvious in Paul's day, as funeral customs were quite different from what was traditional in northern Europe through most of its Christian history, and exported from there to North America. Irrespective of how many other cultures may have used, and continue to use, similar graves for the burial of their dead, this was not the prevailing custom in the world in which Paul wrote Romans. In Rome during the first century, cremation of the dead was normative, and the ashes were placed in monuments generally located above ground. These might be family graves or those of one of the various associations that proliferated in the Roman world, often shaped like a columbarium.[58] In Judaism, on the other hand, subterranean interment was normative, with corpses laid out on shelves carved out of the rock in caves or underground tunnels (cavity graves), such as the Roman catacombs and the smaller burial complexes found in many parts of Palestine; the entrances to these could be closed but the cavity was not filled in with earth.[59] In the eastern Mediterranean regions, customs were much more varied, with cremation and interment in cavity graves both attested, the latter predominating.[60] The analogy between the grave and the baptismal bath would therefore not have been at the level of physical structure and would not have been dependent upon the modalities of corpse disposal. We therefore need to seek a much more profound connection between Baptism and ancient funeral rites.

In the ancient world, interment in holes in the ground, filled in with earth directly over the body, was the fate of the poor. The bodies of executed criminals and other outcasts were routinely dumped in rubbish pits, if not left exposed for scavenging animals to consume. If there is an analogy to be drawn between the shape of the grave and that of the baptismal bath, then the imagery Paul employs is not that of honourable and decent burial in either Jewish or pagan Roman custom but rather of dishonourable burial, as has been argued by Robert Jewett in his recent commentary on Romans.[61] Crucifixion, as a means of executing criminals, was a dishonourable death, and the burial that followed would of necessity be dishonourable. In invoking the image of death and burial, therefore, Paul is identifying the Roman Christians with the dishonourable nature of Jesus' death and burial. However, the pits into which general refuse, including the corpses of executed criminals, were cast were not filled in with earth, and bodies dumped there would be covered only with other rubbish. While this would be a powerful reminder of the circumstances of Jesus' death, to which Paul refers directly in Romans 6.6, the analogy is incomplete. This does not mean that Paul does not intend the readers and hearers of Romans to be reminded of the circumstances of Jesus' death, which clearly he does, but we should seek a more adequate interpretation.

If we are to understand what Paul is saying, we need to appreciate how death was understood in the ancient world and the function of funeral rites in relation to this. These are questions that have scarcely been considered in this context, at least partly because interpreters have been content with an almost visual analogy between a bath in which Baptism could be administered and the vertical shaft grave familiar in many parts of the world, but alien to the societies and cultures in which Paul lived and worked. In the modern world, people of faith, no less than others, tend to understand death as the end of the life of a human or animal body, as clinically defined. Even where there are expectations of salvation or eternity, and the faith that earthly life gives way to eternal life, there remains the notion of death as the point at which a living body becomes a corpse. In the ancient world, death is the state of being that people attain after the demise of their physical bodies, when they begin a transition from one form of life to another, from one sphere of existence to another. While there was a great deal of diversity both in popular belief and in philosophical speculation, we need to approach the Romans passage with an understanding of death that envisages a process whereby the soul vacates the body and undertakes its journey to the netherworld and the life that it continues there.[62] Funeral rites served to expedite this process; not simply a means of disposing of the corpse, the rites that accompanied death were intended to ensure that the deceased reached as congenial an afterlife as possible, as quickly as possible, and would not linger on earth and haunt home and family. The correlation between funeral rites and the quality of existence the deceased might enjoy in the afterlife meant that a great deal of expense was frequently dedicated to funerals and the construction of graves.

In this light we can understand the logic of Paul's statement, 'We were buried with him through baptism into death.' This inverts the sequence of death and burial to which the modern world is accustomed, precisely because the state of death is reached not at the point at which modern medicine would pronounce clinical death but when the body of the deceased has been deposited in the grave, accompanied by the performance of funeral rites, and the soul has departed from the body and completed the journey to the netherworld. Baptism is conceived as the funeral rite whereby the

Christian is symbolically conveyed to the netherworld. Washing the corpse was frequently the first stage in the funeral process, which may have suggested the analogy (cf. Acts 9.37).[63] Ritual washing enabled the deceased to proceed to new life uncontaminated by the impurities of earthly life. Baptism does not merely convey the convert to the state of death, however, it unites the Christian with Jesus in his death. The circumstances of Jesus' death, as a convicted and crucified criminal, could not be ignored. But, more importantly, the conquest of sin Jesus accomplished in his death is realized in the life of the Christian.

The consequence of death with Christ in Baptism is that the Christian attains union with Christ in his resurrection. The transition from dishonourable death to glorious resurrection is quite radical. The link between Baptism and resurrection has been denied,[64] but this ignores the inseparability of the crucifixion and resurrection of Jesus Christ in the defining narrative of the primitive Christian kerygma.[65] There has been a tendency to avoid any analogy between early Christianity and the motif of dying and rising deities in some of the pagan cults of the period, and of rituals in which initiates identified with these dying and rising deities. While there are sound reasons for questioning some of the connections drawn by earlier generations of scholars, in what was commonly known as the History of Religions School, it is nonetheless the case that Christianity emerged from Judaism into a Graeco-Roman world in which such ideas were known and readily understood.[66] Paul's frequent references to 'the cross' certainly refer directly to the crucifixion, but this event is meaningful only in the light of the resurrection. Furthermore, when Paul says that 'Christ was raised from the dead through the glory of the Father', this is to be understood as 'from among the dead'; in other words, from among the souls in hades, those who have died and passed through the grave to the netherworld. That Jesus would have gone to the abode of the dead when he died on the cross and was buried would have been taken for granted in the ancient world. In raising Jesus from the dead, God brought him from the netherworld to the heavenly world, from where he appeared to the disciples (1 Cor. 15.1–8). In Baptism, converts are symbolically transported from terrestrial life to the netherworld, from whence they are raised from the dead with

Christ. Baptism realizes the death of Jesus in the life of the convert and anticipates the eschatological resurrection to which Christians aspire.

Conversion, immersion in the baptismal waters and emergence from them correspond with the death, burial and resurrection of Jesus. This is more than metaphor and analogy, as the rite is understood as effecting the process of death, burial and resurrection in the convert. The rite of Baptism has been concluded, with the death it signifies marking a new beginning and that death continuing to govern the life of the person baptized. In verse 5 Paul describes Christians as having 'become united to the likeness of [Christ's] death', an identification with Christ in his death that is complete in Baptism but has continuing significance and effectiveness for Christian life in the present. This identification with Christ in his death ensures the Christian the same degree of identification with Christ in his resurrection. While the resurrection of Jesus has already been accomplished, the Christian identified with him in Baptism is given the assurance of future participation in his resurrection.

Not only does the Christian anticipate participation in the eschatological resurrection but, as a consequence of having died with Christ in Baptism, he or she has the opportunity to walk 'in newness of life'. In this new life, sin no longer dominates the human will as it does before conversion. The Christian has been granted freedom from sin through Baptism. He or she is therefore no longer controlled by sin and is accordingly able not to commit evil deeds. As well as bestowing salvation, the power transmitted through Baptism enables those baptized to live a new life, free of the dominating and corrupting power of sin. This involves the obligation to strive to lead a sinless life, notwithstanding dependence on the grace of God for salvation. This is integral to dying to sin and living in a manner compatible with the Christian faith. Without this, Baptism is meaningless. The rite is effective only insofar as death to sin, implicit in conversion, is realized in the life of the Christian. The supernatural and eschatological benefits of Baptism are attained only by those whose conversion and incorporation in the Church, and therefore their identification with Christ, are complete. The power of the Holy Spirit invoked and bestowed in Baptism is real, but will not be effective unless the ritual is complemented by the actions on the part of the baptized to complete the conversion and incorporation process. 'The physical actions involved in baptism have no meaning unless they signify that the man [sic] who has submitted to the rite has thereby died to sin and must henceforth walk "in newness of life"'.[67]

Romans 6.3–5 is perhaps the most profound of all Paul's statements on Baptism, and also that which has been most influential in subsequent Christian theology and liturgy. The symbolism of death and burial, followed by resurrection, to which Paul compares the baptismal rite, lent itself to the theological and mystical creativity of subsequent generations of Christians, especially the *descensus ad inferos*, the motif of the descent of the crucified Jesus to hades, destroying the power of Satan and releasing the souls of the righteous from death. While Paul's thought reflects this cosmology,[68] in this passage it is God who raises Jesus from the dead, and by implication those raised with him. More important for Paul than mythological speculation is the immediate moral consequence of Baptism for Christian life in the present. The death of Jesus is realized in the life of the Christian, so that the power of sin is overcome and the resurrection anticipated.

Suggested further reading

For exegesis of this passage in the context of the letter, readers may wish to consult the commentaries on Romans of Barrett, Black, Cranfield, Dunn, Fitzmyer, Jewett, Käsemann and Ziesler. Of these, Barrett and Ziesler are more accessible to the non-specialist reader.

Important recent treatments of this passage include Agersnap, *Baptism and the New Life*; Sabou, *Between Horror and Hope* and Tannehill, *Dying and Rising with Christ*.

I have discussed aspects of the translation of this passage in greater detail in my article 'Dying with Christ in Baptism'.

Another important recent book for understanding Romans is Stowers, *A Rereading of Romans*. A useful and accessible study of the origins of the church in Rome is Brown and Meier, *Antioch and Rome*.

Colossians 2.11–12

With Colossians we come to the letters in the Pauline corpus whose authorship is disputed. The issues surrounding pseudepigraphy have been identified above, and we cannot resolve these here. Without disregarding the important questions that have been raised in scholarship, it is clear that Colossians belongs to the Pauline corpus; if the letter was not written by Paul himself, it represents a conscious attempt to develop and perpetuate his teaching and authority in the Church. What is important for the present purpose is at what stage in the development of the Pauline tradition this letter is to be located. The theology expressed in it needs to be measured against what we read in the undisputed letters, and its continuity with the Pauline tradition thereby ascertained. Therefore when we have considered the passage in which Baptism is mentioned, we will compare it with the teaching on Baptism we have found in the undisputed letters of Paul.

Colossians is not addressed to a church Paul had founded or even visited. The city of Colossae was located on the Lycus river in Phrygia, not far from Hierapolis and Laodicaea in central Asia Minor. By the first Christian century the formerly prosperous city of Colossae was in decline following the rerouting of the Roman road from Ephesus to Pergamum. A major earthquake is reported to have devastated this area during either the seventh or the tenth year of the emperor Nero (i.e. 61 or 64).[69] The letter makes no mention of this catastrophe, after which Colossae was never rebuilt, which would seem to require either a date before the earthquake or a pseudepigraphal letter written many years later.

Colossae is adjacent to areas Paul is known to have evangelized. He does not, however, identify himself as the founding apostle of the church there, and there are several indications that he knew this particular community only by reputation (Col. 1.4, 7–8; 2.1). Tradition associates this letter with that to Philemon, with whom Paul would appear to have been personally acquainted (Philem. 19). It is surmised that Philemon was the leader of the church in Colossae, which met in his home. If this was the case, then we should expect that Philemon was patron or *oikodespotes* of a Christian household. Onesimus was the slave of Philemon and is the subject of Paul's letter to him,[70] and may be the same person as the Onesimus mentioned in Colossians 4.9. Paul's acquaintance with Onesimus, and decision to send him back to Philemon, would in this case provide the opportunity for Paul to address a letter to the church in Colossae at the same time as writing to its leader. This has been the traditional reconstruction of the background to Colossians and Philemon. While it is certainly plausible, it is no more than informed conjecture. In view of the disputed nature of Colossians and its background we will need to be circumspect in discussing its teaching on Baptism. For this reason I will refer to 'the writer' rather than using Paul's name of the author, and defer any conclusions about Paul's teaching on the basis of Colossians to a later stage in the discussion.

It is generally agreed in scholarship that Colossians was written to counteract the influence of a movement whose interpretation of the gospel was inimical to that of the Pauline tradition. It is extremely difficult to ascertain the nature of this movement but it would seem that philosophical speculation, presumably derived from one or more of the Greek schools, defined its approach to the gospel (Col. 2.8). It may be that the degree of philosophical abstraction led, from the perspective of the Pauline tradition, to neglect of the historical and incarnational basis of Christian faith (2.9). Articulating the gospel in the language and conceptual framework of Greek philosophy was a complex and frequently divisive undertaking over the centuries after Paul. It was inevitable that this enterprise would be undertaken once Christianity had become established in the Greek world, and that however Hellenized the Judaism from which Christianity emerged, translating concepts from one philosophical system to another was always likely to be a contested and controversial process, and one towards which Paul had perhaps been somewhat ambivalent (cf. 1 Cor. 1.18–25).

It is clear that the writer of Colossians is concerned to defend the historical and physical foundations of the Christian gospel, God's presence in the human being, Jesus Christ, who lived in the created, material world (2.9). The connection between physical and spiritual, and the nature of each, underlie much of the argument of the letter, not least in the passage in which appeal is made to the common Christian experience of Baptism to illustrate the author's theological points.

[11] In [Christ] you were circumcised with a circumcision not made by hands, in the stripping of the body of flesh, in the circumcision of Christ. [12] You were buried[71] with him in baptism, in which also you were raised with him through faith in the power of God who raised him from the dead.[72]

The interpretation of these verses depends largely on how the analogy between Baptism and circumcision is to be understood. In Judaism, circumcision was the sign of membership of God's covenant with Abraham and therefore of membership of Israel. Boys born into the nation of Israel, and therefore into the covenant, were circumcised, following the pattern of Abraham's circumcision of Isaac (Gen. 21.4), on the eighth day of their lives. Males of gentile origin who joined Israel through conversion underwent circumcision as part of the proselytization rite. This process would almost certainly also have included ritual washing for purification from the contamination of pagan idolatry, even if such washing was not attributed any initiatory significance in itself at this date.[73] In other words, for male gentile converts to Judaism, circumcision was a ritual of initiation into a new identity, symbolizing a disjunction in the life cycle whereby an inherited identity was renounced and a new identity, as a member of Israel, assumed. Male ethnic Jews acquired their identity through birth, and circumcision for them was a rite of passage in which the defining symbol of their identity as Jews was conferred soon after birth; that identity itself was not conferred through circumcision, even if the failure of fathers to have their sons circumcised was deemed a fundamental violation of their covenantal obligations.

The normative rite was that of circumcision of male Jewish babies; the incorporation of proselytes by circumcision was derivative and in significant ways quite different in its function and purpose. Christian Baptism, on the other hand, originated as a conversion and incorporation ritual, representing a radical change of identity and membership of a new community. Baptism was not a rite of passage in the life cycle of an established national or cultural group. The identity conferred through Baptism was not inherited, at least in principle, and Baptism therefore could not confirm or symbolize an identity acquired by birth. Such interpretations might have become possible by the time of writing, if Colossians is a pseudepigraphical letter, and Baptism have become a Christian rite of passage.[74] Such an understanding, however, could not have become established Christian teaching in Asia before the Colossian earthquake. It is therefore unlikely that the historical Paul could have presupposed such an understanding of Baptism in this letter.

Circumcision was a rite of conversion and incorporation, conferring new identity, only for proselytes to Judaism. The rite of passage that followed birth into Israel (for the male) was adapted so that the incorporation of a proselyte into Israel simulated birth, but it was nonetheless a conversion rite. It was this specific usage of circumcision in Judaism that would have been analogous to Christian Baptism during the first century. Baptism certainly became a life-cycle ritual or rite of passage when the Church became essentially a self-perpetuating institution, growing through procreation rather than evangelism, and Christianity became the distinctive culture of its members. Precisely when this change happened is difficult to establish; it is likely that the transition took place very gradually and at different times in different places, and that Baptism functioned simultaneously as a rite of passage for infants born into Christian families and as a rite of incorporation for new converts joining the same community, perhaps over several centuries. Those churches of the early centuries that have left any records seem to have continued attracting and incorporating converts throughout this period, and would therefore have been baptizing both converts and those born into Christian households. But whether this was already the case by the time Colossians was written, to the extent that Baptism of infants born to Christian parents had become normative, is quite another matter. The point of this is that Christian Baptism and Jewish circumcision were not analogous rites during the early years of the Church. Paul nowhere in his polemics against those Christians seeking to impose observance of the law of Moses on gentile Christians cites Baptism as having replaced circumcision. As we noted in our discussion of the passage in Galatians, Paul clearly regarded Christian Baptism as a much more powerful ritual than circumcision, whether of born Jews or of proselytes. Nevertheless, there is no direct correlation between the two, and the comparison drawn between Baptism and circumcision in this passage therefore needs particularly careful consideration.

Circumcision had, at least since the Maccabean revolt, been a defining symbol of Jewish covenantal identity. It is therefore unlikely that this passage is free of anti-Jewish polemic. It is of the nature of polemic, even in Christian documents such as those that have become part of the New Testament canon, that its portrayal of opposing positions is disparaging and often unfair and inaccurate. We therefore cannot expect to learn a great deal about Judaism and Jewish circumcision customs, or even about any particular group within Judaism that this letter is opposing, from a passage such as this. But we can learn something about how the early Christians, in this instance in the Pauline tradition, defined themselves over against Israel and its much larger and more powerful institutions during this period.

The circumcision undergone by the Colossian Christians is described as 'not made by hands'. The opposite of this would of course be 'made by hands'. Such an expression could be used to describe an object, or in this case a process, as the work of human artisanship in a descriptive and morally neutral sense, or even in a highly complimentary sense, implying that the handmade product is distinctive and qualitatively superior to an industrially produced object. However, in Judaism the expression 'made by hands' acquired pejorative connotations in certain contexts. In the Old Testament, idols and the accessories of pagan worship are described as 'made by hands'; in other words, as having been manufactured by the very people who worship them, in contrast to the living God worshipped by Israel, who is no creature of human artistry (cf. Ps. 135.15–18). In the early Church this kind of polemic was on occasion applied to Jewish institutions, an example being Stephen's condemnation of the temple in Jerusalem (Acts 7.48). The letter to the Hebrews uses the same language to contrast the death of Jesus with the sacrificial system of the Jerusalem temple (9.11, 24). Paul similarly uses the word *acheiropoietos* to contrast the earthly, mortal, body and the heavenly, eternal, body (2 Cor. 5.1). If this sense of the word is intended in the Colossians passage, it would suggest that (Jewish) circumcision concerns only the physical, earthly, body and is of no eternal significance, whereas Christian Baptism has a significance that transcends the limitations of earthly life. Baptism is therefore a more powerful ritual than circumcision, conferring entry into the eternal, heavenly, life Christians are promised, which transcends membership of one particular nation on earth.

The description 'not made by hands' suggests that the 'circumcision' indicated is a spiritual transformation rather than a physical ritual, and implies a contrast with the Jewish rite of circumcision. The 'circumcision not made by hands' could be Christian Baptism,[75] but it is only with the derivative rite of proselyte circumcision that Christian Baptism could be compared. Other possible interpretations of this 'circumcision' include an ethical disposition rather than a physical or ritual act, indicating complete obedience to the will of God.[76] According to this understanding, the contrast with Jewish circumcision would be in terms of obedience to God's will as opposed to strict and pedantic observance of the law of Moses. If this is the correct interpretation, we need to be particularly conscious of the polemical nature of the reference. However, 'circumcision not made by hands' could allude much more broadly to renunciation of earthly values. These are associated with the physical body that is cut during circumcision as opposed to a spiritual body whose repudiation of earthly values is depicted as a spiritual circumcision. It is also possible to interpret 'circumcision not made by hands' as participation in the death of Jesus,[77] which, as we have observed, Paul associates with Baptism in Romans and which is implicit in the funerary imagery that occurs also in these verses.

The Christian experience of 'circumcision not made by hands' is described also as, or is an aspect of, a process described as 'the stripping of the body of flesh'. This is clearly another metaphorical expression. 'Flesh' has pejorative connotations in the anthropology of several Hellenistic philosophical schools, in particular those that elevate a spiritual realm above the physical. For Paul and for other early Christians, God, while creator of the physical universe, is associated with the spiritual world, to whose values and whose life Christians are to aspire. The 'flesh' would be identified with human impulses and desires to be repudiated, which leave people vulnerable to temptation and the power of sin, and with the conventions of human society and its rulers who defy the sovereignty of God. The element of dualism in Paul's thought, and in that of the tradition that followed him, cannot be denied, and some later mutations in the tradition were to develop Gnosticizing tendencies.

The metaphor of 'stripping' is suggestive of undressing before entering the baptismal water. We noted that this imagery may be implied or presupposed in the passage from Galatians considered above. Clothing served not only to preserve modesty and protect from the elements but also to indicate identity and status. 'Stripping' would therefore represent the renunciation of a previous identity and status, so that Christian identity could be conferred through Baptism and reflected symbolically in the clothes worn thereafter. If 'the body of flesh' is the identity discarded at Baptism, then all that is associated not only with mortality but also with the values generated and perpetuated in human societies, including the power of sin in the world, is repudiated.

'Circumcision not made by hands' and 'stripping the body of flesh' correspond with a third enigmatic expression, 'the circumcision of Christ'. Historically, Jesus as a Jew would have been circumcised when he was a week old (Luke 2.21), as Paul presupposes when he alludes to the ethnic and cultural heritage of Jesus, and specifically his birth (Rom. 1.3; Gal. 4.4). This has never been in dispute within subsequent orthodox Christianity but it is highly unlikely that the writer is referring here to the rite of passage undergone by Jesus as a male Jewish infant. This is of little theological or salvific relevance, whereas the use of 'Christ' rather than 'Jesus' in this verse could suggest that the 'circumcision' pertains directly to the messiahship of Jesus; however, the tendency to use 'Christ' as a name is well established in the Pauline tradition, indicating the fundamental inseparability of Jesus and his messianic role and status. It has been argued that 'the circumcision of Christ' is his death on the cross,[78] or 'the circumcision that belongs to Christ, which is given by him, which brings forgiveness of sins and thus makes it possible to live ethically in a new way'.[79] The 'circumcision of Christ' somehow connects the Christian convert with the death of Jesus, so that the benefits of that are manifested in the transformation of the person and he or she transcends the limitations of earthly life to enter the spiritual realm. This is a process Paul associates directly with Baptism.

We have noted above that the Baptism rite may, even during the years of Paul's missionary career, have been more complex and potentially more varied than brief allusions in the letters and the accounts in Acts may suggest. The metaphor of 'stripping' indicates that the water rite is the context in which other symbolic acts may have been performed; we should therefore not seek to identify any separate rite but rather to recognize that Baptism may have been accompanied by other ritual acts or by actions that acquired a ritual interpretation. The significance that came to be attached to undressing and clothing, before and after immersion, would be an example of the latter. We have also noted evidence that the cross was being used as a Christian symbol by the third quarter of the first Christian century, much earlier than previous scholarship believed.[80] We know that consignation, or the sign of the cross, formed a part of the baptismal rite of at least some churches by the end of the second century.[81] If visual depiction of the cross was a recognized Christian symbol during the first century, then we need to consider Paul's verbal imagery in his letters and the manual gestures that may have been used during the oral delivery of it and also during the proclamation of the gospel and the administration of Christian rituals that alluded to the crucifixion of Jesus. In Romans 6.3–4, as we have noted, Paul makes a ritual connection between the Christian and the death of Jesus in Baptism, a connection repeated in these verses. The question we need to ask is whether the mode of Jesus' death may have been represented in the ritual, and whether 'the circumcision of Christ' may reflect this.

While the book of Revelation would not commonly be associated with the Pauline tradition,[82] it undoubtedly has an Asian provenance. The letters to the seven churches include those of Ephesus, with which the historical Paul is associated (Acts 19.1–20.1, 17–38; 1 Cor. 15.32; 16.8) and of Laodicaea, a church to which the author of Colossians attributes a close relationship with the church of Colossae (2.1; 4.13–16). If they reflect distinct traditions within early Christianity, as most scholars believe, then it is significant that Paul or his successors, and the seer of Revelation, should claim authority over churches not merely in the same geographical area but in at least two of the same cities, within no more than a few decades of each other. Whatever tensions there may have been between their respective movements,[83] it is unlikely that the Pauline and Johannine traditions would not have held symbols and rituals in common.

Several passages in Revelation speak of marking the forehead as a means of identifying a person's allegiance. The infamous 'mark of the beast' (13.16; 14.9; cf. 17.5) and the tribulations to befall those who refuse to submit to it (20.4) are perhaps the more prominent in contemporary Christian consciousness. The mark that identifies the redeemed is rather more important for our present purpose. In Revelation 7.1–8 an angel uses 'the seal of the living God' to mark 'the servants of our God', the one hundred and forty four thousand from the tribes of Israel, 'upon their foreheads'. In 14.1 this group are described as having 'the name of the Lamb and of his Father inscribed upon their foreheads'. Similarly, in Revelation 22.1–4 'his servants' have 'his name on their foreheads', referring to the Lamb and God as though one.

The scene in Revelation 7, reflected elsewhere in that book, is a reinterpretation of Ezekiel 9, a passage we have considered above in connection with Paul's use of the image of sealing in 2 Corinthians 1.21–22 (the following reiterates some of that discussion). Those who have received 'the seal of God upon their foreheads' (Rev. 7.3) are similarly to be spared the punitive torture meted out on the rest of creation (Rev. 9.4). The Hebrew word for 'mark' (Ezek. 9.4, 6) is *tav*, also the name of the final letter in the alphabet (ת), which in the calligraphy of the period, and until much later, was cruciform (✗ or ✝); even if the square characters of Aramaic script were in increasingly common use in Hebrew by this date, the Paleo-Hebrew script remained in use, particularly for sacred texts. The resemblance between the *tav* and the Greek 'χ' (*chi*) would therefore have been significant. *Chi* is the first letter of *christos*, the anointed one or messiah, which in both the Pauline and the Johannine traditions became as much a name as a title of Jesus. That the seer of Revelation envisages 'the name of the Lamb' as being represented by a cruciform mark is therefore probable. This mark had been interpreted as a sign of eschatological deliverance in Judaism of the Second Temple period,[84] as is the seal in Revelation 7.2–3. Furthermore, in Revelation 22.1–2 the 'water of life' is described as 'flowing from the throne of God and of the Lamb' as a lifegiving and healing river. This is at the very least suggestive of Baptism and of a symbolic connection between a cruciform symbol and saving water.

Revelation reflects a tradition of interpretation of Ezekiel 9 available for Christian appropriation from an early date, and attests its usage in the geographical vicinity of the church to which this letter is addressed. Paul's theology bears eloquent testimony to the transformation of the cross from an instrument of criminal execution to a symbol of triumph and deliverance. An allusion to the crucifixion of Jesus in the Baptism rite could quite naturally have been accompanied by describing the cross on or over the body, and specifically on the forehead. The marking in Ezekiel is not violent or bloody and would not be suggestive of ritual laceration or tattooing, but nonetheless furnished early Christianity with a symbolism that could be appropriated, with or without using oil or water, to link the saving death of Jesus with those ritually incorporated into the community of his body. That the author of Colossians not only had available but also used a Christian tradition of interpretation of Ezekiel 9, in which a ritual inscription of the cross as a covenantal sign, akin to circumcision, formed part of the baptismal rite, is at the very least a tantalizing possibility.

Christians are 'buried' with Christ 'in baptism'; as we have noted in our discussion of Romans 6.3–4, this means that funeral rites have been performed, not simply deposition of the corpse in a grave. We noted also that 'death' cannot simply be equated with the cessation of vital functions in the physical body but designates the state of being to which the person migrates on leaving that body. Irrespective of the type of grave that may have been envisaged or imagined, Baptism has conveyed the converts from one form of existence to another, from terrestrial life to death; the demise of the physical body is represented by at least one, and perhaps all, of the three preceding phrases: 'circumcision not made by hands', 'stripping of the body of flesh', 'circumcision of Christ'. We have noted that in the ancient Greek world the transition from earthly life to the netherworld involved separation of the soul from the body, a notion that could be reflected in 'stripping of the body of flesh', of which circumcision could be a metaphor. Baptism effects this transition and is thus a more powerful ritual than proselyte circumcision, which merely admits converts to an inferior grade of membership of Israel. Their Baptism symbolizes and effects their union with Christ in his death and resurrection, whereby God has overcome hostile powers in the universe, which assures the Colossian Christians of their salvation, apart from observance of the law of Moses.

It is notable that, whereas in Romans 6.5 Paul promises a future resurrection to those who have died with Christ in Baptism, here the Colossian Christians are told that they 'were raised with [Christ] through faith'. It is not merely death, as the place and state of repose of those whose terrestrial lives have come to an end, that is anticipated in Baptism but also the resurrection. Christians have already assumed their resurrection life in their Baptism, even if that process is not complete. Whereas in Romans, Christ's resurrection has ensured the eschatological resurrection of those who die with him in Baptism, in this passage it is implied that the resurrection process has already begun. This understanding of resurrection is remarkably similar to that which Paul seems to be avoiding and cautioning against in 1 Corinthians.[85] In Baptism, Christians enter a union with Christ in his death and resurrection. Faith in the power of God, who raised Christ from the dead, to bring about their eschatological resurrection is the response required of Christians. Faith realizes the union with Christ in his death and resurrection and it is therefore through faith that the eschatological resurrection is to be attained.

There are scholars who believe that this passage is not fully compatible with the ideas Paul expresses in connection with Baptism in his undisputed letters. This would not be the only reason why they believe this letter dates to some time after Paul's ministry, but the notion expressed here that Christians have already experienced resurrection in their Baptism, or at least have begun that process, would be one factor in their arguments. It is certainly the case that this passage represents some development in Paul's theology of the cross. This may represent a deepening of the mystical understanding expressed in Romans, rather than departing from Paul's teaching.[86] Rather than radical innovation, this text would then bring to their logical conclusion ideas already implicit in such passages as Romans 6. We should, furthermore, be wary of placing too much emphasis on the verb tenses. Resurrection is an inherently eschatological concept, and the correlation between temporal history and chronology on the one hand and the eschatological unfolding of God's purposes in history on the other is complex, and the latter cannot simply be equated with terrestrial conceptions of time.[87] We need therefore to be cautious in postulating a significant theological shift between Romans and Colossians. If there is any innovation regarding Baptism and related issues in the latter epistle, this would lie not so much in the notion of resurrection as already under way as in the introduction of circumcision to the discussion of Baptism. Whereas Paul is very concerned in Galatians that gentile Christians should not undergo proselyte circumcision, he does not explicitly state that Baptism replaces circumcision. It could, however, be inferred from Galatians 3.26–28, which we have discussed above, that Baptism serves to incorporate Christians into the covenant God had entered with Abraham, and therefore functions for gentile Christians in the same way as circumcision does for proselytes to other forms of Judaism. Useful as this line of argument could have been in Galatians, Paul does not spell it out in that letter. Similarly, in this passage in Colossians the logical contrast between Christian Baptism and the circumcision of proselytes to other forms of Judaism is at most implicit. While this passage does reflect some development in the understanding of the relationship of the Christian Church with the nation of Israel, the imagery employed does not substantially alter the meaning of Christian Baptism as we have found it reflected in the undisputed Pauline letters.

Colossians 3.9–11

A brief allusion, not so much to the water rite of Baptism as to the stripping and clothing that precede and follow, is worth noting:

> [9] . . . having put off the old nature[88] with its practices, [10] and having put on the new nature, which is being renewed in knowledge according to the image of its creator, [11] in whom there is no gentile[89] and Jew, circumcision and uncircumcision, barbarian, Scythian, slave, free, but Christ is all and in all.

This passage would seem clearly to reflect the same tradition as that transmitted in Galatians 3.26–29. As well as the emphasis on the clothing image, representing moral transformation as well as change in identity, there are conspicuous developments in the list of contrasting identities that are overcome in the 'new nature' that has been acquired in Baptism. Not only is the contrast between male and female omitted but the ethnic and cultural distinctions have been expanded. The primary emphasis remains on Jews and other nations, as is clear from the explicit reference to circumcision which, while not unique to Judaism, nonetheless fundamentally both defined Jewish self-identity and was particularly associated with Judaism by others. The addition of 'barbarians' and, specifically, 'Scythians' emphasizes the inclusion of nations on and beyond the borders of the Graeco-Roman world, who were generally held in contempt as lacking the tenets of civilization.

The notion of Jesus as the 'image' of God recalls the christological hymn quoted earlier in the letter, at 1.15–20. Jesus is described as 'the image of the invisible God, the firstborn of all creation'. He is associated both with the creation of the world and with God's new creation through his death and resurrection. In both these stages of creation, Jesus holds primacy and is also described as 'the head of the body, the Church'. The image of the Church as Christ's body is found in the undisputed letters of Paul, particularly 1 Corinthians 12.12–31, where it is closely associated with Baptism. These verses therefore reflect close continuity with the sections both of Galatians and of 1 Corinthians in which Paul uses the Christian experience of Baptism to illustrate and reinforce his teaching.

Suggested further reading

For exegesis of these passages and discussion of the place of Colossians in the Pauline tradition, readers may wish to consult the commentaries on Colossians of Dunn, Hay, Houlden (*Paul's Letters from Prison*), Lohse, Moule and Schweizer. Of these, Hay and Houlden are more accessible to the non-specialist reader.

Ephesians 1.13–14

Ephesus was one of the most important cities of the Roman Empire and capital of the province of Asia, an area that encompasses much of the south-west of the modern state of Turkey. Located where the river Cayster meets the Aegean, Ephesus was an important trading centre, notwithstanding long-standing problems with siltation that affected access to the harbour, ultimately leading to abandonment of the city some centuries after the New Testament period – as a result of which the archaeological site now lies several miles inland. As well as being a mercantile seaport, which would have attracted a cosmopolitan population, Ephesus was a major centre of Graeco-Roman paganism. The temple to the goddess Artemis or Diana was one of the major pilgrimage destinations of the period, and directly and indirectly its cult played a significant part in the economy of the city. Its location made Ephesus a likely centre in which the Christian gospel would be proclaimed at an early date, and the prominence of the cult of Artemis meant that any Christian or Jewish group that attracted gentile adherents was likely to incur furious opposition from vested interests in the city.

We know from Acts 19 and 20 and from 1 Corinthians 16.8 that Paul operated for some time in Ephesus, and that his associates Aquila, Priscilla and Apollos were also active there. The church in Ephesus nonetheless came to be associated with the Johannine rather than the Pauline tradition in subsequent generations of early Christianity, as is reflected in one of the letters to the seven churches of Asia in the book of Revelation (2.1–7). The apostle John, accompanied by Mary the mother of Jesus and his namesake the seer of Revelation, are all located in Ephesus by various ancient traditions. Paul's influence in the church of Ephesus may therefore have diminished or been assimilated into a Johannine type of Christianity during the late first or early second century.[90] It is also possible that Pauline and Johannine traditions coexisted and eventually coalesced during the first century of Christianity in Ephesus and indeed in other parts of Asia, as we have noted above. Early in the second century, Ignatius of Antioch, who clearly regarded Paul as his model, addressed a letter to the church in Ephesus in which he both alludes to the Pauline origins of the Ephesian church (12.1–2) and conveys traditions about Mary the mother of Jesus (18.2–19.1), which may reflect consciousness of her importance in the Ephesian church. It is therefore not at all unlikely that Paul wrote a letter to the church in Ephesus. It is not for these reasons, however, that many scholars question the date and authorship of the canonical letter to the Ephesians. The theology expressed in the letter clearly belongs to the Pauline tradition; what is in question is whether this document was a letter sent by Paul to the church in Ephesus. Not all the surviving ancient manuscripts of the letter include the opening address to the church 'in Ephesus' (1.1). For this reason it has been argued that this document was not originally a letter addressed to the Ephesian church, but rather an abstraction or epitome of Paul's thought, with material redacted from several letters to create the canonical document. We therefore cannot be certain whether the canonical letter addresses any particular pastoral situation or what this would have been. We can merely study the texts in which Baptism appears and consider how the theology reflected in these passages compares with that in other references to Baptism in the Pauline corpus.

[13] In [Christ] you also, having heard the word of truth, the gospel of your salvation, and having believed, were sealed with the promised Holy Spirit, [14] which is the pledge of our inheritance, until we have taken possession, to the praise of his glory.

These verses resemble in many respects 2 Corinthians 11.21–22. While there is no explicit mention of Baptism, conversion in response to hearing the gospel proclaimed is quite clearly being referred to, and reception of the Spirit is unambiguously associated with Baptism, most notably in 1 Corinthians 12.

It is worth noting, again, that the English words used in translation can be misleading, in that their semantic range can differ from the Greek original and suggest a rather weaker meaning to the statements made in the text. This is true of 'word', where the Greek *logos* denotes much more than a unit of language. Like the English, but even more so, *logos* embraces a wide range of units of speech, from a single term to a statement or oration, including also the thought behind the speech. Rational thought, and the power that makes such thought possible, are also within the semantic range of *logos*. It is worth noting that in the prologue to the Gospel of John, Jesus is identified as the incarnate *logos* of God, not merely the personification of God's creative power in speech but a manifestation of God. This reflects the fruit of the philosophical encounter between Judaism and Greek philosophy over the previous centuries, represented most conspicuously by Philo of Alexandria (*c*.20 BC–AD 45). While there is no question that 'word' here is to be understood as an incarnation of God, the verb 'heard' makes clear that the oral proclamation of the Christian gospel is meant. Nevertheless, we need to recognize that the gospel is communicated in a way that makes it present and powerful in the lives of those who receive it. The 'word' conveys and realizes that of which it speaks.

As with 'word', the English term 'believe' is much weaker than the Greek. The verb *pisteuo* means much more than to hold a particular opinion or assent to a proposition. There are connotations of trust and commitment, reflected also in the related noun *pistis*, rendered 'faith' in English. The recipients of the letter are described as having placed their faith in the gospel, in response to having experienced its power when it was proclaimed to them. It is clear, therefore, that this text is referring to conversion to the Christian gospel, irrespective of how late a date may be ascribed to the letter.

The converts are described as having been 'sealed with the . . . Holy Spirit'. As we have noted above, seals were used to demonstrate ownership and authority. Paul described circumcision as the seal of God's covenant with Abraham, the sign that confirmed the righteousness Abraham had already attained (Rom. 4.11). Similarly, the Holy Spirit inhabits the Christian as a sign of the salvation that has been conferred. We have considered, in respect to previous texts, whether there may have been any ritual counterpart or expression of the sealing within the Baptism rite. While the emphasis in this text is on the reception of the Spirit, this does not imply any separation of ritual from experience. We have noted in 2 Corinthians 1.21–22 that the Spirit is described as a 'pledge' or 'assurance', the anticipation in the present of the salvation that will be attained in the future. The continuing presence of the Holy Spirit in the Christians is the 'assurance' of the 'salvation' of which they have not yet taken full possession.

The author describes 'salvation' as the 'inheritance' of the Christians. We noted in considering the passage in Galatians above that the laws and conventions of inheritance essentially governed the perpetuation of households. In the absence of a natural heir, adoption was a widespread and legally recognized means of ensuring the succession and continuation of the household. In Galatians, Paul is concerned to demonstrate that all Christians inherit that which God had promised Abraham, irrespective of their ethnic origins and status in human households of their day. Some of these concerns are reflected in Ephesians, not least 2.11–22, which seeks to overcome barriers separating Jews and gentiles in the Church. The author shares the concern expressed by Paul in Galatians for the inclusion of gentile Christians in the church on the same basis as Christians of Jewish origin. While the issue of observance of the law of Moses is less apparent, it does seem that the author is concerned to counter claims to privilege on the part of some Jewish Christians: 'So then you are no longer strangers and aliens, but you are citizens with the saints and also members of the household of God' (2.19). This is further reinforced in 3.6, where gentile Christians are described as 'fellow heirs, members of the same body, fellow partakers of the promise'. Irrespective of how Jews and gentiles in the Christian community addressed by this letter were relating to each other, and of precisely how the author wishes to see this rectified, it is important that we recognize the ongoing concern with how Jewish and gentile Christians coexist within a single community. The imagery of the household and of citizenship upholds the essential unity and equality between Christians of diverse origins.

The emphasis on the experience of conversion and reception of the Holy Spirit in this passage is not about individual salvation but about how those who come to faith live in a community defined by that faith. In that the text refers explicitly to conversion, and the letter is addressed to a community who have received salvation, we should understand this passage to allude to the rite of Baptism, whereby the converts are incorporated into the Church. Of greater concern than the modalities of incorporating converts into the community, however, is the life of that community formed through Baptism. That the author is concerned about continuing divisions or barriers between Jewish and gentile members of the church, and perhaps also between Greeks and Romans on the one hand and those considered 'barbarians and Scythians' on the other, suggests that the significance of Baptism has not been fully understood and remains to be realized in the life of the community. This will become clearer when we consider the next passage.

We have asked, in connection with passages from 2 Corinthians and Colossians, whether the symbolism of marking or sealing may have had any ritual counterpart in Baptism. While the church in Ephesus is one of those addressed by the seer in Revelation (2.1–7), we have noted that the manuscript evidence for the address to the church 'in Ephesus' (Eph. 1.1) is weak. We therefore cannot assume that the Ephesian church was the original recipient of this letter. The account of the origins of that church in Acts may accordingly not be relevant to the background of the letter. Paul's discussion of the coming of the Holy Spirit with the disciples of John the Baptist (Acts 19.1–7) would be an intriguing background to the emphasis here on the Spirit's having been 'promised', but the distance in time and location between these texts is too tenuous for any connection to be made.[91]

While we cannot be certain that Ephesians is addressed to Christians in Asia and reflects Christian traditions transmitted there, this does not mean the symbolism of Ezekiel 9 was unknown to the recipients or that it was not reflected in their rituals. However, the emphasis in this text is on the experience of the Christians in their conversion to the gospel and reception of the Holy Spirit, and in the life of the community formed thereby. The rites that symbolized this process are implicit in the text, and we will note in the next section that it becomes much more explicit as the letter progresses that the author considers the full implications of Baptism not to have been realized in the life of the church.

Ephesians 4.4–6

[4] There is one body and one Spirit, just as you were called to one hope in your calling: [5] one Lord, one faith, one baptism. [6] One God and Father of us all, who is over all and through all and in all.

The community addressed in the letter have been called upon to lead their lives in a manner worthy of their faith. Maintaining unity within the Church is an important aspect of this. We have noted some continuity with the issues reflected in Galatians, and there appears also to be some similarity with the problems reflected in 1 Corinthians, where gifts of the Spirit had become the cause of competition and discord in the community. The recipients are reminded that the spiritual gifts are for use in building up the Church, the body of Christ. The unity of the 'body' and of the 'Spirit', and the common faith and hope that unite Christians, form the basis of the appeal for unity in the community. Just as there is one 'Lord', Jesus Christ, there is one 'faith', that which is a response to the gospel of Christ, and one 'baptism' into the one Church. 'Faith' in this context is to be understood as the substance of the doctrines that form the basis of Christian allegiance to God and to Jesus Christ, rather than simply the verbal expression of that allegiance. In other words, 'faith' is the saving work God accomplished through the death and resurrection of Jesus Christ, the dispensation brought about through the faithfulness of Jesus to God, rather than Christian profession of faith in God or in Jesus Christ.[92] In Baptism Christians profess their allegiance to that faith and are incorporated into the 'body' of Christ. The transcendent unity of 'God' the 'Father' is the ultimate source of the unity in the body of Christ, in which the 'one Spirit' is immanent.

Baptism is the rite of incorporation into the Church and therefore into the body of Christ, from which the member derives his or her identity. Baptism is inauguration into the community animated by the Spirit, which acknowledges the one Lord, professes the one faith, anticipates the one hope, baptizes with the one Baptism and, above all, worships the one God. These aspects of the life of the Church are inseparable. Baptism therefore implies membership of the one body, being empowered by the one Spirit, expecting the one hope, acknowledging the one Lord, professing the one faith and worshipping the one God. The corporate nature of Christian identity realized through Baptism is strongly emphasized, in that the initiated Christian becomes a member of the Church united by the Spirit in its worship of God and profession of the Christian faith. Powerful as the rite is, Baptism does not negate human freedom, and Christians have the obligation to conduct themselves in a manner appropriate to their place in the body, maintaining 'the unity of the Spirit in the bond of peace' (4.3). In other words, the unity of the body and harmony within its fellowship should not be undermined by the way members exercise the gifts bestowed on them by the Holy Spirit.

The continuity between 1 Corinthians and this text is clear, and there is no substantial development or departure from the teaching expounded in the undisputed letters of Paul. The teaching is undoubtedly Pauline in ethos, even if the letter itself was not written by Paul. Before reaching conclusions about the relationship of Ephesians to the Pauline corpus, however, there is a further passage we must consider.

Ephesians 5.25–27

Colossians, Ephesians and the Pastoral Letters include passages sometimes described as 'household codes', in which relationships and behaviour in the family or household are regulated. Given the importance of the household in the social structure of the ancient world, and the significant role played by householders in the Church, the concern that household relations be managed so as not to disrupt the life of the Church or harm the interests of those on whose goodwill it depended is hardly surprising. These passages are, by modern standards, patriarchal and authoritarian in their ethos. The absolute subordination of wives to their husbands and of children to their parents, in particular their fathers, which was normative in ancient society, is presumed to be in accordance with the will of God and the order of creation. It is therefore expounded as an unquestioned principle of Christian life in these texts. Moreover, the institution of slavery is presupposed, and there is no hint of insight that this may be contrary to the gospel or to the will of God, still less any recognition that slaves had human rights that were violated by their servitude, however benign. Many scholars are accordingly reluctant to attribute these letters, or at least these sections within them, to the work of Paul.[93] Many Christians consider these passages, if not oppressive in themselves then at the very least as giving licence for repressive conduct and the abuse of power on the part of those who enjoy status and wield authority in society. Some would argue that, far from being the work of

Paul, these passages represent a perversion of Paul's teaching in the service of vested interests in society. It is often suggested that the early Church moderated or even departed from the radical social teaching of Jesus and Paul, and adopted a social ethos in closer harmony with that which prevailed in the surrounding society. As a consequence the Church failed to challenge injustice and abuse in society and instead came to perpetuate and institutionalize in its own structures precisely such injustices and abuses. Some ministers find it difficult to preach on these texts or to offer pastoral counsel on the basis of such teaching. We cannot address all these concerns here but we do need to be aware of them. What is significant for the present study is that in the context of a passage dealing with authority and relationships in the household, we find another potentially significant allusion to Baptism.

[25] . . . Christ loved the Church and gave himself for her, [26] so that he might sanctify her, having cleansed her by the washing of water with a word,[94] [27] so that he might present the Church glorious to himself . . . holy and unblemished.

The image of the Church as the bride of Christ, whom he has won through his death on the cross, is employed in this passage as a model for the love a husband should show to his wife. Marriage is a rite of passage that takes particular forms in different cultural contexts. We must assume that the marital conventions and relationships presupposed in the image are those that prevailed in the Graeco-Roman world of the first century; this does not imply that these customs are normative for all time, simply that they must be taken into account when interpreting this text. Marriage consisted in the transfer of the bride from the household of her birth, and the custody of her father or his heir, to the household of her husband, with the accompanying legal and financial arrangements as well as any festivities.[95] While the marital status of the husband changed, and with it his standing in society, the identity of the bride was transformed, not only in marital status but in her transfer from the household in which she was an unmarried daughter to another in which she was the wife of the householder, or of one of his relations or retainers. The portrayal of marriage implicit in this text is arguably less egalitarian and reciprocal than that presupposed in Paul's discussion of issues relating to marriage in 1 Corinthians 7, but the writer to Ephesians is not concerned with regulating marriage so much as with using a known institution to illustrate his point. Christ's giving himself clearly refers to the crucifixion, and the sanctifying power of his death understood in this text is in clear continuity with undisputed Pauline passages such as Romans 6.

The 'washing of water' whereby the Church is sanctified and cleansed is clearly the rite of Baptism. Whereas Christians are baptized individually or in families, the Church as a whole is baptized corporately, as it were, in Christ's death. If all Christians are baptized into Christ's death on the cross, then it follows that all Christian baptisms are to be identified with that event. Therefore the whole Church, and not just individual Christians, is identified with Christ through Baptism. It is possible that this text is influenced by a nuptial purification rite.[96] In this case the bath that purifies the bride from any contamination in her premarital life serves as a model for Christian Baptism, in which the Church is cleansed of impurity and corruption before the consummation of its spiritual marriage to Christ. The Baptism of the Church is realized in the lives of individual Christians when they themselves are baptized,[97] but an eschatological consummation of this union is still anticipated. In their Baptism, Christians become members of the Church, the bride of Christ, part of the body cleansed of sin and sanctified through his death on the cross. The image of the Church as the bride of Christ may at first sight seem inconsistent with that of the Church as the body of Christ, also employed in this letter. As husband and wife are distinct persons, at least to modern Western perceptions, identifying the Church as the bride of Christ could be understood to imply a less intimate identification between Christ and the Church than is the case with the image of the Church as the body of Christ. The symbolic and mystical nature of these images, however, means that they are not mutually exclusive or incompatible and that they are not intended to be understood in an absolute or literal sense, still less a mutually exclusive one. Furthermore, in his moral teaching Paul presupposes that sexual intimacy realizes complete identification between the two parties, and relates the Christian's membership of Christ's body directly to the conduct of sexual relationships (1 Cor. 6.15–16). We cannot therefore infer from the imagery of the Ephesians text two different degrees of intimacy and identification with Christ. Even if the images of marriage and of the body convey different aspects of the early Christian understanding of this relationship, they are to be understood as complementary rather than contradictory.

The rite of Baptism in water is accompanied by 'a word', and the implication is that sanctification and cleansing are accomplished through the combination of speech and action. Some interpreters argue that the 'word' referred to here is the confession of faith of the individual Baptized, or of the Church as a whole. However, it is clear that 'word' and action alike derive from Christ and not from the recipient of baptism, which would exclude a creedal formulary as the referent in this text. This is not to say that those baptized made no profession of faith but that such an act of profession is not what accomplishes the cleansing and sanctification. Other interpreters accordingly argue that the 'word' is the proclamation of the gospel. If this is the case, it could refer to a sermon or catechetical instruction accompanying the baptismal rite or to the proclamation of the gospel, through which those baptized were converted. This would indicate an essential unity in the conversion–incorporation process, of which the rite of Baptism is the culmination. While this is a possible interpretation, it is more likely that the 'word' is the liturgical formulary that accompanied and interpreted the ritual action of Baptism.[98] Although a Trinitarian formula cannot be excluded (cf. Matt. 28.19), it is more likely that the verse is referring to Baptism 'in the name of Jesus', as is reflected in Paul's earlier references to Baptism 'into Christ' (cf. Rom. 6.3; 1 Cor. 1.13). In either event, the 'word' is the verbal counterpart to the act of administering Baptism and is as such an integral part of the rite.

The relationship between Christ and the Church is conceived eschatologically. Whereas the death of Jesus cleanses and sanctifies the Church, that eschatological body that is to become Christ's bride is anticipated and realized in history through the Baptism of individual Christians and of Christian families. The consummation of the marriage between Christ and the Church follows the process of winning the bride, and takes place when the process of cleansing and sanctification has been completed in the Baptism of Christians.

This refers to the time when Christ returns at some future point to bring the current phase in terrestrial history to a conclusion and to gather the Church into his heavenly kingdom (cf. 1 Thess. 4.13–18; 1 Cor. 15.20–26).

While Paul's authorship of Ephesians is widely disputed, the ideas expressed in connection with Baptism are all previously attested in his undisputed letters. The teaching on Baptism in Ephesians can therefore be regarded as authentically representing Paul's thought. Even if transmitted by another author in Paul's name, the theology is nonetheless clearly in continuity with the teaching reflected in his undisputed letters. The image of the Church as the bride of Christ, while not found in earlier or undisputed Pauline letters, does not substantially alter the conception of the relationship between Christ and the Church attested at least as early as 1 Corinthians. The relationship between the death of Jesus and the condition of baptized Christians is essentially that implied in Romans. The eschatological consummation of the process described is essentially compatible with the eschatology expounded in Paul's earliest letter(s)[99] and implicit in his later writings.

Suggested further reading

For exegesis of these texts, and discussion of the place of Ephesians in the Pauline tradition, readers may wish to consult the recent commentaries of Barth, Best, Kitchen, Lincoln, Muddiman and Schnackenburg. Of these, Kitchen and Muddiman are more accessible to the non-specialist reader.

2 Timothy 2.11–12

Paul's authorship of the Pastoral Letters (1 and 2 Tim.; Titus) has relatively few supporters among modern critical scholars, many of whom regard the purported letters to his colleagues Timothy and Titus as pseudepigrapha written during the second or third generation of Christianity.[100] It is at the very least arguable that the proportion of scholars accepting Paul's authorship of these letters has increased in recent years, but it remains difficult to reconstruct the situations reflected in each letter. Unlike most of Paul's letters, the Pastoral Letters are addressed not to churches but to individuals exercising some kind of pastoral oversight in the Church. Timothy and Titus were companions in Paul's missionary enterprises. As well as being named as a co-author of 2 Corinthians, Philippians, Colossians, the two Thessalonian letters and Philemon, Timothy is mentioned in the texts of several letters (Rom. 16.21; 1 Cor. 4.17; 16.10; 2 Cor. 1.19; Phil. 2.19; 1 Thess. 3.1–10) and in several passages in Acts (16.1–3; 17.14–15; 18.5; 19.22; 20.4). It is clear that Timothy not only shared with Paul in the work of establishing new churches but that he also undertook a significant role in the continuing oversight of already established ones. As well as being a confidant of Paul's, Timothy appears to have been a prominent member of Paul's missionary team who might well have inherited the mantle of leadership after Paul's death. The two letters to Timothy depict a situation in which Paul is entrusting the continued oversight of his churches to him. Such geographical indicators as there are in 2 Timothy (4.19–21) suggest that this letter is concerned primarily with the churches of the Roman province of Asia, in and around Ephesus (cf. also 1 Tim. 1.3).

There is one apparent allusion to Baptism in 2 Timothy. The writer is citing what he describes as a 'trustworthy saying' in Chapter 2.

[11] If we have died with [Christ Jesus], we will also live with him. [12] If we endure, we shall also reign with him . . .

The reference to death with Jesus reflects Paul's analogy of Baptism with the death and resurrection of Jesus in Romans 6.3–5. The 'trustworthy saying' probably derives from the same tradition as Paul creates or cites in Romans but is otherwise unknown to us. We can nevertheless be confident that it was known in the circle of Paul's churches and possibly more widely in Christian communities of the first century. The tradition may well have originated in a baptismal liturgy or catechism of the period, and therefore have been known to the recipient(s) of the letter in that context. If this is correct, the baptismal allusion would have been all the more apparent to a reader familiar with the initiatory rites of the Church of the period. It is in Baptism that Paul taught that Christians had died with Christ and come to live anew with him. Reigning with Christ is to be understood as sharing in his resurrection, the eschatological benefit of Baptism. Whereas in Romans (and Colossians) the emphasis is on the anticipation of the resurrection life in the present world, here the emphasis is on its future consummation. The rite of Baptism symbolized the essence of Christian life, which was to be fulfilled in the ensuing life of the baptized. This very much reflects the spirit of Paul's statements about Baptism in his undisputed letters, in particular Romans. Like the passage in Romans, but unlike that in Colossians, resurrection is depicted in this text as a future event rather than as a state Christians have already assumed. This could indicate the antiquity of the saying, even if we know this rendition of it only from a letter many scholars date to after Paul's death. However, we have already noted that Paul's references to resurrection, particularly in the context of Baptism, reflect eschatological rather than temporal conceptions of time. In any event, the theology of Baptism reflected in this letter is thoroughly Pauline.

Titus 3.5–6

The critical issues surrounding 2 Timothy apply all the more to Titus, and many scholars believe the letter was written after Paul's death to apply his teaching and claim his authority in new situations. Titus is mentioned in the New Testament only in the Pauline corpus (2 Cor. 2.13; 7.6–7, 13–15; 8.6, 16–24; 12.18; Gal. 2.1–5; 2 Tim. 4.10) and is one of the few prominent first-century Christian leaders known to have been of gentile origins. The letter to Titus is concerned with the life of churches on the Mediterranean island of Crete (1.5), about which we have no other information in the New Testament.

There is one passage in which the writer of Titus alludes to Baptism.

[5] [God] saved us . . . through washing of new birth and renewal by the Holy Spirit, [6] which he richly bestowed on us through Jesus Christ our Saviour.

The allusion to Baptism is clear, and the notion of reception of the Holy Spirit in and through Baptism is well attested in the undisputed letters of Paul. The notion of 'renewal by the Holy Spirit' is not mentioned elsewhere explicitly in connection with Baptism, but the concept is certainly Pauline (Rom. 12.2; 2 Cor. 4.16; cf. Eph. 4.23). The closely related but perhaps more radical concept of regeneration or 'new birth' is mentioned only here in the Pauline letters, but Paul does refer to a new creation in Galatians 6.15 and in 2 Corinthians 5.17. The metaphor of 'new birth' is well known to modern Christians from John 3.3–6 and was to become the dominant metaphor of Baptism during the second and third Christian centuries, shaping the development of baptismal liturgies, theology and architecture. The letter to Titus does not introduce a fundamentally new interpretation of Baptism, however, as Paul frequently addresses his converts as his own or God's babies or children.[101] The notion of 'newness of life' is explicit in the imagery of death and resurrection we have found associated with Baptism in Romans 6.4. A new life presupposes a 'new birth' or at least a new beginning of some kind, which could easily be understood or expressed in terms analogous to birth or adoption, as in Galatians 3.26–29. A rigid distinction between the imagery of dying and rising on the one hand and of new birth on the other should not be imposed on the tradition. Therefore while this text may represent some modest development in Pauline theology, it is not incompatible with the teaching of Paul himself.

The passages we have considered in the Pastoral Letters clearly reflect the theology presupposed in Paul's statements about Baptism in his undisputed letters. While new expressions are introduced and images are developed further, the theology of Baptism remains essentially Pauline. The same is true of the other disputed letters, Colossians and Ephesians. While Paul's imagery is employed creatively, the developments in the teaching are in clear continuity with the interpretation of Baptism Paul expounds in his earlier and undisputed letters. So far as teaching on Baptism is concerned, therefore, these letters clearly belong to the Pauline corpus and it is right that we consider them alongside the passages in Galatians, 1 Corinthians and Romans, from which we have sought to identify

the essential elements of Paul's teaching on Baptism. We turn now
to consider the practice of Baptism in Paul's churches.

Suggested further reading

For exegesis of these passages and discussion of the place of these
letters in the Pauline tradition, readers may wish to consult the commentaries on the Pastoral Letters of Dibelius, Fee, Hanson, Houlden,
Johnson (*Letters to Paul's Delegates*), Kelly, Marshall and Quinn.
Of these, Fee and Hanson are more accessible to the non-specialist
reader.

Also important for understanding the Pastoral Letters, particularly
as it differs from what have become uncritically accepted consensus
positions, is Prior, *Paul the Letter-Writer and the Second Letter to
Timothy*. Another important book on issues relating to these documents is Aageson, *Paul, the Pastoral Epistles, and the Church*.

Notes

1 These issues are discussed fully by Meade in *Pseudonymity and
Canon*, as well as more briefly in introductions to the New Testament.
See Johnson, *The Writings of the New Testament*; Kee, *Understanding the
New Testament*; Koester, *History and Literature of Early Christianity, I:
Introduction to the New Testament* and Kümmel, *Introduction to the New
Testament*.

2 The texts of these documents can be found, in translation, in
Hennecke and Schneemelcher (eds), *The New Testament Apocrypha*, Vol.
2. Scholarship on individual documents has developed considerably since
this volume was first published in German in 1959. See e.g. Bremmer (ed.),
The Apocryphal Acts of Paul and Thekla.

3 Sections of Acts, between 16.11 and 28.16, are written in the first person and are commonly known as the 'We' passages. It is sometimes argued
that this reflects Luke's having accompanied Paul during these periods, or
that the author of Acts drew at these points on the written or oral testimony of an eyewitness. See Dunn, *Beginning from Jerusalem*, pp. 73–81.

4 The use of Acts as a source of historical information is treated at
length by Dunn, *Beginning from Jerusalem*, pp. 53–86 and Hengel, *Acts
and the History of Early Christianity*. I discuss it also in my *Paul, Antioch
and Jerusalem*, pp. 49–51.

5 Beker, *Paul the Apostle*, p. 23. This work is a useful treatment of Paul's theology, recognizing the context in which he wrote and to which he addressed his letters.

6 I have argued in *Paul, Antioch and Jerusalem* that Galatia is to be understood to include the churches founded by Barnabas and Paul in Acts 13—14. The early date for the letter (*c*.AD 52) this allows has implications for our understanding Paul's thought on questions of gentile Christians' obligations to the law of Moses, particularly in relation to the later and longer treatment in Romans, but is of little importance for our present purpose.

7 I have treated this issue more fully in 'The Contextualization of Christianity in the Early Church'.

8 As well as my *Paul, Antioch and Jerusalem*, ch. 3, and earlier works cited there, see the more recent books of Zetterholm, *Formation of Christianity in Antioch* and Slee, *The Church of Antioch in the First Century*. More recent still is Dunn, *Beginning from Jerusalem*, pp. 292–321, 416–38. My 'Caligula, the Church of Antioch, and the Gentile Mission' develops some aspects of my earlier work. Of the older material, Brown and Meier, *Antioch and Rome*, is particularly important and accessible.

9 I discuss these events and the issues behind them more fully in *Paul, Antioch and Jerusalem*, chs 4 and 5, as do the various authors cited in the above note. Cummins, *Paul and the Crucified Christ in Antioch*, is another important recent treatment. See also Dunn, *Beginning from Jerusalem*, pp. 416–94.

10 Most translations render the Greek *huioi* 'sons' but the masculine pronoun should in this and many other cases be understood inclusively. In Greek, grammatical and biological gender do not always coincide, and there is no 'common' gender as in English.

11 Faith, *pistis*, should not be understood merely as belief, in the sense of assent to prescribed doctrines. Faith implies trust and commitment, a way of life governed by allegiance to God rather than personal opinion or conviction about questions of doctrine. The faith of Jesus in God, epitomized in his undergoing crucifixion, is as much at issue in Galatians as is the Christian response of faith in Jesus Christ. An important treatment of this issue is to be found in Hays, *The Faith of Jesus Christ*.

12 This is the most obvious translation of this sentence, and is close to the AV, NIV and JB English versions. Greek syntax, however, would allow 'For in Christ Jesus you are all children of God through faith' (NRSV; cf. RSV), or 'For through faith you are all children of God in Christ Jesus' (cf. NEB; REB). While some variations in the relationship between the clauses may be of academic and stylistic significance only, the crucial theological point is the role of faith. If the last translation is that which most accurately reflects Paul's intention, and it is 'the faithfulness of Jesus Christ' to which Paul refers in 3.22 and 24, then it would also be 'the faithfulness of

Jesus Christ' to which this verse refers. However, it would seem more likely that Paul, at this particular point in his argument, is referring here to the Christian response of faith in undergoing Baptism.

13 Most English versions paraphrase at this point, while the RSV renders *hosoi* 'as many . . . as', giving the adjective a quantitative sense. The translation here gives the adjective a qualitative sense, 'as much as', as the passage concerns the consequences of Baptism rather than the number of people baptized. The quantitative point that the statement applies to every baptized Christian is of course true, but not the primary emphasis of this text.

14 Literally 'Greek', but in this phrase Greeks are clearly representative of all gentile, i.e. non-Jewish, races united in Christ through Baptism. Cf. Rom. 2.9–10; 3.9; 10.12; 1 Cor. 12.13.

15 See Longenecker, *New Testament Social Ethics for Today* and my 'Paul for Today'. See also the contribution of Lampe to Balch and Osiek (eds), *Early Christian Families in Context*.

16 For discussion of conversion to Judaism during this period see Cohen, *The Beginnings of Jewishness*; Goodman, *Mission and Conversion* and McKnight, *A Light among the Gentiles*.

17 Mussner, *Der Galaterbrief*, p. 263, translation mine.

18 Christiansen, *The Covenant in Judaism and Paul*, pp. 316–18.

19 For fuller discussion of this issue and in particular the ways Paul addresses it in Galatians and Romans see my 'Conflicting Bases of Identity in Early Christianity'.

20 Some scholars believe the missing letter is preserved in part in 2 Cor. 6.14–7.1. For discussion see my 'The Composition and Chronology of Second Corinthians'.

21 The complex theories regarding the composition of 2 Corinthians need not concern us here, but a review of the various arguments can be found in the commentaries and in my 'The Composition and Chronology of Second Corinthians'.

22 The question could also be rendered, 'Is Christ divided?' The perfect tense refers to completed action in the past, and Paul is referring to the effects of past actions in the present.

23 See e.g. the World Council of Churches Faith and Order Paper, *Baptism, Eucharist and Ministry* and the decree on ecumenism of the Second Vatican Council, *Unitatis redintegratio* 22.

24 For discussion of this issue see Jensen, *Living Water*, pp. 158–68.

25 1 Apology 65.

26 For examples see Finn, *Early Christian Baptism and the Catechumenate*; Johnson, *The Rites of Christian Initiation* and Kavanagh, *The Shape of Baptism*.

27 The translation of the verb *apelousasthe* is problematic. It could be understood in the passive voice, as are the following two verbs, in which case it could be rendered 'you were washed', as is argued by Barrett, *A*

Commentary on the First Epistle to the Corinthians, p. 141, and so rendered in several modern translations. It is more likely, however, to be middle voice, which in Greek grammar means that the verb has both active and passive, as well as reflexive, aspects to its meaning. Hence this translation that incorporates both the sense of converts (actively) presenting themselves for Baptism, and of their (passively) receiving Baptism administered by another. The initiative and responsibility remain with the convert who comes forward for Baptism.

28 For discussion see Willis, *Idol Meat in Corinth* and Winter, *After Paul left Corinth*.

29 The masculine noun *adelphoi* should be understood in an inclusive sense, to include female as well as male members of the Corinthian church.

30 Literally 'fathers', but *pateres* should be understood inclusively, as is clear from the Exodus narrative in which men, women and children alike passed through the Red Sea and experienced God's presence in the pillar of cloud and the pillar of fire during their desert wanderings.

31 The *Life of Moses* of Philo of Alexandria was written during the decades preceding Paul's missions. For discussion see Nickelsburg and Collins, *Ideal Figures in Ancient Judaism*.

32 Moses was revered also in some Graeco-Roman schools. However, none of the extant texts can confidently be dated until after Paul, so it is impossible to be certain what images of Moses may have been in circulation in pagan Corinth at this date. Cf. Gager, *Moses in Greco-Roman Paganism*.

33 Barrett, *A Commentary on the First Epistle to the Corinthians*, p. 221. There are, however, problems with establishing the dates and provenance of documents and the traditions they contain, so this must be regarded as uncertain, cf. Fitzmyer, *First Corinthians*, p. 380. There is also debate in scholarship as to whether Jewish proselyte baptism, an aspect of the initiation ritual of converts to Judaism who wished to become fully incorporated into Israel, was practised during the first century. Circumcision of male converts was the defining ritual of incorporation into Israel, and ritual washing to remove the impurity of paganism was undergone by male and female converts alike. Ritual washing is a well-known form of symbolic cleansing in Judaism and indeed in many other cultures, but these rites are seldom initiatory; rather, they are repeated from time to time as occasion requires. Precisely when the ritual washing that preceded the circumcision of proselytes acquired an initiatory significance is uncertain. It is unlikely that this development would have been introduced in Judaism after Baptism became an established and distinctive Christian initiatory rite. This suggests that Jewish proselyte baptism was already practised by the time this letter was written; or perhaps more accurately, that the ritual washing of proselytes had become part of the conversion–incorporation rite. This does not imply that the metaphorical link with the exodus was

already established. See further Cohen, *The Beginnings of Jewishness*; Goodman, *Mission and Conversion* and McKnight, *A Light among the Gentiles*.

34 Of course for Jews the Covenant between God and Abraham continues to be understood in terms of Israel as a nation. Paul appropriated this image for the Church but we need to be aware of just how sensitive and contentious the notion is in the modern world. Western Christianity has a particular history to which it needs to relate on this issue, concerning centuries of intermittent persecution of the Jewish communities of Europe culminating in the Nazi genocide. Notwithstanding the Christian, as well as pre-Christian origins of this hostility to Judaism and the Jewish people, this does not alter the theological truth Paul perceived and expounded through this image. Nor does it imply that the nation of Israel of the Old Testament can be equated with the modern political and geographical state of Israel and the claims it makes to the land and resources of Palestine. For further discussion see my 'Paul for Today'. Also relevant is Ateek, *Justice, and only Justice*.

35 Najman, *Seconding Sinai*.

36 For examples from contemporary literature see Collins, *First Corinthians*, pp. 458–9 and Martin, *The Corinthian Body*, pp. 3–55.

37 The preposition *en* could alternatively be rendered in a locative sense, 'in one spirit'. E.g. Barrett, *A Commentary on the First Epistle to the Corinthians*, p. 288, renders the phrase 'in one spirit to become one body'. The instrumental sense preferred here understands the Spirit to be the agent of Baptism rather than the substance in which the baptized are (figuratively) immersed. Cf. Fitzmyer, *First Corinthians*, pp. 477–8 and Thiselton, *The First Epistle to the Corinthians*, p. 997.

38 Literally 'Greek', but probably intended to include Christians of all non-Jewish origins, as in Gal. 3.28. See further discussion below.

39 That Paul implies that the Spirit is conferred through Baptism is denied by Dunn, *Baptism in the Holy Spirit*, p. 130; Fee, *1 Corinthians*, pp. 604–6 and Hays, *First Corinthians*, p. 214. Christiansen argues that the Spirit is active in conversion and renders the phrase 'prompted by the one Spirit, we were all baptised', *The Covenant in Judaism and Paul*, p. 305. The response to apostolic preaching that effects conversion is prompted by the Holy Spirit and leads to Baptism into the Church. While not denying the central thrust of this argument or the essential unity (but not uniformity) of the conversion–incorporation process in Paul's thought and early Christian experience, I would nevertheless argue that Paul understands the Spirit to be both the agent of Baptism and the power ritually conferred in Baptism. This is the view of most commentators, e.g. Barrett, *A Commentary on the First Epistle to the Corinthians*, p. 288; Collins, *First Corinthians*, p. 463; Conzelmann, *1 Corinthians*, p. 212; Fitzmyer, *First Corinthians*, pp. 474–8 and Thiselton, *The First Epistle to the Corinthians*, p. 1000. See also Chester, *Conversion at Corinth*, pp. 280–3.

40 No mention is made here of the gender distinction included in the social contrasts abrogated in Christ in Gal. 3.28. Paul's commitment to gender equality in Corinth is a matter of considerable scholarly dispute. For discussion of the issues see Elliott, *Liberating Paul*; Lampe in Balch and Osiek (eds), *Early Christian Families in Context*; Schüssler Fiorenza, *In Memory of Her*; my 'Paul for Today' and Wire, *The Corinthian Women Prophets*. An interesting but not widely accepted variation on scholarly reconstructions of this tradition is offered by MacDonald, *There is no Male and Female*.

41 For discussion see my 'Composition and Chronology of Second Corinthians'.

42 Reconstructions of the precise events are inevitably speculative and inconclusive. For discussion see my *Paul, Antioch and Jerusalem*, pp. 206–14.

43 Irenaeus, *Against Heresies* 1.21.4; Theophilus of Antioch, *Apology to Autolycus* 1.12, both c.AD 180. Early third-century testimony, reflecting quite varied use of oil in Baptism: *Acts of Judas Thomas*; *Didascalia* 16; Hippolytus, *Commentary on Daniel* 3.15; Origen, *On the Passover* 1.73–76; Tertullian, *Baptism* 7; cf. Clement of Alexandria, *Pedagogue* 2.2.19.4.

44 Irenaeus, *Heresies* 1.25.6, states that Carpocratians, whom he condemned as heretics, branded a cross on their right earlobes. Other such practices are mentioned by later church fathers.

45 Circumcision is described as a 'seal' in *Jubilees* 15.26, dating from the second century BC.

46 *Acts of Peter* 5; Tertullian, *Baptism* 8; *On the Resurrection of the Flesh* 8; cf. Cyprian, *Letter* 73.9.

47 Longenecker, *The Cross before Constantine*.

48 Dead Sea Scrolls, *Damascus Document* 19.9–13; *Psalms of Solomon* 15.6. The latter is potentially of particular significance, as it probably originates in a Pharisaic milieu, the movement within Judaism from which Paul was to emerge some decades later. Cf. also 4 Ezra 6.5. See further Longenecker, *The Cross before Constantine*, pp. 55–60.

49 The first Christians, like Jesus himself, were Jews for whom observance of the law of Moses was normative; it was integral to their culture and an obligation of the covenant Israel entered with God at Mount Sinai, as recounted in Exodus. Prophetic traditions such as Isa. 49.6 anticipated that, through the faithful witness of Israel, gentiles would abandon paganism and come to worship the one true God. The conversion of gentiles to the Christian gospel was naturally understood to be a fulfilment of this prophecy. However, Christians for whom *Torah* observance was integral to their culture would naturally suppose that worship of the God of Israel surely entailed obedience to the law of Moses. Paul took a very different position, one that was in due course to become normative in Christianity but was neither self-evident nor dominant in Christian circles during the

first century AD. The issues are complex, and scholars differ considerably in their reconstructions of Paul's theological rationale and of other factors that may have influenced him. See e.g. Dunn, *The Theology of Paul the Apostle*; Gaston, *Paul and Torah*; Gorman, *Cruciformity*; Hübner, *Law in Paul's Thought*; Longenecker, *Eschatology and the Covenant*; Räisänen, *Paul and the Law*; Sanders, *Paul and Palestinian Judaism*; *Paul, the Law, and the Jewish People*; Tomson, *Paul and the Jewish Law*; Watson, *Paul, Judaism and the Gentiles* and Westerholm, *Israel's Law and the Church's Faith*.

50 As with our translation of Gal. 3.27 above, we prefer to render *hosoi* 'as much as' rather than follow those who offer a quantitative or paraphrastic translation. *pantes* would have been a more emphatic and less ambiguous term had Paul wished to make a quantitative point.

51 'Buried' is the most concise rendering available in contemporary English. However, we need to understand that the meaning here is not to do with covering an object with matter. 'Buried' is used in its original sense, concerning the performance of funeral rites, and has a much wider semantic range than one particular mode of corpse disposal. Similarly, *sunetaphemen* denotes the performance of funeral rites, whatever form they might take, and does not mean to cover an object with matter. A translation closer to the sense of Paul's statement would be 'We had funeral rites performed on us'. For more detailed discussion see my 'Dying with Christ in Baptism'.

52 The Greek *ek nekron* means literally 'from (among) dead [people]', the plural adjective referring not to an abstract condition of death but collectively to deceased humanity. See discussion below.

53 Much has been written on this subject in recent years. See Dunn, *The Theology of Paul the Apostle*; Gaston, *Paul and Torah*; Hübner, *Law in Paul's Thought*; Neusner, *Judaic Law from Jesus to the Mishnah*; Räisänen, *Paul and the Law* and Sanders, *Paul and Palestinian Judaism*; *Paul, the Law, and the Jewish People*.

54 This point is emphasized with particular force by Gorman in *Cruciformity*, pp. 32–5.

55 Bornkamm, *Paul*, p. 75. This is perhaps the classic treatment of Paul coming from the Lutheran tradition during the second half of the twentieth century. While scholarly appreciation of Judaism has changed quite radically from that on which this book is based, it continues to be of value.

56 Käsemann, *A Commentary on Romans*, p. 168. This is another work by an influential Lutheran scholar predating the transformation in Christian New Testament scholars' understanding of the Judaism Paul criticized.

57 Beasley-Murray, *Baptism in the New Testament*, pp. 131–2.

58 For further information see Hope, *Roman Death* and Toynbee, *Death and Burial in the Roman World*.

59 For discussion see McCane, *Roll back the Stone.*

60 Garland, *The Greek Way of Death* and Morris, *Death-Ritual and Social Structure in Classical Antiquity.*

61 Jewett, *Romans*, pp. 397–8.

62 For fuller discussion of ancient conceptions of death see Bernstein, *The Formation of Hell*; Johnston, *Shades of Sheol* and Segal, *Life after Death.*

63 Cf. Kavanagh, *The Shape of Baptism*, pp. 28–9.

64 Dunn, *Baptism in the Holy Spirit*, p. 143. For the contrary position see Wedderburn, *Baptism and Resurrection.*

65 This is expounded clearly by Hays in *The Faith of Jesus Christ.* As he himself observes in this book, one does not need to assent to the literary theory he employs to grasp the significance of his argument.

66 For discussion see Wagner, *Pauline Baptism and the Pagan Mysteries* and Wedderburn, *Baptism and Resurrection.*

67 Flemington, *The New Testament Doctrine of Baptism*, p. 60.

68 Cf. Hanson, *The New Testament Interpretation of Scripture*, pp. 123–41.

69 Seventh year of Nero, AD 61 (Tacitus, *Annals* 14.27); tenth year of Nero, AD 64 (Eusebius, *Chronography* 210.4). Tacitus is much earlier and is more likely to have dated the event accurately.

70 The particular case of the slave Onesimus will be considered in Chapter 3. For a more detailed study of the situation behind the letter to Philemon, see my 'Onesimus'.

71 The word *sunetaphemen* rendered 'buried' would more accurately be translated 'had funeral rites performed on us'. It does not mean, literally, to be placed in a hole in the earth, which is then filled in over our bodies, but denotes the entire funeral process, whatever form the disposal of the corpse may take. See fuller discussion in section on Rom. 6.3–4.

72 *ek nekron*, literally 'from [among] the dead'. See further discussion in section on Rom. 6.3–4.

73 Scholars are uncertain as to when and in what circumstances proselyte baptism was introduced in Judaism or, to be more accurate, when the ritual washing for purification from paganism took on initiatory overtones. Some believe this was an innovation of the late first century AD or later, others that proselyte baptism was practised before the ministries of John the Baptist and Jesus. We therefore cannot be certain whether Jewish or Christian baptism is the more ancient rite, or precisely what customs prevailed at the time this letter was written. See further Cohen, *The Beginnings of Jewishness* and Goodman, *Mission and Conversion.*

74 By the mid-second century Justin Martyr described Baptism as Christian circumcision; *Dialogue with Trypho* 14.

75 So Lohse, *Colossians and Philemon*, pp. 101–2.

76 Schweizer, *Colossians*, p. 141.

77 So Dunn, *Baptism in the Holy Spirit*, p. 153; cf. Moule, *The Epistles of Paul the Apostle to the Colossians and to Philemon*, p. 96.

78 Beasley-Murray, *Baptism in the New Testament*, p. 157.

79 Schweizer, *Colossians*, p. 143.

80 Longenecker, *The Cross before Constantine*.

81 Tertullian, *Baptism* 8.

82 An exception is Schüssler Fiorenza, *The Book of Revelation*.

83 Rev. 2.2 could plausibly reflect anti-Pauline polemic and the conflicts over Paul's status as an apostle evident from 2 Corinthians and Galatians.

84 Dead Sea Scrolls, *Damascus Document* 19.9–13; *Psalms of Solomon* 15.6. The latter is potentially of particular significance as it probably originates in a Pharisaic milieu, the movement within Judaism from which Paul was to emerge some decades later. Cf. also 4 Ezra 6.5. See further Longenecker, *The Cross before Constantine*, pp. 55–60.

85 Tannehill, *Dying and Rising with Christ*, p. 10, argues that Col. 2.12 reflects an earlier version of the same formulary Paul also quotes in Rom. 6.4. If this is the case it would suggest that in Romans Paul altered the formulary, perhaps in the light of his experience with the Corinthian church, but that the earlier version has been used in Colossians.

86 For further discussion see Dunn, *Colossians and Philemon*, p. 161.

87 This point is emphasized in a different context by Mbiti in *New Testament Eschatology in an African Background*. See also Collins, *The Apocalyptic Imagination*.

88 *anthropos*, literally 'person', sometimes rendered 'self' in English Bibles, refers to human nature in its unredeemed state.

89 Literally 'Greek', but referring to the division between Jews and others as perceived from a Jewish perspective. See further the discussion of Gal. 3.28 above.

90 Cf. Schüssler Fiorenza, *The Book of Revelation*, who argues that the book of Revelation is a product of a Pauline rather than a Johannine tradition within early Christianity.

91 This passage will be considered in greater detail in the next chapter.

92 An important treatment of this issue is Hays, *The Faith of Jesus Christ*.

93 An important example of this tendency in scholarship is Elliott, *Liberating Paul*. His position is well argued and, while ideologically motivated, does not ignore points where the evidence is equivocal. I question his hermeneutical approach in 'Paul for Today' on the grounds that Paul and other early Christian authorities grappled with many complex theological issues. Some may have been resolved for all time within a single generation but others continued to vex the Church for centuries. It was not until the end of the eighteenth century that the institution of slavery was challenged, and Christians continued to own slaves in parts of the United States of America until the end of the civil war in 1864. Issues of gender

relations in marriage, the workplace, and the Church remain unresolved among Christians to this day. Some would blame this directly on Paul's influence while others seek to universalize selected statements; neither does justice to the contingencies of Paul's situation or to the continuing responsibility of the Church to discern what the gospel requires today. See also the observations of Lampe, Osiek, Levine, Sedgwick and Mitchell in Balch and Osiek (eds), *Early Christian Families in Context.*

94 Although *en hremati* is in the singular, it does not necessarily refer to a single word in the more narrowly defined English sense of that term. It could, and most probably does, refer to a statement rather than to a single word, as is common in English usage, at least in more informal contexts.

95 For discussion see Blundell, *Women in Ancient Greece*; Gardner, *Women in Roman Law and Society*; Pomeroy, *Goddesses, Whores, Wives, and Slaves*; Rawson, *The Family in Ancient Rome* and Rawson (ed.), *Marriage, Divorce, and Children in Ancient Rome.*

96 Kavanagh, *The Shape of Baptism*, p. 29.

97 Cf. Best, *Ephesians*, pp. 542–3.

98 Cf. Best, *Ephesians*, pp. 543–4.

99 This point stands irrespective of whether both Thessalonian letters or 1 Thessalonians only should be considered Paul's earliest writing. See 1 Thess. 4.13 – 5.11; 2 Thess. 2.1–12. For discussion see Wanamaker, *The Letters to the Thessalonians.*

100 Most arguments against Paul's authorship of these letters concern the references to titled office bearers and to rites akin to ordination in the churches in 1 Timothy and Titus. In Protestant scholarship it has become a matter almost of dogma that such offices did not exist during the apostolic period and are contrary to Paul's theology of the Holy Spirit (but cf. Phil. 1.1). In terms of these arguments the establishment of titled offices, and the appeal to Paul's authority to support them, represent a decline from the spiritual purity of the apostolic Church. More recent scholarship has had to recognize the sociological realities of group dynamics and of patronage networks in the ancient world. Authority and influence in the early Church derived at least as much from social position, wealth and patronage as from the spiritual power attributed to any charismatic figure. See discussion in commentaries listed below. See also Blasi, *Making Charisma*; Holmberg, *Paul and Power*; Judge, *The Social Pattern of the Christian Groups in the First Century*; MacDonald, *The Pauline Churches*; Meade, *Pseudonymity and Canon*; Meeks, *The First Urban Christians* and Prior, *Paul the Letter-Writer and the Second Letter to Timothy*. See also my *Lay Presidency at the Eucharist?*, pp. 43–61.

101 *nepios* (baby) Rom. 2.20; 1 Cor. 3.1 (1 Thess. 2.7 – depending on a variant reading of the text); *paidion* 1 Cor. 14.20; *teknon* Rom. 8.16–21; 2 Cor. 6.13; 12.14; Gal. 4.28, 31; Eph. 5.8; 1 Thess. 2.7, 11; *huios* Gal. 3.26; 1 Thess. 5.5.

3

The Practice of Baptism
in the Pauline Churches

We have examined the principal texts in the Pauline letters that allude to Baptism and sought to understand these in terms of their respective contexts. In the extant letters there is no systematic exposition of Paul's theology of Baptism. Rather, Baptism is mentioned in a variety of contexts, always to illustrate a major principle in Paul's pastoral teaching in those letters. To draw together statements of such a nature in order to reconstruct Paul's teaching on Baptism in any comprehensive or systematic way would therefore be inherently problematic. The letters were written to specific churches or church leaders to address specific situations of which our knowledge is very incomplete. The original recipients and the authors would have shared a considerable body of common knowledge concerning Paul's mission preaching, instruction to his converts and the immediate pastoral situations being addressed in the letters. While we simply have no access to this data, we may gain some further insight by considering the practice of Baptism in early Christianity, and in particular in Paul's missions and in the churches established through his work.

Paul says little about the practice of Baptism. The only reference in the Pauline letters to specific occasions on which Baptism was administered is in 1 Corinthians 1.14, 16, which simply lists people whom Paul had baptized in Corinth, with no further details. There is no indication as to how the rite related to the conversion of the individuals mentioned and their households; nor is there any mention of catechumenal instruction before or after Baptism. There is no liturgy described, no venue specified. These details form part of the common knowledge shared by Paul and those to whom he wrote, and in many respects by other of the first generation of Christians also. Paul does suggest that the occasions on which he administered Baptism were the exception rather than his usual practice, so we should not extrapolate too many generalizations from this brief reference.

We have noted in the previous chapter that the relative infrequency with which Paul administered Baptism in Corinth does not indicate any disregard for or disparagement of the rite but merely that the administration of it was normally delegated to his companions. We are not told who, if not Paul, would have been the normal administrator of Baptism, or indeed whether this was a function that belonged to any particular member of his team. We have noted that practicalities such as the availability of water and considerations of propriety may have required that Baptism be administered away from where Paul was preaching or the church gathered. That Paul did not see himself as the only conduit of the Holy Spirit in Baptism is of course fully consistent with the teaching on the gifts of the Spirit in 1 Corinthians 12. Acts 18.8 would seem to provide some further information on the first conversions and baptisms in Corinth, and we shall consider this text shortly. While Stephanas and his household may appear in 1 Corinthians 1.16 to be an afterthought, they must have been part of the first group converted and baptized, as in 1 Corinthians 16.15 the household of Stephanas is described as 'the first-fruit of Achaia'. This implies that they were the first residents of Achaia, the Roman province in which Corinth was situated, to receive the gospel.

It is often inferred, on the basis of Romans 6.3–4 and Colossians 2.12, that Baptism by submersion was normative or even the invariable practice of the ancient Church. Some have argued further that submersion is essential to Baptism today. We have shown that the semantic range of *thapto*, the root verb generally rendered 'bury' in English, has been all but universally misconstrued. Notwithstanding the observations we made above concerning ancient burial customs, we may surmise that the experience of submersion below the surface of the water gave rise to the image of Baptism as burial; burial understood not as interment in a pit grave but as conveyance from earthly life to the netherworld.

We may perhaps infer from the clothing imagery in Galatians 3.27 that dressing after Baptism had acquired some symbolic significance at an early date. This does not necessarily imply that clothing after Baptism was already a liturgical ritual, only that this necessary and functional act was open to symbolic interpretation. Clothing after Baptism would almost certainly imply that there was undressing prior to Baptism, which would confirm the supposition that the rite was normally administered by submersion or immersion, with the candidate naked.[1] It is less likely, in a society accustomed to public bathing in the nude, with conventions governing such issues as segregation of the sexes, and of adults from children, that converts were baptized clothed and that wet clothes were replaced with dry after emerging from the water. The well-known Jewish aversion to public nudity[2] did not apply to ritual washing; purity laws required that the water of the *mikveh* (ritual bath) touch the entire surface of the body and therefore that all clothing, including any jewellery, be removed. Any influence Jewish sensibilities brought to bear on early Christian custom would therefore have required that Baptism be administered with some degree of privacy. It would therefore seem likely that the rite took place out of view of the gathered congregation, with segregation as required by convention. This does not imply that there was uniformity of practice, as Christian churches were established in a variety of multicultural settings in Greece and Asia Minor. Nor does it exclude the possibility that families could have been baptized together. However, it may well have been that women unaccompanied by their husbands would have been baptized by women rather than by men, a custom attested in later Christian practice. Baptism at a different venue from that at which the congregation was gathered would seem to have become customary in at least one congregation in Rome by the middle of the second century at the latest.[3] Clothing after Baptism was to form part of a quite complex initiatory rite, and the association of Baptism with the death and resurrection of Jesus led to the rite's normatively being administered at Easter, at least in some churches.[4] While we may discern the origins of these customs in Paul's letters, and the glimpses they provide into ancient Christian practice, we should not assume that the rite had already developed an elaborate form or acquired consistency in its details, still less that practical actions had acquired symbolic meaning during this early period.

We are told nothing in Paul's letters of the venues in which Baptism was administered, or the source of water. In view of the discussion above, we may surmise that private houses with their own baths may have been the preferred location where available, but this does not exclude the possibility that natural watercourses may have been regarded as purer, and preferred where possible.[5] We cannot exclude the possibility that public baths were used on occasion, notwithstanding the presence of statues of pagan deities and other cultic symbols.[6] Nor can we exclude the possibility that, on some occasions at least, much smaller quantities of water were used, drawn from a public source and carried to a place where Baptism could be administered with decency and decorum.

There is no evidence before the second century of any blessing or exorcism of the water prior to Baptism.[7] Notwithstanding the various symbolic associations of water in the ancient world, and widespread beliefs that matter was inhabited by spiritual beings, the later requirement that the water be purified, or even exorcized and the Holy Spirit become present in it for Baptism, is unattested in the Pauline letters. This does not imply that no such concerns were experienced by Paul and his companions or by their converts, but it does suggest that the power invoked in the rite was deemed sufficient to overcome any hostile power present in the water.

We cannot be certain as to the words that accompanied Baptism, other than that 'the name of Jesus (Christ)' was invoked (cf. Rom. 6.3; 1 Cor. 6.11; Gal. 3.27). Paul clearly associated Baptism with reception of the Holy Spirit (1 Cor. 6.11; 12.13); while there is no explicit reference to invocation of the Spirit, it is highly unlikely that there was no verbal reference to the presence and action of the Holy Spirit in the rite. We can be certain that prayers were addressed to God but there is no evidence in the Pauline tradition of a Trinitarian formulary used in the administration of Baptism. While, in a formulary that has become widespread in Christian liturgical prayer and in private devotions (2 Cor. 13.14), Paul certainly mentions in close association the three persons of the Trinity in later orthodox Christian doctrine, it would be anachronistic to discern any developed Trinitarian doctrine in Paul's theology. We should assume that mention was made, or prayer offered to God, for the Holy Spirit to enter the person being baptized. This would not necessarily imply that the Spirit was understood to be present in the water, which touched the exterior of the body but was not ingested. The same would apply to oil or any other substances that may have been used in the rite.

Even if we can identify as the essentials of the rite an act involving contact with water and the invocation by the officiant of Jesus' name and of the Holy Spirit, it is highly unlikely that in as highly ritualized cultures as those of the ancient Mediterranean world there would have been no further words or actions. We have already noted that symbolic meaning could almost spontaneously become attached to practical actions, such as unclothing and clothing. Physical contact between the parties would be virtually unavoidable in the course of the rite, in particular the use of the officiant's hands to guide the convert in and out of the water. The touching could have acquired a ritual significance of its own, whether or not formal imposition of hands had been intentional from the beginning. While imposition of hands is explicitly mentioned in Acts and the Pauline tradition in connection with commissioning for ministry (6.1–6; 13.1–3; 1 Tim. 4.14; 5.22; 2 Tim. 1.6) rather than with Baptism, it would be difficult to envisage how the attribution of ritual meaning to touching the head or body of the initiate with the hand could have been avoided.

Olive oil was widely used in washing, and we have asked whether oil might have been introduced to baptismal rites and attributed some significance. The association of oil with healing elsewhere in the early Christian tradition (Mark 6.13; John 9.6, 11; James 5.14) confirms that ritual anointing was known in the Church at an early date. Conferral of the Holy Spirit, the lasting consequence of Baptism, undoubtedly came to be associated with post-baptismal anointing during a later period,[8] but there is no evidence that this was the case during the decades in which the Pauline letters were written. Anointing is associated with conferral of God's Spirit in the Hebrew tradition (1 Sam. 16.13; Isa. 61.1), and Paul uses a metaphor of anointing to depict the gift of the Holy Spirit (2 Cor. 1.21–22). However, he also uses metaphors of washing (1 Cor. 6.11) and drinking (1 Cor. 12.13; cf. Eph. 5.18), the latter of which might conceivably involve the wine of the Eucharist but certainly not oil, but not to the exclusion of the water of Baptism. There is therefore no exclusive connection between ritual anointing at Baptism and conferral of the Holy Spirit. This does not imply that oil was not introduced to Baptism at an early date but there is no evidence that this acquired any specific significance, apart from the water rite.

We have enquired whether the sign of the cross, described on the body with or without oil or water, might have become a part of the baptismal rite, reflecting Paul's theology of the cross. Allusions to marking or signing would presumably imply a distinctive and recognizable, even if invisible, image. The evidence that the cross was a pre-Christian Jewish symbol of eschatological deliverance, and was in use as a Christian symbol by the third quarter of the first century, strengthens the likelihood that the Pauline churches made ritual use of the cross at an early date. Paul's association of Baptism with the death of Jesus would powerfully, and quite naturally, have been represented by describing the cross on the body of the convert.

While the imposition of hands, anointing and the sign of the cross would all be consistent with what we know of the rite of Baptism as administered in the Pauline churches of the first century, and would make sense of allusions and imagery Paul employs, there is no explicit statement or other incontrovertible evidence that these rituals formed part of the liturgy at this date. The letters were addressed to people who had undergone the rite and were therefore familiar with it through personal experience and required no detailed description. We can only surmise on the basis of incidental and suggestive phrases. While the minimalism of Protestant anti-ritualism is to be avoided, we cannot assume either that the letters reflect liturgical practices attested at a later date or that the imagery of the letters gave rise to later developments in the ritual. What is clear is that the water rite was the defining, if not uniform, act in the incorporation of converts into the churches established by Paul.

Baptism in the Account of Paul's Mission in the Acts of the Apostles

Acts includes four accounts of baptisms during the course of Paul's independent missionary career (16.15; 16.33–34; 18.8; 19.5–6), and one possible allusion during the course of his partnership with Barnabas (13.52). Whatever the historicity of the specific stories, they must have met the criterion of verisimilitude to the original readers and hearers, if the Acts accounts were to have any credibility at all. In other words, we can assume that these stories reflect, in general terms if not in specific details, the way Baptism was administered in the early Church. We may therefore derive some understanding of Paul's baptismal practice from them.

Philippi

Two of the baptismal narratives include entire households. Both of these are located in Philippi, a Roman colony and the principal city of the province of Macedonia. Located on the Via Egnatia, one of the major thoroughfares of the Roman Empire, Philippi was a prosperous trading centre, with mines and fertile agricultural land in its vicinity. There is no archaeological evidence of a Jewish community in Philippi during this period. This does not in itself imply that there was no Jewish presence in the city, but there is no independent corroboration of the ambiguous evidence in Acts.

The first conversion reported is that of Lydia, a merchant from Asia who is described as 'one who revered God' (Acts 16.14).[9] Paul and his companions were seeking a Jewish gathering[10] outside the city walls, along the banks of the river Kredines, on the Sabbath (Acts 16.13–15). Whether their conversation with the women takes place during or after a Jewish Sabbath service, or is a casual encounter on their way there, is not clear. This is, curiously, described as a meeting of women only, at least until Paul and his companions joined them. Whether or not they ever reached the Jewish gathering, Lydia is clearly identified as having some foundation in the Jewish tradition and as a person able to determine her own religious allegiance. She responds positively to Paul's preaching, and is baptized. The narrative may seem to suggest, but it does not state, that her Baptism was administered in the river, immediately upon her conversion. The narrative is concise and simply does not furnish such details; we therefore cannot be certain as to the precise sequence of events intended. Lydia was baptized 'with her household'; whoever precisely these may have been, we cannot assume they had all accompanied Lydia to the riverside gathering of the Jewish community that particular Sabbath. It is perhaps more plausible to suggest that Baptism followed the company's return to Lydia's house, and took place, there or elsewhere, once the household had been gathered together.

The second Baptism is that of the gaoler and his household (Acts 16.30–34). Paul and Silas had been flogged and imprisoned, following a judicial process in which their status as Roman citizens was violated.[11] An earthquake during the night breaches the security of the prison.[12] The gaoler panics, assuming the prisoners have taken the opportunity to escape, and intends to commit suicide. Paul reassures him that no such escape has taken place. The gaoler thereupon concludes that Paul and Silas, and their imprisonment, are somehow connected to the earthquake, and that they therefore have the power to save him from his predicament. Paul takes the opportunity to proclaim the gospel and invites the gaoler 'and his household' to be baptized. The gaoler takes Paul and Silas to his own quarters, presumably within the prison compound, dresses the wounds of their flogging and gathers his household to hear Paul expound the gospel and be baptized. The narrative is concise but this would seem the most plausible reconstruction of the order of events. It is inconceivable that the quarters of as minor a civic official as a gaoler would have been equipped with a bath or any vessel in which a human adult could be submerged in water. A much more perfunctory ritual must therefore be envisaged. This is, significantly, the only occasion on which pre-baptismal instruction is explicitly mentioned. This cannot be compared with either the rigours or the duration of the later catechumenate, and serves a quite different purpose. Unlike Lydia and others who came to Baptism in response to Paul's mission preaching, the gaoler had responded not to the gospel but to the supernatural power he perceived Paul and Silas to possess. So far as the pre-baptismal instruction can be described as catechesis, therefore, it addresses a clear deficiency in the recipients' conversion, their understanding of the rite they are about to undergo and of the gospel to which they are in process of being converted. There is no suggestion that they were introduced to Lydia and the community formed in her house. It is perhaps significant that the gaoler is nowhere identified by name, which could suggest that he and his family did not become or remain prominent members of the Philippian church to which Paul subsequently addressed a letter.

Corinth

The third reference to Baptism is in Corinth, and simply mentions that several converts were baptized, apparently immediately after following Paul out of the synagogue; principal among these was Crispus, who had been a leader in the synagogue (Acts 18.8). Paul provides some further information in 1 Corinthians 1.14–16, in which he identifies the names of three prominent converts whom he had himself baptized, Crispus, Gaius and Stephanas. Stephanas was baptized together with his household. The Acts account names only Crispus, who is particularly important on account of his office in the synagogue, and intimates that his household was also baptized. It is likely that this was the case with the household of Gaius also, and that in mentioning Crispus and Gaius, Paul intends the entire households rather than the named householders. His reference to 'the household of Stephanas' is an apparent afterthought and cannot be assumed to imply that Crispus and Gaius were baptized without their households. It is significant that these all responded to Paul's proclamation of the gospel in the synagogue in Corinth, even if they made their commitment and underwent Baptism only after Paul had left the synagogue and established his base in an adjacent house. However, the narrative is so concise that we cannot be certain of the sequence of events or even that a precise sequence is intended in the juxtaposition of statements. What is clear is the normativity of household Baptism which, as in the case of Lydia considered above, does not imply that all members of any particular household had been present to hear Paul's preaching or were individually convinced of the truth of the gospel.

Ephesus

The final occurrence of Baptism in the Acts account of Paul's mission is located in Ephesus. This is an anomalous and in many respects problematic episode, which Luke uses to assert the superiority of Jesus to John the Baptist and to indicate how conversions from the Baptist movement to Christianity were to be managed. That John remained a prominent figure in Judaism for decades after his death we need not doubt, nor that the Baptist movement competed with the early Church for the allegiance of eschatologically minded Jews in many places. Nevertheless, questions remain about this particular episode.

Paul encounters 'disciples', whom he apparently assumes to be Christians but in whom he discerns no sign of charismatic empowerment (Acts 19.1–12). On examination he ascertains that these 'disciples' had in fact undergone the baptism of John. When questioned by Paul as to their reception of the Holy Spirit, they seem to deny any knowledge of it. In the light of the teaching of John as recorded in the Gospels (Matt. 3.1–12; Mark 1.2–8; Luke 3.1–20; cf. John 1.19–34), it would seem inconceivable that any of his disciples would have been unaware of the Holy Spirit (Matt. 3.11; Mark 2.8; Luke 3.16). Scholars have long been perplexed about this episode, and the number of variant readings in the textual tradition testifies to the antiquity of the problem.[13] Even if there is room for doubt as to the historicity of the Gospel accounts of John's teaching,[14] the creation narrative in the Pentateuch makes explicit reference to the Spirit of God (Gen. 1.2). The motif of possession by God's Spirit is deeply rooted and widely attested in the prophetic tradition (Judg. 3.10; 6.24; 1 Sam. 10.6, 10; 16.13–16; Isa. 11.2; 42.1; 44.3; 61.1; Ezek. 2.2; 3.12), and a return of such pneumatic inspiration was a known eschatological expectation (Joel 2.28–29). Rather than the existence of the Holy Spirit, it could only have been the fulfilment, through Jesus, of John's prophecy of the outpouring of the Spirit (Acts 1.8; 2.1–13) of which the Ephesian disciples were unaware. This would imply that Acts 19.2 has been misleadingly translated in many English versions; the last clause should more accurately be rendered 'We have not heard that the Holy Spirit is at work' or 'We have not heard that the Holy Spirit has come'.[15] In other words, these disciples of John had heard him preach about the future, eschatological, manifestation of God's Spirit but remained unaware that the manifestation of which John had spoken had taken place. Conversions from the Baptist movement to Christianity outside Palestine would probably have been a relatively rare occurrence, though Apollos, a Jew from Alexandria, is another important example (Acts 18.24–26). In this passage, Paul required that followers of John the Baptist, baptized in his movement, who are converted to the Christian gospel, should be baptized 'in the name of Jesus'. While this is clearly how

Luke expects that such conversions should be managed, it does not follow that this was the general practice in the early Church. Jesus, and presumably several if not all of his disciples, had received John's baptism (Mark 1.9; cf. John 1.35–42; Acts 1.22). There is no indication that the disciples, or other followers of John who had shared in Jesus' historical ministry, subsequently underwent a water rite of baptism 'in the name of Jesus'. This does not mean that the rite of John the Baptist was in some way deemed equivalent to Christian Baptism, but does suggest that for many of the first Christians, John's Baptism represented their incorporation into the community from which Jesus drew his first disciples, who were in turn to become the nucleus of the Church. As Paul mentions John the Baptist nowhere in his extant letters, and in Acts only here and in his sermon in the synagogue at Pisidian Antioch, which clearly reflects the synoptic tradition (Acts 13.24–25), we cannot be certain as to his position on John and the continuing movement of his disciples.

There are few conclusions to be drawn from the accounts in Acts of Paul's administration of Baptism. The significance of household Baptism will be considered further below. The conversion of disciples of John the Baptist in Ephesus seems to be an isolated incident from which no generalizations can be extrapolated. That the venues at which baptismal rites were administered would seem to have varied is no cause for surprise, given that specially designed and constructed church buildings, with or without baptisteries, did not exist during the first Christian centuries. What is significant is that no particular source of water, and no specific occasion other than the conversion of the head of the group to be baptized, seems to have been required.

Suggested further reading

Several commentaries on Acts are available, in which these texts are exegeted in their respective contexts and the historical value of the passages discussed: Barrett, Bruce, Conzelmann, Dunn, Fitzmyer, Haenchen, Hamm and Johnson. Of these, Dunn and Hamm are more accessible to the non-specialist reader.

Also important are Matson, *Household Conversion Narratives in Acts* and Mendez-Mortalla, *The Paradigm of Conversion in Luke.*

We turn now to consider how Paul's teaching on Baptism was implemented in his churches. We will consider three aspects of this: first, the place of Baptism in the conversion–incorporation process; second, household Baptism, under which topic we will consider the question of infant Baptism; third, the reference to Baptism for the dead in 1 Corinthians 15.29.

The Place of Baptism in the Conversion and Incorporation Process

Baptism was integral to conversion and incorporation into the Church, so far as Paul's teaching indicates. He uses 'all' with sufficient frequency in connection with the Christian experience of Baptism (Rom. 6.3; 1 Cor. 12.13; Gal. 3.26–28) for us to conclude that for Paul the rite was essential to incorporation into the Church and into the eschatological salvation founded on the death and resurrection of Jesus, which Christian life anticipated. This understanding is presupposed, but not argued, in at least one letter addressed to a church with which Paul had no previous connection, that in Rome. This leads to the conclusion that Paul was quite uncontroversial on this point and representative of a wider spectrum of early Christianity.

Universal as Baptism was so far as Paul was concerned, there is no indication of any uniformity regarding the place of the rite in the conversion–incorporation process, if this is to be understood in any linear sense of progression. We have argued that conversion is in itself a complex process, entailing a reordering not only of beliefs but, often primarily, of social relationships and identity. Furthermore, in the context of early Christianity, conversion was not always voluntarily undergone. For a slave or a child, or even a wife, conversion may have been no more than compliance with the regime of the householder who had, for whatever reason, decided to join the Church. For a householder or other person able to make an autonomous decision, conversion may have resembled much more closely the experience as perceived in the modern world. The accounts in Acts would represent examples of such occasions, but we need to take care to recognize the silent and invisible human beings in the background of the narratives, who are converted not of their own volition or conviction but through the decision of a principal such as Lydia, the householders in Corinth or the Philippian gaoler. They nonetheless undergo Baptism and become members of the Church. The process and experience of conversion were therefore varied and the realization of conversion in the subsequent life of the Christian would similarly have been diverse, irrespective of the point at which Baptism was administered.

We have noted that there is no evidence of liturgical uniformity beyond invocation of 'the name of Jesus' and some form of contact between the initiate and water. We may suppose that the Holy Spirit was also invoked, even though the evidence is less explicit. Even if submersion of the entire (naked) body beneath the surface of the water was normative, Baptism by immersion (partial submersion), affusion (pouring water over the head) and aspersion (sprinkling) are all attested by the end of the first century.[16] The desire to extrapolate a uniform ritual pattern from the biblical texts may well have more to do with later ecclesiastical controversies than with reconstructing early Christian practice. In reality diverse traditions would have evolved in the light of such circumstances as the availability of water, and in what form and in what places, and of cultural conventions regarding nudity and the segregation of men from women, and whether or not the congregation was gathered to witness the rite. Precedents set at the time a particular church was founded may also have influenced subsequent developments in its customs.

The accounts in Acts discussed above indicate that Baptism was administered with some immediacy after conversion. There is no evidence of any catechumenate preceding Baptism; on the contrary, all the indications are that the rite of incorporation was administered immediately upon conversion. This is the clear impression of all the conversion accounts in Acts, which must have reflected with some plausibility the experience of late-first-century Christian readers and hearers, irrespective of who the intended readers and hearers of the book may have been. We should therefore assume that any detailed instruction in Christian teaching and way of life, beyond the mission preaching of the apostle and his colleagues and any subsequent instruction, followed rather than preceded Baptism. This is not to suggest that such teaching was not given or was not considered essential to forming the way of life of the newly converted Christians; on the contrary, continuing instruction in Christian belief and practice would surely have been crucial, especially for gentile converts unfamiliar with the Scriptures we now call the Old Testament. We have noted that social scientific studies of religious conversion have observed that incorporation into the community generally precedes the process of bringing the convert's beliefs and way of life into conformity with the values of the Church or other organization. Important though teaching of a catechetical nature undoubtedly was, there is no indication that this was a prerequisite to Baptism, still less that the rite merely confirmed a transformation in identity and way of life that had already taken place. Rather, Baptism was followed, and in a sense completed, in the subsequent formation of the converts in their Christian lives in the community of the faithful.

The only account of instruction preceding Baptism is that of the conversion of the Philippian gaoler and his household (Acts 16.30–34). In this case the circumstances would seem to have been exceptional, and the instruction was presumably fairly brief. The gaoler would almost certainly not have heard Paul and Silas preach before their arrest and imprisonment, or not thereby been converted to the gospel. Furthermore, according to the account in Acts the gaoler was converted more through fear at the extraordinary events that had taken place, and relief that the prisoners had not escaped, than through intellectual or moral conviction, still less through contact with and incorporation into a Christian community. In other words, the gaoler surmised that Paul and Silas represented or wielded divine power, and wished to avail himself of it. Some instruction would have been necessary to explain the gospel to him, compensating for his not having heard Paul and Silas's mission preaching rather than furnishing him with any subsequent instruction. Similarly, with the disciples of John the Baptist in Ephesus, what precedes Baptism is not catechetical instruction as such but rather an explanation of the distinction between the rite administered by John the Baptist and Christian initiation 'in the name of Jesus' (Acts 19.1–7).

While Christian doctrine and catechesis had not yet developed to the extent apparent in writings of subsequent centuries, Paul's letters testify to the development, within the first generation of Christianity, of complex and sophisticated traditions of christocentric interpretation of the Hebrew Scriptures. There was therefore no dearth of Christian teaching to impart to converts, particularly those whose familiarity with the Hebrew tradition was limited. Nor was there any reluctance to impart this teaching. That internalizing Christian doctrine and bringing converts' lives into conformity with it was not a prerequisite for Baptism, rather the continuing process of Christian formation that followed it, would seem therefore to have been integral to the missionary strategy of the early Church and certainly of the Pauline movement, so far as we are able to reconstruct this. It is clear from later sources that patterns of formation subsequently changed; nonetheless, we should not ignore the evidence of missionary strategy during the first generation of the Christian Church.

The promptness with which Baptism was administered may be attributed in part to the high level of eschatological expectation that pervaded the early Church and motivated Paul's missionary activities as well as shaping his theology.[17] For Paul, as for other early Christian missionaries, the incorporation of gentile converts into the Church was a prerequisite to the return of Jesus, and their mission was to create conditions in which God's saving work in Christ could be brought to completion without delay. The need to instruct converts in sound doctrine was secondary, not least because incorporation into the Church through Baptism committed converts to the process of learning and internalizing Christian teaching. Churches were expected to continue the formation and nurture of their new members, and while letters such as 1 Corinthians may indicate failings in this regard, it is quite clear that Paul considered his expectations entirely reasonable. The communities may have been young and lacking much of the experience considered essential for contemporary patterns of Christian leadership, but they were communities of the baptized who had been endowed with the Holy Spirit and therefore had the capacity to discern the will of God and act accordingly. Joining the Church through Baptism should lead to acquiescence in Christian doctrine and conformity with Christian moral practice, which could be maintained and enforced through church discipline. There was no expectation that the Church would continue to function for two thousand years before the return of Christ. There was therefore not the need many Christians subsequently felt to establish a clear body of doctrine which, together with the sacraments, could be used to define the identity and boundaries of the community. This is not to say that instruction in the faith was unimportant for Paul, but the establishment of the Christian community, with the inclusion of gentile converts, was his primary and urgent objective. The boundaries of the community were defined through the initiatory rite of Baptism rather than by a distinct body of doctrine. Those categorized as 'within' would have been brought into conformity with the beliefs and practices of the Church through subsequent instruction, reinforced where necessary by church discipline, but the defining moment and the defining ritual was incorporation through Baptism.

A further reason for not delaying Baptism would be the clear link between the rite and reception of the Holy Spirit. Baptism marked the beginning of Christian life as well as entry into the Christian community.[18] Empowerment by the Holy Spirit was essential to Christian life; conferral of the Spirit could therefore not have been deferred until after the transformation, for which it was needed, had already taken place. Even where the Holy Spirit was perceived to be active in a person before Baptism it was nonetheless in the rite that the Spirit was formally conferred and after Baptism that the Spirit would be believed to inhabit and inspire the person permanently, as a member of the Spirit-filled community.

While there is no clear evidence of concerted pre-baptismal instruction of converts in the Pauline mission, it is nevertheless clear that a period of catechumenate became normative in the Church by the middle of the second century. Two factors can be identified that may have influenced this process. We have already made reference to the eschatological climate of the first generation of Christianity, which gradually gave way to a pattern of Christian life in which the return of Christ continued to be expected but no longer so imminently as to define all aspects of Christian life. A second factor, with which Paul is of course closely associated, is the transition of Christianity from a reform movement within Judaism to a universal, non-ethnic religion. Jews steeped in their heritage, and even gentile adherents to the synagogues of the Graeco-Roman world, would have been able to comprehend the basic tenets of early Christian preaching. The Christian gospel was expressed in terms of Jewish prophecy and eschatological expectations, and anyone familiar with what Christians have come to call the Old Testament prophets would have been able to understand the fundamental precepts of Christian teaching. Furthermore, Jews, as well as gentiles who observed Jewish customs through association with synagogues, would have known the moral code enshrined in Scripture, as interpreted in diaspora contexts in their day, and would have governed their lives accordingly. Converts unfamiliar with a Greek translation of the books of the Hebrew Bible, or with the traditions of interpretation of it that informed Jewish and early Christian eschatological expectations, would have required more concerted instruction before they could comprehend the gospel and observe its requirements in their lives.[19]

We can conclude, therefore, that the indications from Paul's writings, corroborated and complemented by the accounts in Acts, are that incorporation into the Church through Baptism followed immediately upon conversion and marked the beginning of the Christian life. By the end of the first century or the beginning of the second, this practice was giving way to a more formal and increasingly lengthy period of catechumenate during which converts occupied a liminal position in the community, governed by its rules but not fully admitted to its worship and community life. The catechumenate became increasingly rigorous and protracted during the second and third centuries, but this development is beyond the parameters of this study.[20]

Household Baptism

Baptism of entire households in the Pauline churches is mentioned in the cases of Stephanas (1 Cor. 1.16) and Crispus (Acts 18.8) in Corinth, and Lydia (Acts 16.15) and the unnamed prison warder at Philippi (Acts 16.33). The household of Crispus is not mentioned in 1 Corinthians 1.14 but there is no occasion to dispute the account in Acts on this point. In the sociocultural setting of the Pauline churches, household Baptism would have been normative. Individuals were generally not autonomous in matters of cultic affiliation and observance, and human identity derived from the social unit of which the person was a member, which in nearly all cases was the household. This is not to deny that there were people displaced from their households, including seafarers, discharged soldiers, escaped slaves and former retainers and others dislocated through the dissolution of households, who are likely to have congregated in trading ports and whose vulnerability may have made the Christian gospel attractive, but we have no direct evidence of these in the early Church.[21] It needs also to be recognized that larger, dispersed households (of which that of the emperor would have been an example, cf. Phil. 4.22),[22] would have been less able to maintain homogeneity and conformity than those concentrated in a single setting. It can nevertheless reasonably be assumed that unless the contrary is indicated, most baptisms reported included the household of the person named or mentioned. Those who are named or merely vaguely and anonymously identified in the texts tend to be the more prominent in society and in the church, which commonly means heads of households. So far as we have been able to reconstruct, the administration of Baptism to the entire household would normally have followed immediately upon the conversion of the head.

The *paterfamilias* (Latin) or *oikodespotes* (Greek) had in most cases the legal right to determine the cultic affiliations and observances of the entire household. Many if not most households had their own domestic cults, with shrines to deities and ancestral spirits located in the house or garden. Devotions would be offered at these shrines daily, and all members of the household were obliged to participate. The freedom of the subordinate members of households to determine their own beliefs, practices and affiliations did increase during the early years of the Roman Empire, especially in larger and dispersed households where it was more difficult to enforce conformity and where common identity could not so easily have been sustained. Such freedom could more easily have been asserted through affiliation to an outside cult than through withdrawal from participation in the devotions of the household cult.

In other words, any voluntary cultic affiliation would usually have been in addition to rather than instead of the household cult. It is apparent from 1 Corinthians 7.12–15 that in Corinth at least, a degree of religious freedom was attained by some wives, even if this liberty was not shared by children, clients (legally free but none-theless dependent retainers) or slaves. This reflects the tendency in Roman marriage contracts of the period for fathers to retain legal custody of their daughters rather than transfer it to their sons-in-law at marriage. Women married under this arrangement obtained some degree of legal autonomy when their fathers died.[23] Marriages across social barriers were becoming increasingly common during the first century, even though such unions were officially discouraged. A woman married to a man of lower status would enjoy greater freedom than one whose husband was of her own or a higher social order. Some women were able even to become the dominant partners in marriages to men of lower status. Wives of heads of households were not entirely restricted and often could adhere to cults of their choice outside the home, while remaining loyal to the household through adherence to the civic and other cults favoured by their husbands.[24] Exclusive cultic allegiance was a dis-tinctive feature of Judaism and Christianity[25] and was a corollary of their monotheism. Even here, however, exclusivity was not always maintained.[26] A plurality of cultic affiliations and observances was normative in the Graeco-Roman world, and any incompatibility in beliefs, as moderns might perceive them, would have occasioned no difficulties in households,[27] except where the exclusive claims of Judaism or Christianity were involved. In other words, only where exclusive belief in and worship of one god was involved would adherence to several cults be in any way problematic.

In the cosmopolitan and relatively tolerant Corinthian society, many heads of households may not have required cultic conform-ity from their subordinates, or rather may have permitted them to participate in additional cults of their choice, provided their observances did not affect their duties in and to the household or in any way undermine the prestige of the householder. In other words, provided the household deities and their cults were honoured, members were free to pursue additional devotions of their own choice. This would have been a problem for Jews and Christians but not for other subordinate members of households. The household itself, with its domestic shrines to ancestral and other protecting spirits, was the primary context for the religious devotions of slaves and children and to a lesser extent of legally free subordinate adults.[28] Public religion was largely an activity of citizens, and in particular of householders and magistrates (public office bearers). So long as domestic cults were observed and their ancestral spirits respected, householders would generally not have been concerned at any further cultic observances undertaken by their dependants, unless these became somehow disruptive of order in the home or otherwise undermined their interests. It is in this context that any religious freedom apparent in Paul's letters or elsewhere in the New Testament is to be understood.

Paul nowhere suggests that Christian householders should exercise their legal rights to compel subordinate members of their households to conform to their Christian beliefs and observances (cf. 1 Cor. 7.10–16). There were legal restrictions on the forcible conversion of gentile slaves by Jewish owners, and during this period Christianity would have been regarded as a form of Judaism. Furthermore, civil courts would not willingly have supported householders seeking to prevent their dependants from worshipping the pagan gods, who were regarded as guardians of the city and whom the magistrates themselves would have worshipped in public ceremonies. Christian householders would therefore have had great difficulty in suppressing pagan practices by members of their households.[29] There is, however, no indication that the liberty reflected in 1 Corinthians 7 extended beyond the wife of the head to other members of the household. It is unlikely that a man would elect not to compel his wife to conform to his religion, and then contemplate divorce when she exercised that freedom. We should therefore suppose that wives in such marriages enjoyed legal autonomy.

In a situation where a wife, able to act independently of her husband, converted to Christianity on her own, she would presumably have been baptized on her own or possibly with any of her slaves she had brought into the household and now brought with her into the Church. However, if it was the householder who had converted, it is almost certain that the subordinate members of the household would have been baptized with him.

His wife, once again, could have been legally independent of him and therefore may or may not have undergone Baptism. Paul's clear hope is that in such situations the Christian partner might in due course be able to bring the unconverted spouse, and by implication the rest of the household, to Baptism (1 Cor. 7.12–14). This does not mean that Baptism is contingent upon an individual declaration of faith but that there were legal and social obstacles to the enforcement by Christian householders of conformity to the gospel on the part of their dependants.

The case of Onesimus is often regarded as an example of a slave who was not compulsorily baptized on the conversion of his owner. That this was the case is far from certain, however. Paul's having become Onesimus's 'father' (Philem. 10) is not necessarily the same occasion as Onesimus's conversion and Baptism, as is widely assumed in scholarship. Furthermore, when Onesimus left Philemon's house, in whatever circumstances, he could have repudiated any cultic allegiance imposed on him by his owner, if he was at the same time rejecting his servile position in the household. While Paul apparently formed an intimate relationship with Onesimus, he does not mention having baptized him. It is quite possible that whatever his personal beliefs may have been, Onesimus was baptized on Philemon's conversion to Christianity. Paul persuaded Onesimus to return to Philemon's house as a member of the Christian community that worshipped there, and appealed to Philemon not only to pardon him but also to welcome him as a 'brother' in Christ. This does not imply that Onesimus had not previously been a member of the church. Rather, Paul is demanding that Philemon acknowledge Onesimus first as a fellow Christian and receive him back into the church, and second, at most, regard him as a slave and treat him accordingly.[30] Paul demands the restoration of Onesimus to both the church and the household.

Household Baptism was normative in the Pauline churches. The conversion of the head of the household resulted in the incorporation of the entire household into the Church. Although some women were able to exercise independence of their husbands in religious and other matters, in most cases the right of the head to pronounce on cultic matters prevailed, particularly for the servile members of the household. This is not to say that some such members, where the head was not Christian, could not have been converted. However, even if baptized into the Church they would not have been able to avoid conformity with the cultic practices of the head of the household. In other words, such converts would not have been able to make an exclusive commitment to the Christian gospel and the Church.[31] It is therefore possible that Baptism may have been withheld from such adherents to the Church, unless and until such time as they could make an exclusive profession of faith in Christ.[32] The delay in Baptism was not to make time for catechetical preparation but to await an opportunity when the convert was free to make an exclusive commitment to the Christian gospel.

Suggested further reading

An important book on the role of the household in early Christian mission and church life is Gehring, *House Church and Mission*. Gehring's thesis has been disputed by Adams in *The Earliest Christian Meeting Places*. While Adams correctly identifies a variety of venues for Christian worship, particularly from the second century onwards, this overlooks the pervasiveness of the household, which was a social unit that transcended the architectural setting of the home.

The following treatments of family life in the world of early Christianity are useful for considering the question of household conversion and Baptism:

Osiek and Balch, *Families in the New Testament World*.

Balch and Osiek (eds), *Early Christian Families in Context*. This collection has several important and relevant contributions on the place of women, slaves and children in the Graeco-Roman household.

Moxnes (ed.), *Constructing Early Christian Families*. Several chapters of this are concerned specifically with questions of sexuality, but the contribution of Barclay, 'The Family as the Bearer of Religion in Judaism and Early Christianity', is particularly useful.

Infant Baptism?

The question of infant Baptism can be considered only in the context of household Baptism. Many arguments on this issue depend on whether the specific households mentioned in Paul's letters or in Acts, and which corporately underwent Baptism, included children. There is no explicit evidence in any of the recorded cases but it would have been remarkable indeed were every household so identified in Acts or by Paul to have been without children, whether the offspring of the householder or of his or her adult dependants. There can be no doubt that, in principle, children were regarded as members of the household to which they belonged.[33] There is no extant guidance from Paul or any other Christian source of the first century as to which members of households were to be baptized and which not, or the criteria to be used; all the sources indicate that households were normally baptized collectively and by implication entirely.

It has been objected that the household of Stephanas (1 Cor. 1.16) cannot have included children, as in 1 Corinthians 16.15 Paul calls upon the Corinthian Christians to be submissive to this household; it is inconceivable Paul should envisage the church being submissive to children; any children of Stephanas or his dependants could therefore not have been regarded as members of his household or of the church.[34] It is clear that in 1 Corinthians 16.15 Paul is referring quite specifically to those of the household actively engaged in the work of the church, which would imply that they had been delegated for such work by Stephanas and were acting on his authority. Paul does not urge submission to every member of that household but to those whom Stephanas has seconded to the service of the church.

As can be seen from the above example, no useful purpose can be served by dismantling every reference to household Baptism in Paul's letters and in those sections of Acts that deal with Paul, in order to establish whether those particular households included children. The results of such efforts would inevitably be inconclusive, as there is no evidence outside the biblical texts to complement the silence of Paul and Luke on this subject. Nor is there any purpose in forcing a solution to the problem from the link between Baptism and circumcision in Colossians 2.11. We have already noted the critical problems associated with Colossians, and the significant functional difference between Baptism and circumcision during the earliest years of the Church. Furthermore, 'the belief that circumcision has been replaced by baptism by no means automatically involves the corollary that the two rites have identical significance or identical administration'.[35] The same principle would apply to any link between Christian Baptism and Jewish proselyte circumcision which, we have argued, is the more appropriate analogy. The issue is to be seen in terms of Paul's teaching, in the light of the social and cultural context in which he and his associates proclaimed the Christian gospel.

It has been shown that household Baptism was normative in Pauline Christianity. The conversion of the head was in most circumstances followed by the Baptism of the entire household. It is clear from 1 Corinthians 7.12–16 that this was not always the case in Corinth, and we have noted the legal and socio-economic circumstances of some marriages of the period that enabled wives to exercise greater autonomy than was usual. In cases where a woman was able to assert her own religious freedom, she would not necessarily have been able to determine her children's religious affiliation, as they would have been her husband's heirs and under his guardianship. Nevertheless, Paul is able to describe such children as 'holy', which does not imply that they had been baptized, as he describes unbelieving spouses, who presumably are not baptized, as 'having been made holy' (1 Cor. 7.14). The sanctification of which Paul speaks here is derived from the marriage and reflects Jewish *halakhah* that protected the Jewish identity of children born to Jewish women in mixed marriages, irrespective of whether the boys had been circumcised (cf. Acts 16.1).

Religion for the subordinate members of the household was a matter of belonging, not of believing in the sense of independent personal conviction. The children of the householder would almost invariably have been brought up in conformity with his (or her) cultic beliefs and practices. Other children in the household would usually have been brought up to conform to the domestic cult of the head, to which their parents would also have adhered. There is no reason to suppose that, on the occasion of the conversion of the head to Christianity, any member of the household was excluded from Baptism, except where legal provisions to protect slaves from forcible conversion to Judaism applied. The household was a religious unit just as it was a social unit, and all members were involved either directly or merely through belonging to the household. The conversion of the head was the prerequisite to the Baptism of the entire household: in the conversion of the head was presumed to take place the conversion of the entire household. Slaves and freedmen and freedwomen, as well as children and infants, may have differed in intellectual capacity and in physical and mental maturity but they enjoyed and exercised much the same degree of personal freedom. It is clear from Paul's teaching that Baptism was essential to the conversion and incorporation process; therefore none would have been excluded from it. Knowledge of the events of the gospel was not regarded as fundamental to Baptism; understanding the meaning and significance of Baptism was not seen as essential to its reception.[36]

Given the high birth rates in the ancient world, it is highly unlikely that the question of the status of children born into Christian households did not arise at a very early date, and well within the period of Paul's mission to Corinth if not always elsewhere. There is no evidence at all that the custom established when the Church was formed was at all controversial, as there is no response to any issues in this connection in any of the letters. Letters addressed to the congregation as a whole would have been directed principally to the adult members and perhaps especially to householders and others with the authority to implement Paul's directives. These would all have been relatively recent adult converts, and any allusions to conversion and Baptism are accordingly framed in terms of the normative rite of incorporation, rather than of the derivative use of Baptism as a rite of passage. We are simply not told whether the rite of passage was administered at birth or at puberty, or indeed at any other specific moment in the life cycle.

Public health in the world of early Christianity fell short even of the standards prevalent in most parts of the developing world today. Infant and child mortality rates are difficult to estimate, as we are dependent upon surviving archaeological evidence.[37] Tombstones and other informative artefacts are likely to reflect the lives (and deaths) of the wealthiest members of society and therefore the most adequately nourished and those with easiest access to such medical treatment as was available. The most privileged are of course likely to have lived longest. Even such incomplete and unrepresentative records as do exist indicate a very high infant mortality rate, and of the children who survived childbirth and infancy, fewer than half are likely to have reached adulthood. Given the low proportion of live births that led to adulthood, it is inherently unlikely that Christians would have deferred Baptism, with its eschatological and soterio- logical benefits, to a stage in life that most infants and children were statistically unlikely to reach. Rather, they would have been incorpo- rated without delay into the Church, so that if they died they would die 'in Christ' and rise also to new life with him (cf. 1 Thess. 4.13–18).

Jews and Christians were distinctive in the Graeco-Roman world in attaching high value, and even sanctity, to the lives of children, born and unborn. Not only were children in the Roman Empire sub- ject to the risks attached to poor levels of public health, they were subject also to wilful destruction through abortion, infanticide and exposure (abandonment in a public place where they might or might not be rescued, to be reared as a slave or adopted into another house- hold). Families sought to restrict the number of children in order to avoid division of the estate at the death of the householder, which would have implications for the social status of the heirs. In addition, girls took some of the family wealth with them when they married. Unborn children were frequently aborted, and babies, especially girls, abandoned at birth in order to restrict the number of heirs and dow- ries and keep estates intact. Jews and Christians, on the other hand, prohibited abortion and raised all children who survived childbirth.[38] The sanctity Christians ascribed to the lives of children would have been expressed forcefully in and through their Baptism.

It is often argued that the Baptism of infants is incompatible with Paul's teaching. Scholars from the Baptist and Pentecostal trad- itions in particular base their conclusions on their exegesis of pas- sages in which Paul discusses Baptism, and assume on that basis that every Christian Baptism must have been of an adult convert. They fail to appreciate the social context of the Pauline churches, where the head of the household determined the religious affiliation and observance of his or her dependants. The autonomous, volun- tary and informed profession of faith demanded of candidates for Baptism in some Christian denominations today was not an option in the early Church, whether for an adult slave or a young child. While the head would undoubtedly, to a greater or lesser degree, be an autonomous adult who could freely convert to Christianity and abandon public and private profession and observance of other cults, this did not apply at any stage of their lives to dependent and subordinate members of households. Furthermore, a child brought up in a Christian home and nurtured in the faith can never be a convert to Christianity, especially in a society where identity was derived from the social unit to which one belonged.

The determining factor in conversion and incorporation in the Pauline churches was the conversion of the head of a household or other autonomous adult. Paul accordingly bases his teaching concerning Baptism on the conversion and integration into the Church of such individuals. Others participated in or submitted to the conversion and incorporation process as subordinate and dependent members of the converting household, and conformed to the devotional and moral life that was consequent upon conversion to Christianity.

There is no reason to doubt that juvenile members of the household were baptized with the other subordinate and dependent members on the conversion of the head. By virtue of belonging to the head and to the social unit identified with him or her, they belonged by implication and extension to his lord. In the case of a Christian household, all members were baptized in the name of that Lord, Jesus Christ. By virtue of their membership of a Christian household, they were members of the Church. They were brought up as Christians, so that they would live out the obligations of their Baptism and membership of the Church.

While all members of the household, unless exempted or exercising limited autonomy, would normally have been baptized on the conversion of the head, the question remains as to the incorporation into the Church of those who joined the household by birth, purchase as a slave, engagement as a servant or client or by marriage to any member of the household, subsequent to this Baptism. We might surmise that servants, and especially slaves, brought into the household would probably have been baptized on entry, just as in non-Christian households they may have been initiated into the cults practised there. Marriage of a woman to a subordinate member of the household, which could involve engagement as a servant, might include Baptism into the church of which the household formed a part. Paul does require that Christians who contract marriages do so only with other members of the Church (1 Cor. 7.39). Paul must have been referring to a particular case or cases of Christians able to exercise autonomy in this matter, who are likely to have been householders or the legally autonomous widows of householders. But most members of early Christian communities would not have been able to exercise such autonomy, and unions between slaves enjoyed no legal recognition or protection. In the case of marriage to the head of the household, the religious implications would have depended upon the nature of the marriage contract and the relative social status of the couple. Marriage without transfer of legal custody of the wife would not necessarily have involved her conforming to her husband's cultic observances, although the children of the marriage would have been brought up according to the husband's beliefs and commitments. Children born into a Christian household, especially the children of the head, may have been baptized soon after birth. While marriages between slaves were not recognized in law, there is no evidence that this was an impediment to Baptism for the offspring of such unions.[39]

These and all other arguments on this issue are far from conclusive. We cannot assume that practice was uniform or that the customs established by Paul were continued unaltered in any of the churches he founded. The example of Baptism for the dead in Corinth, which we will consider below, is an example of an early development of the tradition, in a church in which Paul had spent a considerable period during his founding mission. This innovation presumably came about to address a pastoral situation for which there was no precedent and for which an appropriate ritual was needed. It is highly unlikely that infant Baptism could have originated in comparable circumstances, simply in view of the unlikelihood that many families or households would have been without children at the time of their conversion. Nevertheless, while we cannot assume uniformity of practice in the Pauline churches, neither is there any evidence of controversy on this subject before or after the Pauline tradition became fully integrated in emergent Catholic Christianity.

Among the arguments marshalled against infant Baptism during the first Christian century are evidence of the Baptism of adults, after a prolonged catechumenate, at a later period. We have noted that there is no evidence of a pre-baptismal catechumenate during the first Christian century, and contrary evidence that Baptism followed immediately upon conversion. It is far too easily assumed that 'believers' Baptism' was the original, authentic, Christian practice, and that Baptism of infants was a deviation, if not aberration, of this. As we have argued in the preceding pages, this represents a misreading of the biblical texts, founded upon a misunderstanding both of social structure and relationships, and of religious conversion and affiliation, in the world in which Christianity first took root. There is no evidence that the practice of baptizing the children of Christian families was questioned before Tertullian (late second, early third century).[40]

Increasing concern at the consequences imputed to post-baptismal sin, first attested in the early-second-century *Shepherd of Hermas* (*Vision* 3.7.3–6), became a major factor, together with diminished urgency in eschatological expectations, in both deferred Baptism and the development of the catechumenate. The *Apostolic Tradition*, in its various recensions, restricts access to Baptism for those whose way of life is deemed incompatible with Christian profession. This includes serving soldiers, reflecting an ancient conviction that to kill was sin.[41] As Christianity expanded both numerically and in the social status of its adherents, the same principle would have come to apply to civic officials whose authority included office in the cults and the administration of capital punishment.

There are a variety of reasons, therefore, to believe that the tendency, particularly in the western parts of the Roman Empire, during the second and subsequent centuries was away from infant Baptism. Varied practice is attested throughout this period as adults and their households continued to be incorporated into the Church and Baptism of children born into Christian families became increasingly deferred, largely on account of anxieties surrounding post-baptismal lapses and the dilemmas of life and work in the pagan world in which the Church and Christian profession were no more than tolerated. It would be anachronistic to read these concerns and considerations into the practice of the Church during the eschatologically charged years of Paul's missions. The letters and Acts provide no evidence of any restriction on admission to the Church through Baptism on grounds of age.

While this study has argued for the practice of infant Baptism in the churches of the first century established by Paul, this does not in itself identify the appropriate sacramental and pastoral practice for the contemporary Church. This is an issue that will be discussed in the final chapter, after attention has been given to the phenomenon of Baptism for the dead.

Suggested further reading

Much has been written about the question of infant Baptism. Not all treatments of the subject are founded upon exegesis of relevant scriptural passages or knowledge of the religious environment of the time. However, the following, which reach very different conclusions, are essentially sound:

Aland, *Did the Early Church Baptize Infants?*

Jeremias, *Infant Baptism in the First Four Centuries* and *The Origins of Infant Baptism.*

The debate between Jeremias and Aland is in many ways a classic of dispassionate academic exchange, with Jeremias arguing for infant Baptism in the early Church, and Aland maintaining the opposite position.

Beasley-Murray, *Baptism in the New Testament*, is firmly committed to a 'believers' Baptism' position and presents perhaps the strongest case for this on the basis of sound exegesis. The development of historical and cultural knowledge since this book was written has made his assumptions about the background somewhat dated and inadequate. This has implications for the conclusions drawn from his exegesis, but the book remains a valuable contribution to the discussion.

A more popular treatment committed to a 'believers' Baptism' position is Jewett, *Infant Baptism and the Covenant of Grace.*

For the point of view of a long-standing critic of infant Baptism, writing from the Reformed tradition of the Church of Scotland, see Wright, *Infant Baptism in Historical Perspective* and *What has Infant Baptism done to Baptism?*

Bakke, *When Children became People*, argues that infant Baptism was normative in the early Church until the time of Tertullian. It was only during the fourth century that deferral of their children's Baptism by Christian parents was widely practised. This book draws on anthropological studies of children in the Graeco-Roman world but is stronger in treating Patristic material than the relevant New Testament texts.

Among the books that vindicate the practice of infant Baptism are the following:

Bromiley, *Children of Promise*.
Marcel, *The Biblical Doctrine of Infant Baptism*.

Not all who argue for the Baptism of the children of committed Christian parents are willing to see the rite administered indiscriminately. A more restrictive approach is argued by Buchanan, Owen and Wright in *Reforming Infant Baptism*, and a more open policy by Dalby in *Open Baptism*.

Baptism for the Dead

In 1 Corinthians 15.29 Paul poses a rhetorical question:

> What, then, will those do who are baptized for the dead?[42] If the dead are not raised, why are they baptized for them?

The context is Paul's treatment of resurrection in 1 Corinthians 15. There were evidently within the Corinthian church some who disputed Paul's teaching on the resurrection of the dead. Scholars differ as to precisely what they did believe, and it is likely to have been a matter of interpretation or emphasis rather than of outright denial of any life beyond physical death. In other words, the theological differences between Paul and those whose teaching he opposes probably concern the way life beyond physical death is conceptualized and how the physical and non-physical aspects of the person, body and soul in the language of some Greek philosophical schools, relate to this. What is clear is that it is precisely those who, from Paul's point of view, deny the resurrection who are being 'baptized for the dead'.

At face value, Paul is referring to a practice involving members of the Church undergoing Baptism on behalf of people who have died. No such rite is mentioned anywhere else in the New Testament or other early Christian literature, but two writings of the late fourth century allege such a practice among Gnostics and Marcionites.[43] Similar rituals are known from some Greek mystery cults, so vicarious rituals on behalf of certain dead people were not entirely unknown in the world of early Christianity.

The absence of any other evidence of a vicarious baptismal or quasi-baptismal rite in the records of early Christianity has quite naturally led scholars to explore alternative interpretations of this verse. While an instinctive wish to avoid any practice that conflicts with notions of justification by faith may have played some part in this, the lack of corroboration from other sources, and of evidence that such a rite was more widely practised, or even that it endured in Corinth, make such inquiries essential to reaching any secure understanding of this text. Some estimates place the number of possible explanations offered as high as forty, which reflects the degree of uncertainty with which scholarship is working. While not all interpretations can be considered, or even listed, it may be helpful to be aware of the uncertainties in the exegesis of this text.

It is generally assumed that 'the dead' are people who have died in the literal, physical sense, but arguably it could refer to living people who are deemed to be in some sense spiritually dead. Some scholars argue that the reference is not to dead people but to the inevitable future deaths of members of the Church, in anticipation of which some are undergoing Christian Baptism, and that Paul is alluding simply to the normative rite of Christian initiation.[44] The corollary is that these people's conversions are motivated not by conviction regarding the Christian gospel but by fearful anticipation of death, and Paul is pointing out that Baptism is of no benefit if there is no resurrection. Another possibility could be that Paul is upholding the example of those who undergo Baptism in anticipation of resurrection, against those who deny it.[45] This interpretation is founded on a less likely translation of the Greek text, and it is more likely that Paul is referring here to people already deceased.

To the modern Christian, Baptism refers obviously to the sacrament of initiation into the Church. However, in the ancient world the Greek verb *baptizo* could apply to any form of immersion in water and only later acquired the technical sense of the Christian rite of incorporation. Moreover, the word was used in a variety of figurative senses, suggestive of destruction analogous to drowning in water or a ship sinking. In this case, 'baptism' could be a reference to people being overwhelmed or destroyed. It has even been argued that Paul is referring to himself as being consumed in the work of the gospel, which would be futile if there were no resurrection of the dead. However, the overwhelming majority of usages of *baptizo* in early Christian writings, as in the Greek version of the Hebrew Scriptures, are literal in meaning and ritual in their sense. Unless the context indicates a figurative sense, we should therefore understand the term in a literal sense, denoting a water rite practised in the Corinthian church. The issue is whether it is normative Christian Baptism or a derived rite.

The majority of scholars believe that there is no plausible alternative to interpreting this verse as an allusion to an otherwise unknown ritual administered in the Corinthian church. What form this rite took and what purpose it was intended to accomplish are more difficult to establish. It is clear that Paul regards the practice as incompatible with the beliefs of at least some of those who underwent it, but he does not seem to condemn the rite as such. If the dead do not rise, then, from Paul's point of view, they cannot benefit from the ritual being performed on their behalf in Corinth. This suggests that very different understandings of death and resurrection are involved in the dispute. For Paul, resurrection was eschatological; just as Christ had risen from the dead, so dead Christians would rise from the dead at his return in glory; body and soul are integral and, while the body is transformed at the resurrection, it continues to exist (1 Thess. 4.13–18; 1 Cor. 15.12–28; cf. Eph. 5.25–27). Paul's understanding is deeply rooted in the Old

Testament and in Pharisaic Jewish beliefs of his day. Most of the Corinthian Christians were not Jews, and their thought may have been influenced more by Greek ideas they had inherited or otherwise derived from their native culture. For many Greeks, physical death separated the soul from the body. While the body died, the soul was liberated from the physical world and continued its immortal existence in a superior, spiritual world. There may therefore have been in the Corinthian church some members who did not believe that the continued life of the soul required the resurrection of the body or even that physical resurrection was at all desirable. While their position was clearly not acceptable to Paul, we can see that from their point of view a ritual carried out on behalf of people who had already died could still make sense.

What this ritual was intended to accomplish is more difficult to ascertain. Some scholars believe that Paul is referring to Baptism undergone in order to obtain union beyond death with deceased Christian relations. In other words, the ritual was Christian Baptism but the motivation behind conversion was not conviction but a desire to be reunited with deceased Christian relatives. This interpretation has been quite widely supported but it is neither the most obvious rendering of the Greek text nor is the Greek phrase the most obvious or clearest way of expressing the sense of such conversions.

It is possible that the expression 'baptized for the dead' refers not to Christian initiation but to a funeral rite. As noted in the discussion above, the eschatological framework in which Baptism is referred to in Ephesians 5.25–27 could reflect an interpretation of Baptism in terms of which such a ritual could be meaningful. It has been suggested that the ritual was undergone by some of the Corinthian Christians in order to expedite the transition of deceased members of the community to eternal life.[46] In terms of the imagery found in Ephesians, this rite would prepare Christians for their part in the eschatological consummation of the marriage of Christ and his bride, the Church.[47] Such a rite was presumably not performed on the bodies of the deceased but on living members of the community acting as their proxy. A rite understood to free the soul from the body would probably not have met with Paul's approval, but if this interpretation is correct it did not meet with his condemnation either.

The most obvious interpretation, in terms of the Greek language of the text, is the one some exegetes have been most concerned to avoid. This is that some members of the Corinthian church underwent Baptism in order to make its benefits available to people who had died. This does not conform with highly individualistic conceptions of Baptism that have come to prevail in Western Christianity, and certainly not with the notions of 'believers' Baptism' or of justification by faith as traditionally understood in Western Protestantism. But it may not have been so incompatible with the way Baptism was understood in the early Church. The desire to incorporate deceased persons into the body of Christ would have been entirely logical in such a context.

The most likely interpretation of the rite alluded to in 1 Corinthians 15.29 is that some members of the church were undergoing Baptism on behalf of deceased relatives and friends. Whether these were people who had died before Paul's mission to Corinth and had therefore not heard the gospel proclaimed, or whether they had died more recently, we cannot be certain. The rite involved the mediation of salvation by proxy, without the incorporation of those on whose behalf it was undergone into the living and active earthly community of the Church. This implies an understanding that incorporation into the Church and eschatological salvation could be bestowed beyond death. This idea is attested elsewhere in the New Testament in 1 Peter 3.19–20 and 4.6,[48] which alludes to the tradition that Jesus between his death and resurrection descended to hades and preached to the spirits of the deceased, an episode alluded to also in the Apostles' Creed and therefore an entirely orthodox Christian belief. This idea may be reflected also in John 5.25 and Ephesians 4.8–10,[49] and other early Christian texts suggest a conviction that salvation could be bestowed after death.[50] Two texts go as far as to relate the administration of Baptism to the souls of the deceased, in conjunction with their resurrection.[51]

While the notion of Baptism on behalf of deceased relatives and friends may seem foreign to the mindset of the modern Western Christian, it was not nearly so alien to the world of early Christianity. Furthermore, in a missionary context it may have met a specific pastoral need. New converts to Christianity would have had forebears, other relatives and friends who had died without hearing the gospel proclaimed, and questions would have been raised about their fate in the light of the Christian expectation of divine judgement. In addition to wishing to save loved ones from the impending judgement, Christians undergoing this baptism may also have been seeking to transform domestic cults in which ancestral spirits had previously been worshipped. By incorporating their ancestors into the Church, they could continue to honour them without offering any form of cultic worship.

In addition to forebears who had had no contact with the Christian gospel, the Corinthian church may have had unbaptized adherents who had died. While we have seen that the records indicate that Baptism followed conversion, normatively that of the head of a household, immediately or almost immediately, there are several reasons why some converts may have died unbaptized. Some prominent householders may have held public office or have been of the social order from which magistrates were drawn. Unless they were Jews, and thereby exempt from civic obligations, they would have been required to participate in public ceremonies that included pagan cultic observances. They would therefore not have been able to make any exclusive allegiance to Christianity. This was clearly a problem in Corinth, as in 1 Corinthians 8 – 10 Paul deals extensively with the problems of eating the meat of animals that had been offered in pagan sacrifices and the related issues of public activities in the temples and moral behaviour surrounding social occasions. It was impossible for men of social eminence to conduct their business without involvement in the pagan cults of the city and empire, and dining publicly or semi-publicly with others of similar standing in society. Some may therefore have decided not to undergo Baptism into the Church, and to remain on the fringes of the Christian community, until they had fulfilled their political obligations. Similarly, at the other end of the social spectrum there may have been slaves and other dependent members of pagan households who had somehow become involved in the life of a Christian congregation. Compulsory daily participation in domestic cults could have precluded any exclusive commitment to Christianity and therefore their incorporation into the Church through Baptism.

There may well have been Christians who, at the deaths of such unbaptized adherents, would have sought to resolve their ambiguous status in the Church and to procure for them the eschatological benefits of full membership of the body of Christ through posthumous and vicarious Baptism.

While there is no indication that Paul was in any way the instigator of the ritual of Baptism for the dead, we are nonetheless able to learn something both of the environment in which he operated and the cultural presuppositions that influenced the first Christians' understanding of Baptism. Most significantly, ritual was understood to be efficacious and not merely symbolic. Baptism was not contingent upon the consent or the understanding of the one baptized. Divine power was understood to be transmitted in the ritual, for the salvation of the one baptized or on whose behalf Baptism was received in the case of posthumous vicarious initiation. As a way of procuring eschatological salvation for the deceased, Baptism for the dead would seem not to have been a widespread practice, as it is attested only in Corinth. Furthermore, the practice must have fallen into abeyance at an early date, as there is no later record, and by the end of the second century the allusion in 1 Corinthians 15.29 could no longer be explained on the basis of any direct or reliable knowledge. The traditions of Christ's descent to hell or hades (1 Pet. 3.18–22), and deliverance from there of the righteous departed would seem to have answered the theological questions and addressed the pastoral concerns more adequately than the Corinthian ritual. By the early-second-century at the latest, this was the accepted Christian belief concerning how salvation in Christ could reach those who had died without hearing the gospel.

Suggested further reading

For a more detailed treatment of the subject see my 'Baptism for the Dead (1 Cor 15:29)?' and the references there to earlier treatments of the issue. For a more recent study with a very different position on the question see Hull, *Baptism on Account of the Dead (1 Cor 15:29)*.

Notes

1 For discussion see Jensen, *Living Water*, pp. 158–68.

2 Poliakoff, '"They Should Cover their Shame"'.

3 Justin, *I Apology* 61.

4 An account of this is found in *Apostolic Tradition* 21.11, 20. The textual tradition is quite complex. Translations with commentary have been published by Bradshaw et al. in *The Apostolic Tradition*. Epiphany was another ancient date for Baptism, particularly in the East, where the rite was associated with the baptism of Jesus by John rather than the crucifixion and resurrection.

5 Cf. *Didache* 7: 'Now concerning Baptism, baptize as follows: after you have reviewed all these things, baptize in the name of the Father and of the Son and of the Holy Spirit in running water. But if you have no running water, then baptize in some other water; and if you are not able to baptize in cold water, then do so in warm. But if you have neither, then pour water on the head three times in the name of the Father and Son and Holy Spirit.'

6 In Scythopolis in Palestine, part of a public bathhouse was during the fourth century converted into a Christian baptistery, the remains of which can be seen today.

7 Cyprian, *Letters* 70.1.3 is the earliest recorded prescription that the water be purified through ritual action that could be carried out only by the bishop. The second-century Valentinian *Excerpts of Theodosius*, preserved by Clement of Alexandria, stipulate that water should be exorcized prior to Baptism (*Excerpts* 82). There is no antecedent for either practice in the Pauline letters.

8 This anointing was integral to the Baptism liturgy as it continues to be in the Orthodox tradition. The separation of anointing from Baptism, and reservation of the former to the bishop, ultimately developed into the distinct sacrament of Confirmation in the Western Church. The theological, liturgical, pastoral and ecumenical issues this raises are beyond the immediate scope of this study, but some reflections will be offered in the final chapter.

9 *sebomenē ton theon* implies that Lydia worshipped the God of Israel but was not a Jew. There was no single, clearly defined category of 'God-fearer', and patterns of allegiance and adherence to the God of Israel and to Jewish communities and institutions varied considerably. See especially Cohen, *The Beginnings of Jewishness*. We cannot, on the basis of this brief pericope, locate Lydia with any confidence on Cohen's paradigm, and she is mentioned nowhere else in early Christian literature.

10 *proseuchē* means 'place of prayer' and could denote a dedicated building. However, most scholars understand the term in this context to refer to a place where the Jewish community of Philippi gathered, out of doors on the river bank.

11 Scholars dispute whether or not Paul was a citizen of Rome. While crucial to the narrative here, this question is not relevant to our subject.

12 Scholars dispute the historicity of the earthquake. What is important for our purposes is that this provides the narrative context for a conversion account that can assist our understanding of early Christian baptismal practice.

13 As the text of Acts was transmitted during the centuries before the invention of the printing press, copyists amended the text of Acts 19.2 because the version they had received did not make sense and they sought to recover an original version. See Barrett, *The Acts of the Apostles*, pp. 892–6; Metzger, *A Textual Commentary on the Greek New Testament* and Webb, *John the Baptizer and Prophet*, pp. 273–6.

14 The Jewish historian Josephus includes a brief account of John the Baptist in *Antiquities of the Jews*, 18.116–19. In this he makes no mention of the or a Holy Spirit, but his account of John's teaching is brief and the concept would have been difficult to explain to his intended Roman readership.

15 Cf. Johnson, *The Acts of the Apostles*, p. 337 and Webb, *John the Baptizer and Prophet*, pp. 273–4.

16 While not written by Paul or even directly influenced by him, the mid- to late-first-century *Didache* explicitly provides for various forms of Baptism depending on circumstances, though with a clear preference for Baptism in rivers where possible (*Didache* 7). It may be relevant that in Judaism, running water was considered purer and less liable to contamination than still water. This text is discussed in Niederwimmer, *The Didache*.

17 For discussion of the nature of early Christian expectations and the ways they changed with the passing of time, see my 'Early Christian Expectations concerning the Return of Jesus'.

18 Chester, writing within an evangelical Protestant tradition, has observed the extent to which anti-ritual dogmatism within that tradition has shaped scholarly interpretations of Paul on this issue; see his *Conversion at Corinth*, pp. 280–3. He refers pointedly to 'the uncomfortable fact that Paul held views concerning the sacraments, and indeed the demonic, which they would find distasteful and primitive' (p. 342).

19 Hartman argues that the pre-baptismal catechumenate can be traced back to the Pauline mission; see his '*Into the Name of the Lord Jesus*', p. 142. His reconstruction is based on precisely this point, but in his view incorporation of gentiles unfamiliar with the Jewish heritage into the Church already required catechetical instruction before Baptism in Paul's day. However, there would seem to be in Paul's letters more evidence of a lack of comprehensive orientation into Christian life than of systematic instruction in it. The moral and pastoral issues that arose in Corinth are the most graphic example of this.

20 Some scholars argue that passages in the New Testament, including at least some of the Pauline texts we have considered, reflect early Christian

catechetical instruction, but there is no indication that this precedes Baptism. Sections of 1 Peter are also often interpreted as catechetical instruction, whether before or after Baptism. But the institution of the catechumenate, and pre-baptismal instruction and preparation, is more evident from later texts such as *Didache* 1–6; 7.4, and the mid-second-century writings of Justin, *Apology* 1.61, the *Apostolic Tradition* 20, and the late-second-century work of Tertullian, *On Baptism*. See the discussion in Finn, *Early Christian Baptism and the Catechumenate* and Kelly, *Early Christian Creeds*.

21 There has been considerable debate in recent scholarship regarding the socio-economic conditions of the Graeco-Roman cities and the location in them of the earliest Christians. See esp. Meeks, *The First Urban Christians*; Still and Horrell (eds), *After the First Urban Christians* and Longenecker, *Remember the Poor*.

22 The household was not confined to a single geographical location but was present wherever the head held property or other interests.

23 For discussion of this point see Osiek and Balch, *Families in the New Testament World*, p. 61.

24 Meeks, *The First Urban Christians*, pp. 24–30.

25 On this issue see Cohen, *The Beginnings of Jewishness* and my 'The Social Nature of Conversion in the Early Christian World'.

26 See e.g. Harland, *Dynamics of Identity in the World of the Early Christians*.

27 See Klauck, *Magic and Paganism in Early Christianity* and MacMullen, *Paganism in the Roman Empire*.

28 See especially the article by Barclay in Moxnes (ed.), *Constructing Early Christian Families*.

29 An incidence of this is reported, somewhat later, by Tertullian in *Idolatry* 15.7–8.

30 Many complex issues surround this case, which would be beyond the scope of this study. For example, it is far from clear that Paul demands the manumission of Onesimus. For fuller discussion see my 'Onesimus' and works cited there.

31 For fuller discussion see my 'The Social Nature of Conversion in the Early Christian World'.

32 In my 'Baptism for the Dead (1 Cor 15:29)? I explore the possibility that deaths of such persons may have occasioned the rite mentioned in 1 Corinthians 15.29, which is discussed below.

33 Jeremias, *Infant Baptism in the First Four Centuries*, pp. 20–2; see also Theissen, *The Social Setting of Pauline Christianity*, pp. 84–5.

34 So argues Aland, *Did the Early Church Baptize Infants?* p. 88.

35 Beasley-Murray, *Baptism in the New Testament*, p. 157.

36 Cullmann, *Baptism in the New Testament*, p. 31.

37 This issue has been discussed by Frier, 'Roman Demography' and Wiedemann, *Adults and Children in the Roman Empire*.

38 Stark argues that this was a major factor in the resilience of Judaism and the growth of Christianity during this period; see his *The Rise of Christianity*.

39 Cullmann argues that children born into Christian households, and therefore into the Church, did not require Baptism; see his *Baptism in the New Testament*, p. 44. He interprets 1 Cor. 7.14 to mean that the benefits of Baptism are transmitted to children born to Christian parents, rather than indicating that children of mixed marriages could potentially be brought up in the faith. He argues also that Christian Baptism was modelled on Jewish proselyte baptism and would therefore not have been administered to children born into the Church. This is plausible to a point but unlikely in view of Paul's explicit statement that all Christians were baptized (1 Cor. 12.13).

40 While immensely significant, Tertullian is an enigmatic figure and by no means representative of the Church of the late second century. His *On Baptism* and *Apology* nonetheless contributed greatly to concerns about post-baptismal sin and its consequences, leading many converts and parents to defer their and their children's Baptism until after their passions, i.e. their sex drive, had diminished with age. For discussion see Osborn, *Tertullian* and Rankin, *Tertullian and the Church*.

41 *Apostolic Tradition* 16. The textual history behind, and relationship between, the various texts containing *Apostolic Tradition* are extremely complex and beyond the range of this study. Nevertheless, the development of the tradition reflects adaptation to changing conditions for Christians in the Roman Empire. For discussion of this section, see Bradshaw et al., *The Apostolic Tradition*, pp. 87–95.

42 The expression *uper ton nekron* has some breadth of possible meaning, and for the present purpose the verse has been rendered in a similarly broad sense.

43 John Chrysostom, *Homily on 1 Corinthians* 40.1; Epiphanius, *Against Heresies* 28.6.4.

44 This is the interpretation of Winter in *After Paul left Corinth*, p. 104.

45 Hull, *Baptism on Account of the Dead (1 Cor 15:29)*.

46 De Maris, 'Corinthian Religion and Baptism for the Dead (1 Corinthians 15.29)'.

47 I am grateful to Dr Ellen Juhl Christiansen for pointing out the possible significance of the Ephesians passage for understanding Baptism for the dead.

48 For discussion see Horrell, *Becoming Christian*, pp. 73–99 and Trumbower, *Rescue for the Dead*, pp. 44–7.

49 Cf. Hanson, *The New Testament Interpretation of Scripture*, pp. 122–6.

50 *Gospel of Peter* 10.41; *Acts of Pilate* 25–26; Justin, *Dialogue with Trypho* 72.4; Irenaeus, *Against all Heresies* 3.20.4; Clement of Alexandria,

Stromateis 6.6.44–46. These writings all date to before the end of the second century AD. The texts of the first two documents cited can be found in Hennecke (ed.), *New Testament Apocrypha*, vol. 1. Justin, Irenaeus and Clement's writings are available in such collections as the *Ante-Nicene Fathers*. The *Gospel of Peter* and the *Acts of Pilate* have never been acknowledged as Scripture, except perhaps in the circles in which they were written. Justin, Irenaeus and Clement, on the other hand, exercised a formative influence on the development of Christian doctrine during the second century.

51 Hermas, *Similitudes* 9.16.5–6; *Acts of Pilate* 27. The former text is published in collections of the *Apostolic Fathers* edited by Lightfoot, Lake or Ehrman. This dates not later than the early-second-century and is therefore ancient, although not of any authority in the Church.

4

Pauline Baptism and Contemporary Issues

We have considered the teaching in the Pauline letters on the subject of Baptism, or rather those passages in which Baptism is used to illustrate or reinforce teaching on various aspects of Christian life and doctrine. Paul and his circle were of course not the only authoritative teachers of Christian doctrine and ethics during the earliest period of the Church, nor were they the only effective missionaries of the Christian gospel. Nevertheless, the Pauline tradition has been particularly influential in shaping the Church of succeeding centuries. Furthermore, the letters of the Pauline corpus have preserved theological reflection on pastoral issues of their day, and thereby provide a unique, if incomplete, insight into ways the gospel was brought to bear upon practical aspects of Christian life in the early years of the Church.

Insofar as Romans and Colossians are any indication, Paul and his circle were able to presuppose a considerable degree of common ground on the subject of Baptism with churches he and his companions had not founded. This does not mean that the early Church was entirely united in its teaching and practice on Baptism, still less on the issues on which Paul and his followers appealed to their converts' experience of Baptism to reinforce their teaching. There nevertheless clearly was some degree of commonality, at least in the geographical regions in which Paul operated. We can conclude, on the basis of our study in the preceding chapters, that Baptism played an important role in defining and expressing a common Christian identity. This extended beyond the networks of churches established by the various missionary movements of the period, to embrace all Christians and all communities in a single Church.

We noted at the outset that Paul's letters were written during the course of an active career in Christian mission, and oversight of the new communities of believers that were formed as a result of it. The theology expressed in the letters reflects this. Paul's writings undoubtedly proved to be of enduring value and inspiration to succeeding generations within what came to be orthodox Christianity, and became a major source of doctrine for the Catholic Church. This does not imply that his teaching passed unaltered into Christian tradition, but does reinforce the significance of the figure of Paul for subsequent Christian generations. While the Church in the Roman Empire did not cease to expand, mission gradually evolved into the continuing life of established Christian communities, alongside the continuing spread of the gospel to new centres and into the hinterland of the urban centres in which the first churches were founded. Paul's letters provide a unique insight into the earliest phase of this movement, when Christian missionaries began to establish churches in the Graeco-Roman world.

The Church in many parts of the world today reflects with some ambivalence upon the legacy of its founding missionaries. The period of European expansion saw the Christian gospel proclaimed alongside, and frequently in collusion with, economic exploitation, military occupation and colonization. The educational and health-care institutions established by many missionaries reflect their ambiguous position within the imperial system and their role in the cultural domination of colonized people. Few questioned the identification of their own culture with the gospel and Christian values and way of life. Notwithstanding the protection – not always effective – afforded by the Roman citizenship attributed to Paul in Acts, he did not have the power of the empire behind his missionary ventures. Nor did he have the resources to establish institutions such as those that characterized European missions during the modern period and served as vehicles of cultural imperialism. However bitter and potentially divisive the issues that beset the early Church, Paul's missions were not compromised by the scandal of institutionalized schism and denominational rivalries.

An early critic of the approach that predominated in European mission agencies, of all denominations, during the nineteenth and early twentieth centuries was Roland Allen, an Anglican missionary to China who also conducted field research in India, Canada and east Africa. In his classic work *Missionary Methods: St. Paul's or Ours*, Allen explicitly contrasted the missionary methods of his contemporaries and predecessors with those of Paul.[1] While Allen's reading of the sources is in many respects debatable, and he is not immune from the cultural assumptions of his day, he nevertheless makes some trenchant observations that this study would corroborate. Like Paul, he had no qualms about proclaiming the Christian gospel to people of other races, cultures and religions.

It is perhaps in his reliance on Acts that the modern critical scholar would most particularly take issue with Allen, but his central arguments, so far as they pertain to the subject of this study, are fundamentally sound. Paul, in forming his converts into communities who would continue not only in prayer and worship but in the proclamation of the gospel to others, established local churches rather than outposts of foreign missionary agencies. Allen's portrayal of Paul's continuing oversight of the churches he had founded undoubtedly requires some refinement,[2] but the communities founded by Paul were nevertheless able to sustain their common lives, celebrate what came to be known as the sacraments and incorporate new converts into their fellowship, in the absence of their founding apostle and his associates. While we may question whether Paul administered any rite we might call ordination,[3] authority and ministry were clearly vested in recognized local leaders at an early date.

Allen observed that Paul seems to have baptized his converts without delay. Whether Paul baptized the converts himself or directed they be baptized, this contention is supported by this study. Catechetical instruction and integration in the community began with Baptism. We have noted that studies of religious conversion by contemporary social scientists have confirmed that integration in the community is the most effective means of changing the convert's beliefs and way of life. This contrasts with the extended pre-baptismal catechumenate attested from the second century onwards, which was also to become the dominant model during the period of European missionary expansion into other continents. Irrespective of confessional discipline and whether children of Christian families were baptized in infancy or on attaining adulthood, converts were subjected to a period of probation during which their way of life and family structures were subjected not merely to scrutiny but to regulation in accordance with patterns that had evolved in northern and western European cultures. The catechumenate became an endurance test, not only for converts but also for children and adults born into Christian families which, in effect if not in intention, redefined the function of Baptism. Allen's observation is worth quoting in full:

> We have taught [converts] that union with Christ is the source of strength, we have taught them that baptism is the sacrament of unity, then we have told them that they must prove their sincerity by practising virtue in their own strength before they can be admitted to the sacrament by which they are to receive strength to be virtuous. In other words, we have taught them that the one great need of men is Christ, and then that they must attain to righteousness by themselves in order to receive Christ.[4]

The question whether Baptism is defined by God's grace or the human response of faith lies at the root of some of the deepest divisions among Christians. Rather than rehearsing these arguments or attempting to resolve them, we simply note at this point the evidence concerning Paul's missionary practice, which did not concern the tradition or discipline of any established denomination.

We have noted that Paul operated in a world in which spiritual powers were perceived to be omnipresent and in which rituals were the established means of seeking the intervention of these powers for protection or advantage. Neither Jewish monotheism nor the philosophical monotheism common among the intellectual elites of the Graeco-Roman world ameliorated the popular beliefs many in the modern world would consider superstitious; nor did monotheistic Jews and many Graeco-Roman philosophers doubt the operation of divine power in rituals. In this world Baptism was experienced as effecting fundamental transformation in the identity of the convert, precisely because divine power was transmitted in the rite, redefining converts' relationships with both the spiritual powers and their terrestrial counterparts. Whether symbolized in terms of death and resurrection, adoption or rebirth, Baptism represented rupture with past relationships, allegiances and way of living, and the acquisition of new relationships in the body of Christ, marking the beginning of life in allegiance to God and empowered by the Holy Spirit.

In Baptism the change was effected and realized as fact. Baptism was not a mere formal external act, a symbol of a spiritual fact which was already complete without it . . . Faith without Baptism and all that Baptism involved was consequently no part of St. Paul's teaching.[5]

For Paul and his converts, Baptism was a powerful ritual in which the Spirit of the one God entered people and communities. Modern Western rationalism in no way informed their thinking. Monotheism, the doctrine of divine sovereignty, and a strong tradition of moral teaching militated against too mechanistic or magical a conception of ritual in Judaism and Christianity. That Paul may have found it necessary to caution his converts against presumption that the rite alone would secure their salvation (1 Cor. 10.1–5), confirms their shared conviction that the operation of the Holy Spirit was integral to Baptism, even if it provided no guarantee against divine judgement.

Western rationalism and Protestant anti-sacramentalism have alike been hostile to acknowledging the social function and power of rituals in modern societies, and to recognizing that symbolic but transformative acts lie at the heart of the Christian gospel. The persistence of religious and quasi-religious beliefs and superstitions, and the power of national and other quasi-cultic symbols – such as those associated with football teams – to evoke not only loyalty and courage but also chauvinism and violence, suggest that those who deny the power of rituals and symbols have failed to appreciate something of the nature of human society and the world we inhabit.[6] The pastoral value of ritual is increasingly appreciated but tends to be expressed in the language of the social sciences and to emphasize individual emotional needs rather than the corporate life of the Church. It remains a challenge to maintain the link between pastoral care, liturgical act and theological principle.

In the Western world, supernaturalistic interpretations of Baptism may well be more prevalent on the fringes of and outside Christian communities than among clergy and their regular congregations. While clergy and theologians struggle to discern any connection between the liturgy of Baptism and the operation of the Holy Spirit, and many reduce the rite to an act of obedience to a dominical injunction (Matt. 28.19), parents who seek Baptism for their children may well believe there are supernatural benefits to be derived by it, even if they have no wish to become active or committed members of a church.[7] While such attitudes are theologically aberrant, the crude ascription of insincerity to such parents[8] may reflect a serious misunderstanding of popular culture. A more adequate response to the pastoral and missiological challenges such situations present might be to recognize the residual religiosity, and to assist those seeking Baptism both to connect their beliefs and desires more adequately to the rite they are seeking, and to discover its fulfilment in the corporate and worshipping life of the Church. Paul, in his speech on the Areopagus, identifies 'the unknown god' of popular Athenian religiosity with the one whom he proclaims (Acts 17.22–31). He may not have persuaded many, but he used the opportunity to proclaim the gospel. We have noted also the story of the Philippian gaoler who reacts in panic, superstition and fear to an earthquake that might have enabled his prisoners to escape and who sought the counsel and assistance of Paul and Silas (Acts 16.25–34). They offer instruction in the gospel and bring the gaoler and his household to Baptism.

However differently post-Enlightenment Christians may understand the operation of the Holy Spirit in Baptism today, we fail as stewards of the sacraments if we do not recognize the power of the rites we administer to transform the lives of those who seek our ministry and if we do not respond creatively and sensitively to the pastoral and missionary, as well as liturgical opportunities presented to us. If we pander to a demand for cheap grace and free magic, we simply service consumers passing along a conveyor belt without experiencing or appreciating the commodity they sample. In this connection it may be worth noting that Roland Allen resigned as vicar of Chalfont St Peter in the Diocese of Oxford, at least partly in frustration with this approach to Baptism in the Church of England. We have noted that as a missionary he opposed the imposition of obstacles to Baptism, decried probationary periods and lengthy catechumenates, and identified 'spiritual change' or conversion as the criterion on which the sacrament was to be administered. Conversely, if we replace God's prevenient grace with an expectation of prevenient understanding of the faith and commitment to the life of the Church, then we waste the opportunity to proclaim the gospel and draw into the fellowship of the Church people who seek but do not understand what it is our calling to offer; and so we become an obstacle to the realization of our own expectations.

The Church today, particularly in Western cultures that have been influenced by rationalism and secularism, needs to interpret theologically the religious needs and experiences of people who have received little Christian education or liturgical formation, and to articulate the connection between its sacraments and the operation of the Holy Spirit. This is not a matter of perpetuating superstition, nor of dismissing experiences and desires, but of affirming people and relating spiritual aspirations, however uninformed, to the gospel in such a way that commitment may be sustained in the life of the Church. The power of rituals, observed and documented by social scientists, needs to be theologically scrutinized and disciplined, so that it is appropriated responsibly and ethically in pastoral ministry and in the corporate worship of the congregation.

While some modern or postmodern Christians have scruples about actively seeking converts from among people of other faiths or none, it is not in itself controversial that the Church continues to incorporate into its fellowship, through Baptism, people who have chosen to profess the faith of Christ. The disputes within as well as between Christian denominations concern the derivative role of Baptism as a rite of passage that gradually became normative. Children would almost certainly have been born into Christian households fairly soon after the foundation of most churches. There is no evidence in Paul's letters or in any other extant Christian writing of the period that the ritual incorporation of the next generation was at all contentious, or required direction from the founding apostle in letters written some years after the establishment of the Church. We have shown that the analogy drawn between Baptism and circumcision in the disputed letter to the Colossians does not necessarily reflect a development whereby Baptism has become a rite of passage; the original analogy between the two rites would specifically have been between Baptism and proselyte circumcision, and it is not clear that Colossians draws an analogy between Baptism and circumcision as life-cycle rites. If this development were presupposed, it would seem to imply that children born into Christian households were baptized in infancy.

That Baptism acquired the derivative role of a rite of passage at a very early date would seem certain, irrespective of the point in the life cycle at which the ritual was customarily administered. While this function of Baptism is never directly addressed by Paul, it cannot be wished away, either from the liturgical life of the early Church or from that of the Church today.

When Baptism is administered as a rite of passage, it simulates the conversion–incorporation rite, but when the outsider who becomes an insider through the rite has been born and nurtured in a Christian family, he or she was in effect never an outsider except for the purposes of the liturgies of the Church. Even if, during the first generation of Christianity, those not yet baptized were excluded from some acts of worship, such as the celebration of the Eucharist (as came to be the custom at a later date), those born into Christian households would nonetheless have been integrated in the social networks of the household and of the local church, and nurtured in the Christian faith. In this respect the incorporation into the Church of children born into Christian families, and therefore in a sense already a part of the 'church family', is nothing new and is perhaps the least vexed aspect of Baptism as a rite of passage.

The derivative role of Baptism as a rite of passage perhaps explains at least partly why there is no clarity on this issue in the surviving literature of the earliest Christian centuries; on the contrary, there is evidence of varied approaches. The question cannot be reduced to 'paedobaptism' versus 'credobaptism', and the reservations experienced by some moderns and postmoderns about parents' committing their children to the Christian or any other faith simply did not apply. Concerns about post-baptismal sin and its consequences were a major factor in deferring Baptism, both for converts and for those born into Christian families, particularly in the Western (Latin) church until and beyond the time of Augustine of Hippo. The incompatibility of holding public office with Christian profession was another factor until the time of Constantine, by which time deferred Baptism had become an established custom, particularly in those orders of society liable for public office. Baptismal teaching and practice evolved in varied ways as the Church negotiated its position in Roman imperial society.

The Church today lives and works in a world with enormous diversity of cultures, in which religious consciousness and belief vary considerably. Baptism, as a rite of incorporation, defines the boundary between the Church and the various societies in which its members live and work, and in which its institutions play a recognized or unacknowledged public role. Christian faith continues to be transmitted – or not – through families in this variety of cultural contexts. When Baptism functions as a rite of passage, the person to be baptized is somewhat artificially placed outside the community in order to be ritually incorporated.

The boundary between Church and society has become indistinct or no longer recognized in many places, where Christianity or a particular denomination has enjoyed a privileged position and official status has led to a coalescence of political, cultural and religious identity. Baptism has become a rite of passage, no longer even simulating incorporation from the outside, and expresses an expectation of continuity in the life cycle of the culture. This does not in itself imply any lack of Christian commitment on the part of those who seek or those who administer Baptism. However, when social change gradually erodes the previously inextricable identification of Church and society, this in time raises questions about the nature and function of Baptism; a violent rupture between Church and state, on the other hand, might clarify the matter more quickly. In seeking to interpret differences in Christian approaches to society, H. Richard Niebuhr constructed a helpful paradigm in *Christ and Culture*. He identifies five different approaches to society in Christian teaching and in the life of the Church, which may help us to understand differences in the theology and practice of Baptism.

The 'Christ against culture' approach defines the Church in terms of its active, worshipping community and regulates members' way of life as integral to their Christian commitment. There is no space for ambiguity or for less than fully committed membership: the Church 'affirms the sole authority of Christ over culture and resolutely rejects culture's claims to loyalty'.[9] The host society is perceived as hostile, idolatrous and depraved, and a rigid boundary is maintained against it. While Niebuhr himself does not do so, there are scholars who would attribute to Paul an approach to Roman imperial society and its cults and deities that would most closely approximate the 'Christ against culture' position.[10] Niebuhr identifies Tertullian with this approach,[11] and the same could be argued for the *Didache*, the *Apostolic Tradition* and other liturgical texts as well as much of the apocalyptic literature. What is important is that with the possible exception of some apocalyptic texts, these figures and writings all reflect a Church that is missionary, proclaiming the gospel to the world and not isolating itself from contamination by the world. While Tertullian is an early critic of infant baptism, this does not account for how boundaries are to be maintained and the faith transmitted to the next generation. What it does explain, though, is that such a group would have a clear sense of when a member lapses from the faith and separates from the community.

The 'Christ of culture' approach is the polar opposite of 'Christ against culture', and characteristic of established denominations where religious, cultural and national identity are inextricably linked. It is assumed that society as a whole is Christian and therefore that the culture is inherently Christian. Membership of the Church is inherited and not contingent upon any personal commitment or profession. Baptism is therefore as much a cultural as a religious rite of passage and is administered to all members of the society indiscriminately. There is no sense of lapsing from the faith or of separation from the community, as Church and society are coterminous and non-observance does not constitute apostasy. This has been normative wherever there is a state Church, and persists to the present day even where secularization and other social changes have rendered the close identification of Church and society anachronistic. This can also occur where a particular form of Christianity is the religion of an ethnic subculture within an empire, as has been the case with many of the Orthodox churches for much of Christian history. The resilience of these communities under intensified pressure from various Islamist forces in recent years testifies to the tenacity of Christian faith that is possible while identifying closely both with the ethnic culture and with the state and regional culture. Where Baptism is understood not as a rite of the Church but one to be administered by the Church, on demand, to those who seek it, and on the terms on which they seek it,[12] this represents a quite fundamental redefinition of the ancient Christian rite. The uncritical equation of Christian values with prevailing popular culture, or the subordination of the former to the latter, would be difficult to defend with theological integrity in secularized societies. Most proponents of an 'open Baptism' policy, whereby the rite is administered without any expectation of Christian commitment on the part of those who seek it, would wish to maintain at least some critical distance from the prevailing culture, and argue a theological basis for Baptism in such circumstances.[13] As well as emphasizing God's prevenient grace and expressing a reluctance to hurt or reject people, arguments can include a somewhat surprising confidence in the supernatural effects of the rite.

The 'Christ above culture' approach sees the gospel incarnated in but always distinct from human culture. While recognizing human limitations and sinfulness, and moral responsibility, potential is also seen for an ecclesiastical and cultural synthesis. The gospel is interpreted and applied to life in a manner congenial to the host culture while remaining the standard against which cultural observances and attitudes are measured. Niebuhr assigns the early Christian apologists Justin and Clement to this category.[14] This approach would seem to reflect the idealism of an intellectual elite rather than the experience and outlook of the Church as a whole, if surviving liturgies and apocalyptic literature of the period provide any indication of Christian popular religiosity. While inviting society, and in particular the intellectual elites, to accept the gospel, this approach would tend nonetheless to maintain a clear boundary between Church and society and to advocate a discipline that nurtured those born into the Christian community.

The 'Christ and culture in paradox' approach engages critically with the prevailing culture; in negotiating the tensions between the gospel and prevailing culture, this approach is missional, seeking to bring people, families and society as a whole into Christian fellowship and into conformity with Christian beliefs, values and observance, as these are understood. Niebuhr assigns Paul to this category.[15] As we have noted, there are scholars who, if using Niebuhr's paradigm, would probably argue that he underestimates Paul's radicalism. Where there is palpable tension between Christian and cultural values, and no avoiding integration in society, the Church will define a clear boundary between itself and the world. Baptism marks that boundary, and is restricted to converts and committed and active families in the worshipping community. Enquirers and the uncommitted are to be drawn into the fellowship of the Church, whether from the periphery or from outside, and then, on the basis of commitment, invited to Baptism. This correlates with the recommendations of the World Council of Churches Faith and Order Paper, *Baptism, Eucharist and Ministry*,[16] reflecting wide support across the spectrum of Christian traditions. The 'post-Christendom' position of this document, and the debate it stimulated, provided an impetus for reform in baptismal practice, particularly in the national churches of Europe that have tended to operate on a 'Christ of culture' basis.[17]

The final category, 'Christ transforming culture', seeks to move beyond drawing people into the fellowship of the Church, and aspires to change the character of society. In aspiring to be the 'salt of the earth', Christians hope to influence society and culture without directly or overtly seeking to convert people to the gospel. So far as baptismal discipline is concerned, there would be awareness of a boundary between Church and society, albeit vague and contested. How the objective of transforming society is to be accomplished is also likely to be contested, but Baptism may be seen as a means of preserving and extending Christian influence and identity in secularized societies and cultures.

If these categories were to be considered, rather than in the order in which Niebuhr presented them, as tendencies along a continuum from 'Christ against culture', through 'Christ and culture in paradox', 'Christ above culture' and 'Christ transforming culture' to 'Christ of culture', then they can helpfully illuminate many of the contested issues surrounding Baptism. The same group may take a position on a particular issue that reflects one point in this spectrum, while on other issues holding a position that would suggest a different position in its relationship to the local society and culture. This ambivalence is particularly likely where the church forms or defines a subculture with an ambiguous or vacillating relationship with the dominant culture. There may be some diversity of views of a church's relationship with its host society within a particular community. Where church structures include congregations in different social, cultural and political contexts, very different views may be held within that polity. The position of a particular church along this continuum may shift, consciously or unconsciously, in response to internal or external developments. Changes in society, without any corresponding development or response from the Church, can similarly generate a dissonance between the inherited position of the Church and its present reality. This has been seen most clearly in the secularization of much of Europe and indeed of other parts of the world, with some time passing before the prevailing 'Christ of culture' assumptions have been challenged, especially within established and national churches. Many of the disputes of the present day can usefully be understood as concerning whether the 'Christ of culture' approach is tenable and theologically justifiable in a post-Christendom society, and how the churches are most effectively to engage with those on the fringes of and beyond its regular worshipping congregations.

Wherever it is located and whatever the nature of its relationship with surrounding societies, the Church in its various manifestations needs to find ways it can both proclaim the gospel to the world, incorporating through Baptism those drawn into Christian fellowship, and baptize and nurture those born into the community so that they are sustained in the faith and remain committed members of Christ's body. Mission, however effective, without retention simply creates a proverbial revolving door and perpetuates if it does not hasten the decline of the Church.

In his analogy of Baptism as an adoption rite (Gal. 3.26–29), Paul does not merely emphasize a Christian identity that transcends all human divisions founded on race, class and gender but also identifies the Church as the family of God. There is little need to rehearse in detail the ways the Church has assimilated to societal and cultural patterns of domination and exploitation rather than transforming Christian societies in the light of the gospel. That Paul did not fully realize the profundity of his vision, still less implement it in his own day, in no way diminishes the obligation of the Church today to bring its life and values into conformity with the gospel.[18] Baptism is not merely a matter of incorporating individuals into the Church but of the earthly body of Christ ordering its life in accordance with God's purposes. Being the family of God requires that the barriers of race, class and gender be overcome, as well as other forms of institutionalized violence, discrimination and exploitation that have all too easily been imported into the Church. The family of God must be a place in which human families can flourish and in which people whose family lives have been damaged and damaging may find healing and wholeness within the fellowship of the Church.

Paul associates Baptism unequivocally and inextricably with the reception of the Holy Spirit, manifested in the complementary gifts Christians are given for the service of the Church (1 Corinthians 12). The authenticity of gifts is not measured by dramatic effect or sensational experience but embraces what in secular societies would be considered quite mundane competencies. These gifts do not function apart from human responsibility for the ways they are used. Nor is the Holy Spirit a substitute for competence and appropriate training and formation. Baptism requires that the Church should not merely expect its members to be empowered by the Holy Spirit but also should encourage them to discern and to exercise their gifts and to mature in faith through learning to use them in the service of Christ and the community. Baptism is integral to Paul's vision of a living body in which all members are active and the gifts of the Spirit are used collaboratively in and for the mission of the Church and in living in accordance with the gospel in the world.[19]

This impacts directly on questions of church order and ministry. Paul recognizes that within the Church there are people called to particular roles and leadership (1 Cor. 12.28; Phil. 1.1; 1 Thess. 5.12) and endowed with the Holy Spirit accordingly. There is no precedent for charismatic anarchy. Nevertheless, those exercising leadership are to serve in such a way as to enable the entire body to function, with each member exercising the gifts of the Spirit received at their Baptism. Whatever ecclesiastical structures and orders of ministry have emerged in different Christian traditions, the body as a whole is empowered with the Holy Spirit. Whether Christians exercise their gifts within the life of the church or in service to the community, this is the realization of their Baptism.

Baptism defines the Church and Christian identity. For Paul, as for the culture of the societies in which he proclaimed the gospel, this identity was primarily corporate. This did not mean that individuals did not matter, but they lived their lives within a network of social relationships that reinforced their identity. This had implications for the ways Baptism was administered and the gifts of the Spirit exercised in the life of the Church. In cultures that have become much more individualistic, this raises quite fundamental questions about the nature of Christian identity. These concern the ways the Church relates to families and to individual members. The Liturgical Movement has emphasized the presence and role of the gathered congregation in the celebration of Baptism, and identified the Eucharist as the most appropriate setting for the rite. This represents a significant departure from what had been customary in most parts of the Church for centuries, where a private ceremony in the church building or in the family home had been normative, with only the immediate family and close friends present.[20]

We have noted the evidence that the immersion rite would frequently have been administered away from the gathered congregation during the early Christian centuries, and for reasons of decorum and practicality this may well have been the prevailing custom during Paul's day. The privacy with which converts were stripped, immersed and clothed does not constitute a private ceremony, however, as the newly baptized were immediately integrated after Baptism into the Christian community and shared in the Eucharist. The administration of private Baptism, apart from the worship of the gathered congregation, is favoured where there is no intention that those baptized would become part of the worshipping community of the church. While this custom is defended, particularly in national churches with a 'Christ of culture' outlook, in terms of Paul's theology the practice is aberrant and serious questions need to be asked as to how the mission of the Church is furthered by it. At best it sustains the most tenuous of links with the Church and Christian values, at worst it panders to superstition and, in denuding Baptism of much of its meaning, makes it less likely that those baptized will experience Christian life to the full, discover the gifts bestowed on them by the Holy Spirit and be encouraged to exercise these in the life of the Church.

Baptism is an occasion when the life of the Church can engage creatively with that of the family. Given the sanctity the Christian tradition has always attached to marriage and family life, notwithstanding the exaltation of celibacy to spiritual pre-eminence in the Catholic and Orthodox traditions, it is entirely proper that the Church should support families, not least in the nurture of children.

Whether providing an officiant and a venue for a family ceremony is the most appropriate way to do so, or represents capitulation to a consumerist and secular culture, is another matter. When there have been centuries of precedent, a more missional approach to care for those on the fringes of the Church may be difficult to conceive. However, when family life has in many cases and in many ways become complicated, leaving some of the most broken and vulnerable of people on the margins of society as well as of the Church, this requires rather more than a sentimental occasion that can temporarily conceal the pain.

Paul speaks of Baptism as dying with Christ in order to share in the promise of his resurrection (Rom. 6.4). Christian ministry cannot with integrity offer anything less. If death is the place to which the baptized symbolically travel, then Baptism ought to be the occasion on which all that is tarnished and disfigured, all that has been degraded through human sinfulness and misfortune, can be laid to rest and a new life begun. The limitations of human existence cannot be discarded but the sacraments of the Church can and must be occasion for finding healing and wholeness, and integration in a community in and through which the enduring consequences of past mistakes, misfortune and sin can be managed – not only and not necessarily for those baptized but also for those who seek Baptism for their loved ones.

The demands of the gospel proclaimed by Paul are undoubtedly costly but the Church cannot be true to the heritage of the apostolic preaching and community formation unless and until it is willing to use its human and material resources to realize its spiritual resources in the lives of those who seek its ministry. This undoubtedly involves offering more than many people seek, or know to seek, and calling upon them to take into their lives the gifts of God entrusted to the Church, and to find fulfilment in discovering and using the particular gifts they have been given.

The pastoral and missional task of the Church is to administer Baptism so that the rite releases the spiritual potential in those incorporated into the community. Baptism begins a lifelong process of growth in the Christian faith, empowered by the Holy Spirit and discovering and using the gifts of that Spirit in the life of the Church. This is not a matter of instant gratification or of cheap thrills but of perseverance, nurture, learning and discipline. Worship, with the reading of Scripture and celebration of the Eucharist, sustains spiritual growth so that the mystery of Baptism is constantly being realized in the lives of Christian believers and of the communities of which they are members.

We have noted that the ritual use of water and invocation of the name of Jesus are the clearly attested elements of Baptism in Paul's missions and the churches he founded. We have observed that God would certainly have been addressed in prayer and that the Holy Spirit was intimately associated with Baptism. Therefore the Trinitarian formula that came to be regarded as essential to Christian Baptism is not incompatible with its Pauline antecedent, whatever customs may have prevailed in other traditions in the apostolic Church.

We have noted also that stripping before and clothing after immersion may have acquired a ritual significance at a very early date, and were to be integral to Baptism for several centuries. The custom of white clothing at Baptism is a residue of this, and stripping for immersion continues to be practised with infants in many places, particularly in the Orthodox churches. With an increasing proportion of adult converts seeking Baptism in churches that have traditionally practised infant Baptism, ritual clothing after immersion is being revived, and the potential of the Pauline image invites exploitation. Clothing as a symbol of identity and of representation of Christ and the gospel in the world would reinforce the ritual experience and invite its fulfilment in Christian life in the world.

We considered the possibility that anointing, imposition of hands and consignation may have formed part of the Baptism rite in the churches of Paul's mission. It is difficult to conceptualize how Baptism could have been administered without some contact between the hands of the officiant and the body of the person being baptized, or to imagine that this would not have acquired some ritual significance at an early date, not least in order to avoid inappropriate contact. The use of oil and the sign of the cross are much less certain but would be consistent with imagery used by Paul and with known ritual customs of the day. Anointing, with oil consecrated for the purpose by the bishop, and consignation have remained integral to the Baptism rite in the Orthodox churches. In the Western churches the liturgical history has been rather different, and this is worth considering briefly.

The separation of the rite that became confirmation from Baptism in the Latin Church is attributed to a number of factors. While immersion was generally delegated to presbyters and deacons, anointing thereafter came to be reserved to the bishop. With the growth of the Church and the geographical scale of many dioceses, it ceased to be possible for the bishop to preside at every Baptism. This led to disintegration of the rite, with anointing postponed until such time as the candidate could be presented to the bishop. That catechesis should intervene between immersion and anointing was a much later development, after the fraction of Western Christendom at the Reformation.

The disintegration of Baptism was accompanied or followed by association of empowerment by the Holy Spirit with the anointing rite, or with imposition of hands without the use of oil. This in effect removed the reception of the Holy Spirit from Baptism, in a significant departure from the apostolic doctrine. For Paul Baptism was an integrated rite, and water rather than oil the essential medium. There has in recent years been widespread ecumenical recognition that Baptism, in water, with invocation of the Trinity confers membership of the Church and the gifts of the Holy Spirit.[21] This is not to deny that there may be value in rites subsequent to Baptism that accompany Christian nurture and enable deepening maturity in the faith to be expressed and affirmed, and responsibility accepted for the discernment and exercise of the gifts of the Spirit received at Baptism. Nor is it to deny that the role of the bishop or an equivalent representative of the wider Church in such a rite may be appropriate and meaningful. But there can be no justification for regarding Baptism as less than complete ritual incorporation into the Church or for reserving conferral of the Holy Spirit to any ecclesiastical dignitary.

Notwithstanding the undoubted value of catechesis in Christian nurture, neither intellectual knowledge of the gospel nor the endurance of instruction in it, nor even evidence of spiritual growth, is a valid prerequisite to Baptism or to sharing in the Eucharist. The evidence is that Paul baptized converts immediately and that ritual and social integration in the community is the most effective means of encouraging people to grow in the faith of the Church. Intellectual and spiritual growth in the faith begin with Baptism. Christian nurture and catechesis, and sharing in the Eucharist and in the spiritual and corporate life of the community, enable those incorporated into the body of Christ to realize their Baptism in worship and service and to discern and exercise their gifts in the life of the Church.

We have in this chapter covered a wide range of issues, and the relevance of statements in the Pauline letters may not always have been apparent. What is clear from Paul's explicit statements is that in Baptism the Church receives into the fellowship of Christ's body new members, confers a Christian identity upon them, and indeed a new life free of the power of evil. In the name of God the Church invokes on those baptized the Holy Spirit to guide and empower them in their Christian lives. To apply this in contemporary pastoral contexts and in the face of contemporary challenges to Christian mission and ministry requires a far broader awareness of the context in which the apostle Paul proclaimed the gospel, established churches and wrote letters of pastoral advice and admonition than has too often been the case with traditional modes of exegesis. Many an ecclesiastical controversy and schism has been occasioned by an incomplete and inadequate understanding of the biblical texts, not least the letters of Paul. But these same letters have also provided the inspiration and the theological imperative to address those issues anew and to realize in this day and age his vision of 'one God, one Church, one Faith, one Baptism'.[22]

Suggested further reading

There is a vast and growing body of literature on issues relating to secularization. Specialists agree neither as to the theory nor in their analysis of trends in society. For recent examples see Bruce, *Secularization*; Gill, *The Myth of the 'Empty Church'* and Heelas et al. (eds), *Predicting Religion*.

There has been increasing appreciation, particularly among theologians informed by the social sciences, of the pastoral value of ritual. For major contributions in this area see Driver, *Liberating Rites*; Grimes, *Deeply into the Bone*; Ramshaw, *Ritual and Pastoral Care* and Smith, *Christian Ritualizing and the Baptismal Process*.

Notes

1 This and other of Allen's writings have been reprinted several times, several including this book by a publishing house ironically known as World Dominion Press. For a recent treatment of Allen, see Goldsmith, 'The Genius of Roland Allen' and Payne, *Roland Allen*. It is conspicuous that these and other appreciations of Allen emanate from a theological position very different from Allen's Anglo-Catholicism. A more recent reflection on approaches to mission, from a Roman Catholic missionary working in east Africa, is Donovan, *Christianity Rediscovered*.

2 In common with most scholars of his and the present day, Allen overlooks the nature of Barnabas and Paul's relationship with the church of Antioch during the period reflected in Acts 13—14, commonly known as the first missionary journey. For further discussion see my *Paul, Antioch and Jerusalem*.

3 For discussion see my *Lay Presidency at the Eucharist?*, pp. 36–63.

4 Allen, *Missionary Methods: St. Paul's or Ours*, p. 129.

5 Allen, *Missionary Methods: St. Paul's or Ours*, p. 100.

6 An important study of this and related issues is Berger, *A Rumor of Angels*.

7 Cf. Carr, *Brief Encounters*, pp. 52–6; Davie, *Religion in Britain since 1945*, pp. 74–116 and Percy, *The Salt of the Earth*, pp. 60–80.

8 Buchanan, *Infant Baptism and the Gospel*, pp. 175–81; Crowe, *Christian Baptism*, pp. 83–4 and Owen, *Baptise Every Baby?*, pp. 150–4.

9 *Christ and Culture*, p. 45.

10 Cf. Elliott, *Liberating Paul*.

11 *Christ and Culture*, pp. 51–5. The martyrdom of Perpetua and Felicitas took place in Carthage during Tertullian's time, c.AD 203.

12 A position defended by Carr, *Brief Encounters*, pp. 49–57.

13 Cf. Dalby, *Open Baptism* and Osborn, *Forbid Them Not*.

14 *Christ and Culture*, pp. 123–8.

15 *Christ and Culture*, pp. 159–67.

16 Several volumes of official responses to this document by member churches and others were published by the WCC between 1986 and 1988.

17 Baptismal Integrity, formerly the Movement for the Reform of Infant Baptism, has advocated this position in the Church of England and more widely. Bishop Colin Buchanan is the President of this organization and has published extensively on this subject; most recently, *Infant Baptism and the Gospel*. The website of Baptismal Integrity can be accessed at www.baptism.org.uk; it appears not to have been updated since 2010.

18 Cf. my 'Paul for Today'.

19 Cf. Pickard, *Theological Foundations for Collaborative Ministry*.

20 When Baptism had been administered as soon as possible after birth, against the eventuality of neonatal death, and mothers were isolated for 40 days from giving birth, they would not have attended the Baptism of their own children unless this was administered in their homes.

21 This is clearly reflected in *Baptism, Eucharist and Ministry* and in the volumes of responses to this document.

Concluding Remarks

The aim of this book has been to make the fruits of scholarship available to the pastoral minister. Even within the relatively narrow field of the apostle Paul's teaching on Baptism, this has been incomplete. More detailed exegesis of the texts might have been academically satisfying but it is doubtful whether this would have been of much assistance to clergy confronted with practical pastoral issues on a daily basis. It is hoped, however, that readers will have acquired a broader understanding of the context in which Paul wrote, as well as of the letters themselves, and so be better able to understand the points he is making when he refers to Baptism. Christians committed to some confessional positions on Baptism will have found this treatment unconvincing and may find some of the corollaries drawn for contemporary ministerial practice unacceptable. But I hope that all will be convinced of the importance of the Church as the community of Christ's body into which new Christians are received. And I hope that baptismal practice will increasingly take into account the social and cultural dimensions of Christian life in the world. Above all, I hope that the teaching and practice of Baptism will be more effective in building the body of Christ, and that the Church will thereby become a more powerful force in bringing about God's saving purpose in the world.

References and Further Reading

Aageson, James W., *Paul, the Pastoral Epistles, and the Church* (Peabody, MA: Hendrickson, 2008).

Adams, Edward, *The Earliest Christian Meeting Places: Almost Exclusively Houses?* (London: Bloomsbury, 2016).

Agersnap, Søren, *Baptism and the New Life* (Aarhus: Aarhus University Press, 1999).

Aland, Kurt, *Did the Early Church Baptize Infants?* (London: SCM Press, 1963).

Allen, Roland, *Missionary Methods: St. Paul's or Ours: A Study of the Church in the Four Provinces* (London: Robert Scott, 1912).

The Ante-Nicene Fathers (10 volumes; Grand Rapids, MI: Eerdmans, 1980).

Ateek, Naim S., *Justice, and only Justice* (Maryknoll, NY: Orbis, 1989).

Bakke, O. M., *When Children became People: The Birth of Childhood in Early Christianity* (Minneapolis, MN: Fortress Press, 2005).

Balch, David and Carolyn Osiek (eds), *Early Christian Families in Context: An Interdisciplinary Dialogue* (Grand Rapids, MI: Eerdmans, 2003).

Baptism, Eucharist and Ministry (Geneva: The Faith and Order Group of the World Council of Churches, 1982).

Baptism, Eucharist and Ministry 1982–1990 (Geneva: The World Council of Churches, 1990).

Barclay, John M. G., *Jews in the Mediterranean Diaspora: From Alexander to Trajan* (Edinburgh: T. & T. Clark, 1998).

Barclay, John M. G., *Obeying the Truth* (Edinburgh: T. & T. Clark, 1988).

Barrett, C. K., *The Acts of the Apostles* (International Critical Commentary; Edinburgh: T. & T. Clark, 1994 and 1998).

Barrett, C. K., *A Commentary on the Epistle to the Romans* (Black's Biblical Commentary; London: A. & C. Black, 1962).

Barrett, C. K., *A Commentary on the First Epistle to the Corinthians* (Black's New Testament Commentary; London: A. & C. Black, 1968).

Barrett, C. K., *A Commentary on the Second Epistle to the Corinthians* (Black's New Testament Commentary; London: A. & C. Black, 1979).

Barth, Markus, *Ephesians* (Anchor Bible; New York: Doubleday, 1974).

Beasley-Murray, George R., *Baptism in the New Testament* (Exeter: Paternoster Press, 1962).

Beker, J. Christiaan, *Paul the Apostle* (Edinburgh: T. & T. Clark, 1980).

Bell, Catherine M., *Ritual: Perspectives and Dimensions* (Oxford: Oxford University Press, 2009).

Bell, Catherine M., *Ritual Theory, Ritual Practice* (Oxford: Oxford University Press, 1992).

Berger, Peter L., *A Rumor of Angels: Modern Society and the Rediscovery of the Supernatural* (New York: Doubleday, 1969).

Bernstein, Alan, *The Formation of Hell: Death and Retribution in the Ancient and Early Christian World* (London: Routledge, 1993).

Best, Ernest, *Ephesians* (International Critical Commentary; Edinburgh: T. & T. Clark, 1998).

Best, Thomas F. (ed.), *Baptism Today: Understanding, Practice, Ecumenical Implications* (Collegeville, MN: Liturgical Press, 2008).

Best, Thomas F. and Dagmar Heller (eds), *Becoming a Christian: The Ecumenical Implications of Our Common Baptism* (Geneva: The World Council of Churches, 1999).

Betz, Hans Dieter, *Galatians* (Hermeneia Commentary; Philadelphia, PA: Fortress Press, 1979).

Black, Matthew, *Romans* (New Century Bible Commentary; Grand Rapids, MI: Eerdmans, 1973).

Blasi, Anthony J., *Making Charisma* (New York: Peter Lang, 1991).

Blundell, Susan, *Women in Ancient Greece* (Cambridge, MA: Harvard University Press, 1995).

Bornkamm, Günther, *Paul* (London: Hodder & Stoughton, 1969).

Bradshaw, Paul F., Maxwell E. Johnson and L. Edward Phillips, *The Apostolic Tradition* (Hermeneia Commentary; Minneapolis, MN: Fortress Press, 2002).

Bremmer, J. N. (ed.), *The Apocryphal Acts of Paul and Thekla* (Kampen: Kok Pharos, 1996).

Bromiley, Geoffrey W., *Children of Promise* (Grand Rapids, MI: Eerdmans, 1979).

Brown, Raymond E., *The Gospel According to John* (Anchor Bible; New York: Doubleday, 1966).

Brown, Raymond E., *An Introduction to the New Testament* (New Haven, CT: Yale University Press, 1997).

Brown, Raymond E. and John P. Meier, *Antioch and Rome* (London: Chapman, 1983).

Brownson, James V., *The Promise of Baptism* (Grand Rapids, MI: Eerdmans, 2007).

Bruce, F. F., *The Acts of the Apostles* (New International Commentary; Leicester: Inter-Varsity Press, 1976).

Bruce, F. F., *Galatians* (New International Greek Text Commentary; Grand Rapids, MI: Eerdmans, 1982).

Bruce, Steve, *Secularization* (Oxford: Oxford University Press, 2013).

Buchanan, Colin O., *Infant Baptism and the Gospel* (London: Darton, Longman & Todd, 1993).

Buchanan, Colin O., Clifford Owen and Alan Wright, *Reforming Infant Baptism* (London: Hodder & Stoughton, 1990).

Carr, Wesley, *Brief Encounters: Pastoral Ministry through Baptisms, Weddings and Funerals* (London: SPCK, 1994).

Chester, Stephen J., *Conversion at Corinth* (London: T. & T. Clark, 2003).

Chow, John K.-M., *Patronage and Power: A Study of Social Networks in Corinth* (Sheffield: Sheffield Academic Press, 1992).

Christiansen, Ellen Juhl, *The Covenant in Judaism and Paul* (Leiden: Brill, 1995).

Cohen, Shaye J. D., *The Beginnings of Jewishness: Boundaries, Varieties, Uncertainties* (Berkeley, CA: University of California Press, 2001).

Collins, John J., *The Apocalyptic Imagination* (New York: Crossroad, 1984).

Collins, John J., *Between Athens and Jerusalem: Jewish Identity in the Hellenistic Diaspora* (Grand Rapids, MI: Eerdmans, 1999).

Collins, Raymond F., *First Corinthians* (Sacra Pagina; Collegeville, MN: Liturgical Press, 1999).

Collins, Raymond F., *Introduction to the New Testament* (New York: Doubleday, 1987).

Collins, Raymond F., *Second Corinthians* (Paideia Commentaries; Grand Rapids, MI: Baker Book House, 2013).

Conzelmann, Hans, *1 Corinthians* (Hermeneia Commentary; Philadelphia, PA: Fortress Press, 1975).

Conzelmann, Hans, *The Acts of the Apostles* (Hermeneia Commentary; Philadelphia, PA: Fortress Press, 1987).

Cranfield, C. E. B., *The Epistle to the Romans* (International Critical Commentary; Edinburgh: T. & T. Clark, 1975 and 1979).

Cross, F. L., *1 Peter: A Paschal Liturgy* (London: Mowbray, 1954).

Crowe, Philip, *Christian Baptism* (London: Mowbray, 1980).

Cullmann, Oscar, *Baptism in the New Testament* (London: SCM Press, 1950).

Cummins, Stephen A., *Paul and the Crucified Christ in Antioch* (Cambridge: Cambridge University Press, 2002).

Dalby, Mark, *Open Baptism* (London: SPCK, 1989).

Daniélou, Jean, *The Bible and the Liturgy* (Notre Dame, IN: University of Notre Dame Press, 1956).

Davie, Grace, *Religion in Britain since 1945: Believing without Belonging* (Oxford: Blackwell, 1994).

Dibelius, Martin, Hans Conzelmann and Helmut Koester, *The Pastoral Epistles* (Hermeneia Commentary; Philadelphia, PA: Fortress Press, 1972).

Dickie, Matthew W., *Magic and Magicians in the Greco-Roman World* (New York: Routledge, 2001).

Dillistone, Frank W., *Christianity and Symbolism* (London: SCM Press, 1955).

Dillistone, Frank W., *The Power of Symbols* (London: SCM Press, 1986).

Donovan, Vincent, *Christianity Rediscovered: An Epistle from the Masai* (Maryknoll, NY: Orbis, 1982).

Douglas, Mary, *Purity and Danger* (London: Routledge & Kegan Paul, 1966).

Driver, Tom F., *Liberating Rites: Understanding the Transformative Power of Ritual* (Oxford: Westview, 1998).

Dunn, James D. G., *The Acts of the Apostles* (Epworth Commentary; Peterborough: Epworth Press, 1996).

Dunn, James D. G., *Baptism in the Holy Spirit* (London: SCM Press, 1970).

Dunn, James D. G., *Beginning from Jerusalem. Christianity in the Making*, Vol. 2 (Grand Rapids, MI: Eerdmans, 2009).

Dunn, James D. G., *Colossians and Philemon* (New International Greek Text Commentary; Grand Rapids, MI: Eerdmans, 1996).

Dunn, James D. G., *Galatians* (Black's New Testament Commentary; London: A. & C. Black, 1993).

Dunn, James D. G., *Romans* (Word Biblical Commentary; Waco, TX: Word, 1988).

Dunn, James D. G., *The Theology of Paul the Apostle* (Grand Rapids, MI: Eerdmans and Edinburgh: T. & T. Clark, 1998).

Ehrman, Bart D., *The Apostolic Fathers* (London: Heinemann and Cambridge, MA: Harvard University Press, 2003).

Elliott, Neil, *Liberating Paul* (New York: Crossroad, 1994).

Fee, Gordon D., *1 and 2 Timothy, Titus* (New International Biblical Commentary; Peabody, MA: Hendrickson, 1988).

Fee, Gordon D., *1 Corinthians* (New International Commentary on the New Testament; Grand Rapids, MI: Eerdmans, 1987).

Ferguson, Everett, *Baptism in the Early Church: History, Theology, and Liturgy in the First Five Centuries* (Grand Rapids, MI: Eerdmans, 2009).

Ferguson, Everett (ed.), *Conversion, Catechumenate, and Baptism in the Early Church* (New York: Garland, 1993).

Finn, Thomas M., *Early Christian Baptism and the Catechumenate* (Collegeville, MN: Liturgical Press, 1992),

Finn, Thomas M., *From Death to Rebirth: Ritual and Conversion in Antiquity* (New York: Paulist, 1997).

Fitzmyer, Joseph A., *The Acts of the Apostles* (Anchor Bible; New York: Doubleday, 1998).

Fitzmyer, Joseph A., *First Corinthians* (Anchor Bible; New Haven, CT: Yale University Press, 2008).

Fitzmyer, Joseph A., *Pauline Theology* (Englewood Cliffs, NJ: Prentice Hall, 1989).

Fitzmyer, Joseph A., *Romans* (Anchor Bible; New York: Doubleday, 1998).

Flemington, W. F., *The New Testament Doctrine of Baptism* (London: SPCK, 1948).

Fontaine, J. S. la, *Initiation: Ritual Drama and Secret Knowledge* (Harmondsworth: Penguin, 1985).

Fowler, James W., *The Stages of Faith* (New York: HarperCollins, 1981).

Frier, Bruce W., 'Roman Demography', in D. J. Potter and D. J. Mattingly (eds), *Life, Death, and Entertainment in the Roman Empire* (Ann Arbor, MI: University of Michigan Press, 1999), pp. 85–109.

Furnish, Victor Paul, *II Corinthians* (Anchor Bible; New York: Doubleday, 1984).

Gager, John G., *Moses in Greco-Roman Paganism* (Nashville, TN: Abingdon, 1972).

Gardner, Jane F., *Women in Roman Law and Society* (Bloomington, IN: Indiana University Press, 1991).

Garland, Robert, *The Greek Way of Death* (Ithaca, NY: Cornell University Press, 2001).

Gaston, Lloyd, *Paul and Torah* (Philadelphia, PA: Fortress Press, 1979).

Gaventa, Beverley Roberts, *From Darkness to Light: Aspects of Conversion in the New Testament* (Philadelphia, PA: Fortress Press, 1986).

Gehring, Roger W., *House Church and Mission: The Importance of Household Structures in Early Christianity* (Peabody, MA: Hendrickson, 2004).

Gennep, Arnold van, *The Rites of Passage* (London: Routledge & Kegan Paul, 1960).

Gill, Robin M., *The Myth of the 'Empty Church'* (London: SPCK, 1993).

Goldsmith, Martin, 'The Genius of Roland Allen', *Evangel* 7.3 (1989), pp. 11–13.

Goodman, Martin D., *Mission and Conversion: Proselytizing in the Religious History of the Roman Empire* (Oxford: Clarendon Press, 1994).

Gorman, Michael J., *Cruciformity: Paul's Narrative Spirituality of the Cross* (Grand Rapids, MI: Eerdmans, 2001).

Green, Michael, *Baptism* (London: Hodder & Stoughton, 1987).

Grimes, Ronald L., *Deeply into the Bone: Re-Inventing Rites of Passage* (Berkeley, CA: University of California Press, 2000).

Haenchen, Ernst, *The Acts of the Apostles* (Oxford: Blackwell, 1971).

Hamm, Dennis, *The Acts of the Apostles* (New Collegeville Bible Commentary; Collegeville, MN: Liturgical Press, 2005).

Hanson, Anthony Tyrrell, *The New Testament Interpretation of Scripture* (London: SPCK, 1979).

Hanson, Anthony Tyrrell, *The Pastoral Epistles* (New Century Bible Commentary; Grand Rapids, MI: Eerdmans, 1982).

Harland, Philip A., *Associations, Synagogues, and Congregations: Claiming a Place in Ancient Mediterranean Society* (Minneapolis, MN: Fortress Press, 2009).

Harland, Philip A., *Dynamics of Identity in the World of the Early Christians: Associations, Judeans, and Cultural Minorities* (London: T. & T. Clark, 2010).

Hartman, Lars, '*Into the Name of the Lord Jesus*': Baptism in the Early Church (Edinburgh: T. & T. Clark, 1997).

Hay, David M., *Colossians* (Abingdon New Testament Commentary; Nashville, TN: Abingdon, 2000).

Hays, Richard B., *The Faith of Jesus Christ* (Chico, CA: Scholars Press, 1983).

Hays, Richard B., *First Corinthians* (Interpretation; Louisville, KY: Westminster John Knox Press, 1997).

Heelas, Paul, Grace Davie and Linda Woodhead (eds), *Predicting Religion* (London: Routledge, 2003).

Hengel, Martin, *Acts and the History of Early Christianity* (London: SCM Press, 1979).

Hennecke, Edgar, Wilhelm Schneemelcher and R. McL. Wilson (eds), *The New Testament Apocrypha*. Vol. 1 (Cambridge: James Clarke, 1991). Vol. 2 (Cambridge: James Clarke, 1992).

Holmberg, Bengt, *Paul and Power* (Philadelphia, PA: Fortress Press, 1980).

Holmberg, Bengt (ed.), *Exploring Early Christian Identity* (Tübingen: Mohr Siebeck, 2008).

Holmberg, Bengt and Mikael Winninge (eds), *Identity Formation in the New Testament* (Tübingen: Mohr Siebeck, 2008).

Hope, Valerie M., *Roman Death: The Dying and the Dead in Ancient Rome* (London: Continuum, 2009).

Horrell, David G., *Becoming Christian: Essays on 1 Peter and the Formation of Christian Identity* (London: Bloomsbury, 2013).

Horrell, David G., *An Introduction to the Study of Paul* (London: Continuum, 2000).

Horrell, David G., *The Social Ethos of the Corinthian Correspondence: Interests and Ideology from 1 Corinthians to 1 Clement* (Edinburgh: T. & T. Clark, 1996).

Horsley, Richard A., *1 Corinthians* (Abingdon New Testament Commentary; Nashville, TN: Abingdon, 1998).

Houlden, J. Leslie, *The Pastoral Epistles* (TPI New Testament Commentary; London: SCM Press, 1989).

Houlden, J. Leslie, *Paul's Letters from Prison* (SCM Pelican New Testament Commentary; London: SCM Press, 1977).

Hübner, Hans, *Law in Paul's Thought* (Edinburgh: T. & T. Clark, 1984).

Hull, Michael F., *Baptism on Account of the Dead (1 Cor 15:29): An Act of Faith in the Resurrection* (Atlanta, GA: SBL, 2005).

Jensen, Robin M., *Baptismal Imagery in Early Christianity: Ritual, Visual, and Theological Dimensions* (Grand Rapids, MI: Baker Book House, 2012).

Jensen, Robin M., *Living Water: Images, Symbols, and Settings of Early Christian Baptism* (Leiden: Brill, 2010).

Jeremias, Joachim, *Infant Baptism in the First Four Centuries* (London: SCM Press, 1960).

Jeremias, Joachim, *The Origins of Infant Baptism* (London: SCM Press, 1963).

Jervis, L. Ann, *Galatians* (New International Biblical Commentary; Peabody, MA: Hendrickson, 1999).

Jewett, Paul K., *Infant Baptism and the Covenant of Grace* (Grand Rapids, MI: Eerdmans, 1978).

Jewett, Robert, *Romans* (Hermeneia Commentary; Minneapolis, MN: Fortress Press, 2008).

Johnson, Luke Timothy, *The Acts of the Apostles* (Sacra Pagina; Collegeville, MN: Liturgical Press, 1992).

Johnson, Luke Timothy, *Letters to Paul's Delegates* (Valley Forge, PA: Trinity Press International, 1996).

Johnson, Luke Timothy, *The Writings of the New Testament* (London: SCM Press, 2010).

Johnson, Maxwell E., *The Rites of Christian Initiation: Their Evolution and Interpretation* (Collegeville, MN: Liturgical Press, 1999).

Johnston, Philip S., *Shades of Sheol: Death and Afterlife in the Old Testament* (Downers Grove, IL: InterVarsity Press, 2002).

Jones, Cheslyn et al., *The Study of Liturgy* (London: SPCK, 1978).

Judge, Edwin A., *The Social Pattern of the Christian Groups in the First Century* (London: Tyndale, 1960).

Käsemann, Ernst, *A Commentary on Romans* (Grand Rapids, MI: Eerdmans, 1980).

Kavanagh, Aidan, *The Shape of Baptism: The Rite of Christian Initiation* (New York: Pueblo, 1978).

Kee, Howard Clark, *Understanding the New Testament* (Englewood Cliffs, NJ: Prentice Hall, 1993).

Kelly, J. N. D., *Early Christian Creeds* (London: Longman, 1972).

Kelly, J. N. D., *The Epistles of Peter and of Jude* (Black's New Testament Commentary; London: A. & C. Black, 1969).

Kelly, J. N. D., *The Pastoral Epistles* (Black's New Testament Commentary; London: A. & C. Black, 1963).

Kim, Yung-Suk, *Christ's Body in Corinth: The Politics of a Metaphor* (Minneapolis, MN: Fortress Press, 2008).

Kitchen, Martin, *Ephesians* (New Testament Readings; London: Routledge, 1994).

Klauck, Hans-Josef, *Magic and Paganism in Early Christianity* (Minneapolis, MN: Fortress Press, 2003).

Klauck, Hans-Josef, *The Religious Context of Early Christianity: A Guide to Graeco-Roman Religions* (Minneapolis, MN: Fortress Press, 2003).

Koester, Helmut, *History and Literature of Early Christianity, I: Introduction to the New Testament* (Berlin: De Gruyter, 1982).

Kreider, Alan, *The Change of Conversion and the Origin of Christendom* (Valley Forge, PA: Trinity Press International, 1999).

Kuhrt, Gordon W., *Believing in Baptism: Christian Baptism – Its Theology and Practice* (London: Mowbray, 1987).

Kümmel, W. G., *Introduction to the New Testament* (London: SCM Press, 1975).

Lake, Kirsopp, *The Apostolic Fathers* (London: Heinemann and Cambridge, MA: Harvard University Press, 1970).

Lambrecht, Jan, *Second Corinthians* (Sacra Pagina; Collegeville, MN: Liturgical Press, 1999).

Lee, Michelle V., *Paul, the Stoics, and the Body of Christ* (Cambridge: Cambridge University Press, 2006).

Leeuw, Gerhardus van der, *Religion in Essence and Manifestation* (London: Allen & Unwin, 1964).

Lightfoot, J. B., *The Apostolic Fathers* (Grand Rapids, MI: Baker Book House and Leicester: Apollos, 1990).

Lincoln, Andrew T., *Ephesians* (Word Bible Commentary; Waco, TX: Word, 1990).

Lohse, Eduard, *Colossians and Philemon* (Hermeneia Commentary; Philadelphia, PA: Fortress Press, 1971).

Longenecker, Bruce W., *The Cross before Constantine: The Early Life of a Christian Symbol* (Minneapolis, MN: Fortress Press, 2015).

Longenecker, Bruce W., *Eschatology and the Covenant* (Sheffield: Sheffield Academic Press, 1991).

Longenecker, Bruce W., *Remember the Poor: Paul, Poverty, and the Greco-Roman World* (Grand Rapids, MI: Eerdmans, 2010).

Longenecker, Bruce W., *The Triumph of Abraham's God* (Edinburgh: T. & T. Clark, 1998).

Longenecker, Richard N., *Galatians* (Word Bible Commentary; Waco, TX: Word, 1990).

Longenecker, Richard N., *New Testament Social Ethics for Today* (Grand Rapids, MI: Eerdmans, 1981).

McCane, Byron R., *Roll back the Stone: Death and Burial in the World of Jesus* (Harrisburg, PA: Trinity Press International, 2003).

McKnight, Scott, *A Light among the Gentiles* (Minneapolis, MN: Fortress Press, 1991).

MacDonald, Dennis R., *There is no Male and Female* (Philadelphia, PA: Fortress Press, 1987).

MacDonald, Margaret Y., *The Pauline Churches* (Cambridge: Cambridge University Press, 1988).

McDonnell, Kilian and George T. Montague, *Christian Initiation and Baptism in the Holy Spirit: Evidence from the First Eight Centuries* (Collegeville, MN: Liturgical Press, 1991).

MacMullen, Ramsay, *Paganism in the Roman Empire* (New Haven, CT: Yale University Press, 1981).

Malina, Bruce J., *Christian Origins and Cultural Anthropology* (Louisville, KY: Westminster John Knox Press, 1986).

Malina, Bruce J., *The New Testament World* (London: SCM Press, 1981).

Malina, Bruce J. and Jerome H. Neyrey, *Portraits of Paul: An Archaeology of Ancient Personality* (Louisville, KY: Westminster John Knox Press, 1996).

Marcel, Pierre Ch., *The Biblical Doctrine of Infant Baptism* (London: James Clarke, 1953).

Maris, Richard E. de, 'Corinthian Religion and Baptism for the Dead (1 Corinthians 15.29): Insights from Archaeology and Anthropology', *Journal of Biblical Literature* 114 (1995), pp. 661–82.

Maris, Richard E. de, *The New Testament in its Ritual World* (London: Routledge, 2008).

Marshall, I. Howard, *A Critical and Exegetical Commentary on the Pastoral Epistles* (International Critical Commentary; Edinburgh: T. & T. Clark, 1999).

Martin, Dale B., *The Corinthian Body* (New Haven, CT: Yale University Press, 1995).

Martin, Ralph P., *2 Corinthians* (Word Biblical Commentary; Waco, TX: Word, 1986).

Martyn, J. Louis, *Galatians* (Anchor Bible; New York: Doubleday, 1997).

Matson, David L., *Household Conversion Narratives in Acts: Pattern and Interpretation* (Sheffield: Sheffield Academic Press, 1996).

Mbiti, John S., *New Testament Eschatology in an African Background* (London: SPCK, 1971).

Meade, David G., *Pseudonymity and Canon* (Grand Rapids, MI: Eerdmans, 1986).

Meeks, Wayne A., *The First Urban Christians* (New Haven, CT: Yale University Press, 1983).

Mendez-Mortalla, Fernando, *The Paradigm of Conversion in Luke* (London: Bloomsbury, 2004).

Metzger, Bruce M., *A Textual Commentary on the Greek New Testament* (Stuttgart: Deutsche Bibelgesellschaft, 1994).

Milavec, Aaron, *The Didache* (Mahwah, NJ: Newman Press, 2003).

Mol, Hans J., *Identity and the Sacred* (Oxford: Blackwell, 1976).

Morris, Ian, *Death-Ritual and Social Structure in Classical Antiquity* (Cambridge: Cambridge University Press, 1992).

Moule, C. F. D., *The Epistles of Paul the Apostle to the Colossians and to Philemon* (Cambridge Greek Text Commentary; Cambridge: Cambridge University Press, 1957).

Moxnes, Halvor (ed.), *Constructing Early Christian Families* (London: Routledge, 1997).

Muddiman, John, *The Epistle to the Ephesians* (Black's New Testament Commentary; London: Continuum, 2001).

Mussner, Franz, *Der Galaterbrief* (Freiburg: Herder, 1977).

Najman, Hindy, *Seconding Sinai: The Development of Mosaic Discourse in Second Temple Judaism* (Leiden: Brill, 2012).

Neusner, Jacob, *The Idea of Purity in Ancient Judaism* (Leiden: Brill, 1973).

Neusner, Jacob, *Judaic Law from Jesus to the Mishnah* (Atlanta, GA: Scholars Press, 1993).

Neyrey, Jerome H., *Paul, in Other Words* (Louisville, KY: Westminster John Knox Press, 1990).

Neyrey, Jerome H. (ed.), *The Social World of Luke–Acts* (Peabody, MA: Hendrickson, 1991).

Ng, Wai-Yee, *Water Symbolism in John* (New York: Peter Lang, 2001).

Nickelsburg, George W. E. and John J. Collins, *Ideal Figures in Ancient Judaism* (Chico, CA: Scholars Press, 1982).

Niebuhr, H. Richard, *Christ and Culture* (New York: Harper & Row, 1951).

Niederwimmer, Kurt, *The Didache: A Commentary*, trans. Linda M. Maloney, ed. Harold W. Attridge (Hermeneia Commentary; Minneapolis, MN: Fortress Press, 1998).

Osborn, Eric, *Tertullian* (Cambridge: Cambridge University Press, 1997).

Osborn, R. R., *Forbid Them Not: The Importance and History of General Baptism* (London: SPCK, 1972).

Osiek, Carolyn and David Balch, *Families in the New Testament World: Households and House Churches* (Louisville, KY: Westminster John Knox Press, 1997).

Owen, Clifford, *Baptise Every Baby?* (Eastbourne: Marc, 1991).

Payne, J. D., *Roland Allen: Pioneer of Spontaneous Expansion* (Birmingham, AL: J. D. Payne via CreateSpace, 2012).

Percy, Martyn, *The Salt of the Earth: Religious Resilience in a Secular Age* (Sheffield: Sheffield Academic Press, 2001).

Pickard, Stephen K., *Theological Foundations for Collaborative Ministry* (Farnham: Ashgate, 2009).

Poliakoff, Michael, '"They Should Cover their Shame": Attitudes to Nudity in Greco-Roman Judaism', *Source* 12.2 (1993), pp. 56–62.

Pomeroy, Sarah, *Goddesses, Whores, Wives, and Slaves: Women in Ancient Greece* (New York: Schocken, 1995).

Price, S. R. F., *Religions of the Ancient Greeks* (Cambridge: Cambridge University Press, 1999).

Prior, Michael, *Paul the Letter-Writer and the Second Letter to Timothy* (Sheffield: Sheffield Academic Press, 1989).

Quinn, Jerome D., *The Letter to Titus* (Anchor Bible; New York: Doubleday, 1990).

Radcliffe, Timothy, *Take the Plunge: Living Baptism and Confirmation* (London: Bloomsbury, 2012).

Räisänen, Heikki, *Paul and the Law* (Philadelphia, PA: Fortress Press, 1986).

Rambo, Lewis R., *Understanding Religious Conversion* (New Haven, CT: Yale University Press, 1993).

Ramshaw, Elaine, *Ritual and Pastoral Care* (Philadelphia, PA: Fortress Press, 1987).

Rankin, David, *Tertullian and the Church* (Cambridge: Cambridge University Press, 1995).

Rawson, Beryl, *The Family in Ancient Rome* (Ithaca, NY: Cornell University Press, 1987).

Rawson, Beryl (ed.), *Marriage, Divorce, and Children in Ancient Rome* (Oxford: Oxford University Press, 1991).

Robinson, H. Wheeler, *Corporate Personality in Ancient Israel* (Philadelphia, PA: Fortress Press, 1980).

Rogerson, John W., *Anthropology and the Old Testament* (Oxford: Blackwell, 1978).

Root, Michael and Risto Saarinen, *Baptism and the Unity of the Church* (Grand Rapids, MI: Eerdmans, 1998).

Roy, Kevin, *Baptism, Reconciliation, and Unity* (Carlisle: Paternoster Press, 1997).

Sabou, Sorin, *Between Horror and Hope: Paul's Metaphorical Language of Death in Romans 6.1–11* (Downers Grove, IL: InterVarsity Press, 2006).

Sanders, E. P., *Judaism: Practice and Belief* (London: SCM Press, 1992).

Sanders, E. P., *Paul* (Oxford: Oxford University Press, 1991).

Sanders, E. P., *Paul and Palestinian Judaism* (London: SCM Press, 1977).

Sanders, E. P., *Paul, the Law, and the Jewish People* (London: SCM Press, 1983).

Schmemann, Alexander, *Of Water and the Spirit: A Liturgical Study of Baptism* (New York: St Vladimir's Seminary Press, 1974).

Schnackenburg, Rudolf, *Baptism in the Thought of St Paul* (Oxford: Blackwell, 1961).

Schnackenburg, Rudolf, *The Epistle to the Ephesians* (Edinburgh: T. & T. Clark, 1991).

Schüssler Fiorenza, Elisabeth, *The Book of Revelation: Justice and Judgement* (Minneapolis, MN: Fortress Press, 1998).

Schüssler Fiorenza, Elisabeth, *In Memory of Her* (Philadelphia, PA: Fortress Press, 1983).

Schweizer, Eduard, *Colossians* (Minneapolis, MN: Augsburg, 1982).

Scott, James M., *2 Corinthians* (New International Biblical Commentary; Peabody, MA: Hendrickson, 1998).

Segal, Alan F., *Life after Death: A History of the Afterlife in Western Religion* (New York: Doubleday, 2004).

Segal, Alan F., *Paul the Convert: The Apostasy and Apostolate of Saul the Pharisee* (New Haven, CT: Yale University Press, 1990).

Slee, Michele, *The Church of Antioch in the First Century* (London: Sheffield Academic Press, 2003).

Smith, Jonathan Z., *To Take Place: Toward Theory in Ritual* (Chicago: University of Chicago Press, 1987).

Smith, Susan Marie, *Christian Ritualizing and the Baptismal Process: Liturgical Explorations toward a Realized Baptismal Ecclesiology* (Eugene, OR: Pickwick, 2012).

Snow, David A. and Richard Machalek, 'The Convert as a Social Type', in Randall Collins (ed.), *Sociological Theory 1983* (San Francisco: Jossey-Bass, 1983).

Snow, David A. and Richard Machalek, 'The Sociology of Conversion', *Annual Review of Sociology* 10 (1984), pp. 167–90.

Soards, Marion L., *1 Corinthians* (New International Biblical Commentary; Peabody, MA: Hendrickson, 1999).

Spinks, Bryan D., *Early and Medieval Rituals and Theologies of Baptism: From the New Testament to the Council of Trent* (Aldershot: Ashgate, 2006).

Spinks, Bryan D., *Reformation and Modern Rituals and Theologies of Baptism: From Luther to Contemporary Practices* (Aldershot: Ashgate, 2006).

Stark, Rodney, *The Rise of Christianity: A Sociologist reconsiders History* (Princeton: Princeton University Press, 1996).

Still, Todd D. and David G. Horrell (eds), *After the First Urban Christians* (London: Continuum, 2009).

Stowers, Stanley K., *A Rereading of Romans* (New Haven, CT: Yale University Press, 1994).

Strange, William A., *Children in the Early Church: Children in the Ancient World, the New Testament, and the Early Church* (Carlisle: Paternoster Press, 1996).

Suggit, John, *Down to Earth and Up to Heaven: The Gospel of John and Life Abundant* (Grahamstown: College of the Transfiguration, 2003).

Tannehill, Robert C., *Dying and Rising with Christ* (Eugene, OR: Wipf & Stock, 1996).

Taylor, Joan E., *John the Baptist within Second Temple Judaism* (London: SPCK, 1997).

Taylor, Nicholas H., 'Baptism for the Dead (1 Cor 15:29)?', *Neotestamentica* 36 (2002), pp. 111–20.

Taylor, Nicholas H., 'Caligula, the Church of Antioch, and the Gentile Mission', *Religion and Theology* 7 (2000), pp. 1–22.

Taylor, Nicholas H., 'The Composition and Chronology of Second Corinthians', *Journal for the Study of the New Testament* 44 (1991), pp. 67–87.

Taylor, Nicholas H., 'Conflicting Bases of Identity in Early Christianity', in Anthony J. Blasi et al. (eds), *Handbook of Early Christianity: Social Science Approaches* (Walnut Creek, CA: Alta Mira, 2002), pp. 577–97.

Taylor, Nicholas H., 'The Contextualization of Christianity in the Early Church', in Ethel R. Johnson (ed.), *Reflections on Christian Faith: An African Context* (Mutare: Africa University Press, 2002), pp. 41–54.

Taylor, Nicholas H., 'Dying with Christ in Baptism: Issues in the Translation and Interpretation of Rom. 6.3–4', *The Bible Translator* 59 (2008), pp. 38–49.

Taylor, Nicholas H., 'Early Christian Expectations concerning the Return of Jesus', *Journal of Theology for Southern Africa* 104 (1999), pp. 32–43.

Taylor, Nicholas H., *Lay Presidency at the Eucharist? An Anglican Approach* (London: Mowbray, 2009).

Taylor, Nicholas H., 'Liturgy and Identity: Conversion-Initiation in Galatians 3.26–29', *Anaphora* 6.2 (2012), pp. 1–18.

Taylor, Nicholas H., 'Onesimus: A Study in Slavery and Conversion in Early Christianity', *Religion and Theology* 3 (1996), pp. 159–81.

Taylor, Nicholas H., *Paul, Antioch and Jerusalem: A Study in Relationships and Authority in Earliest Christianity* (Sheffield: Sheffield Academic Press, 1992; London: Bloomsbury, 2015).

Taylor, Nicholas H., 'Paul for Today: Race, Class, and Gender in Light of Cognitive Dissonance Theory', *Sociological Interpretation of the New Testament and Contemporary Christian Life. Listening: Journal of Religion and Culture* 32.1 (1997), pp. 22–38.

Taylor, Nicholas H., 'The Social Nature of Conversion in the Early Christian World', in Philip F. Esler (ed.), *Modelling Early Christianity* (London: Routledge, 1995), pp. 128–36.

Theissen, Gerd, *The Social Setting of Pauline Christianity* (Edinburgh: T. & T. Clark, 1982).

Theissen, Gerd, *A Theory of Primitive Christian Religion* (London: SCM Press, 1999).

Thiselton, Anthony C., *The First Epistle to the Corinthians* (New International Greek Text Commentary; Grand Rapids, MI: Eerdmans, 2000).

Thrall, Margaret E., *A Critical and Exegetical Commentary on the Second Epistle to the Corinthians* (International Critical Commentary; London: T. & T. Clark, 1994, 2000).

Tomson, Peter J., *Paul and the Jewish Law* (Assen: Van Gorcum, 1990).

Toynbee, Jocelyn C. M., *Death and Burial in the Roman World* (Ithaca, NY: Cornell University Press, 1971).

Trebilco, Paul R., *Jewish Communities in Asia Minor* (Cambridge: Cambridge University Press, 1991).

Trumbower, Jeffrey A., *Rescue for the Dead: The Posthumous Salvation of Non-Christians in Early Christianity* (Oxford: Oxford University Press, 2001).

Turner, Victor W., *The Ritual Process* (London: Routledge & Kegan Paul, 1969).

Uro, Risto, *Ritual and Christian Beginnings* (Oxford: Oxford University Press, 2016).

Wagner, Günther, *Pauline Baptism and the Pagan Mysteries* (Edinburgh: Oliver & Boyd, 1967).

Walsh, Liam G., *The Sacraments of Initiation* (London: Geoffrey Chapman, 1988).

Wanamaker, Charles A., *The Letters to the Thessalonians* (New International Greek Text Commentary; Grand Rapids, MI: Eerdmans, 1990).

Watson, Francis, *Paul, Judaism and the Gentiles* (Cambridge: Cambridge University Press, 1986).

Webb, Robert L., *John the Baptizer and Prophet* (Sheffield: Sheffield Academic Press, 1991).

Wedderburn, A. J. M., *Baptism and Resurrection* (Tübingen: Mohr, 1987).

Westerholm, Stephen, *Israel's Law and the Church's Faith* (Grand Rapids, MI: Eerdmans, 1988).

Whitaker, E. C., *The Baptismal Liturgy* (London: SPCK, 1981).

Whitaker, E. C., *Documents of the Baptismal Liturgy* (London: SPCK, 1964).

Wiedemann, Thomas, *Adults and Children in the Roman Empire* (London: Routledge, 1989).

Willis, Wendell L., *Idol Meat in Corinth* (Chico, CA: Scholars Press, 1985).

Winter, Bruce W., *After Paul left Corinth* (Grand Rapids, MI: Eerdmans, 2001).

Wire, Antoinette Clark, *The Corinthian Women Prophets* (Minneapolis, MN: Fortress Press, 1990).

Wood, Susan K., *One Baptism: Ecumenical Dimensions of the Doctrine of Baptism* (Collegeville, MN: Liturgical Press, 2009).

Wright, David F., *Infant Baptism in Historical Perspective* (Milton Keynes: Paternoster Press, 2007).

Wright, David F., *What has Infant Baptism done to Baptism?: An Enquiry at the End of Christendom* (Milton Keynes: Paternoster Press, 2005).

Zetterholm, Magnus, *The Formation of Christianity in Antioch* (London: Routledge, 2003).

Ziesler, John, *Paul's Letter to the Romans* (TPI New Testament Commentary; London: SCM Press, 1989).

CPSIA information can be obtained
at www.ICGtesting.com
Printed in the USA
FFOW04n1905040317
33101FF

9 780334 054764